DAN KILEY

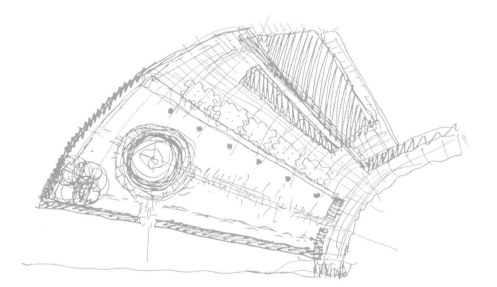

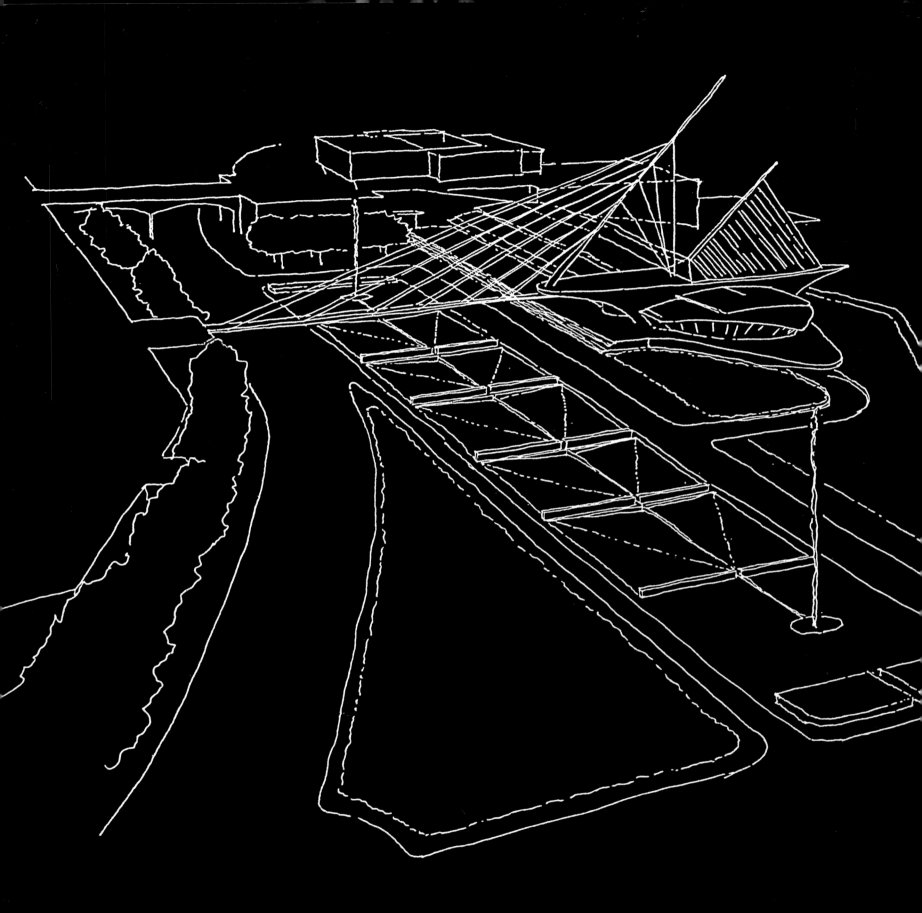

DAN KILEY IN HIS OWN WORDS

AMERICA'S MASTER LANDSCAPE ARCHITECT

Dan Kiley and Jane Amidon

with 382 illustrations, 152 in colour

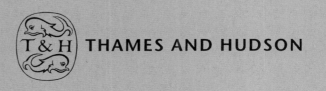
THAMES AND HUDSON

To Anne Sturges Kiley

ACKNOWLEDGEMENTS

With the publication of this book I send my deepest appreciation to all the wonderful people who have worked with me, in my office and afield, in the past sixty years. Without you all, our design exploration would not have been possible. There are many outstanding associates whom I wish to thank for their sensitive approach and strong design skills.

In particular, I thank my past partners: Henry Arnold, Jack Smith, Ian Tyndall and Peter Ker Walker. I applaud my current studio staff: Peter Meyer, Jane Amidon, Terence Lee and Joachin Kiley.

I have been fortunate over the years to have had the opportunity to work with many architects and other designers of the highest level, beginning with Louis Kahn and Eero Saarinen. I am always inspired by their ideas and find that the fruit of collaboration is rich.

I have had grand times with many clients. My appreciation for your enthusiasm and open minds is true.

My family and our life on the land always has been the deepest well of energy: Caleb, Aaron, Grace, Timothy, Chris, Antonia, Kathleen, Kor and especially my wife, Anne.

Many thanks to my son Pusstoe for his excellent photography and especially to my son Gus, who worked on the early development of the book and guided us through to the end.

HALF-TITLE PAGE Mashantucket Pequot Museum

TITLE PAGE Milwaukee Art Museum Expansion

British Library Cataloguing-in-Publication Data: A catalogue record for this book is available from the British Library.

ISBN 0-500-34170-2

Printed and bound in Hong Kong

CONTENTS

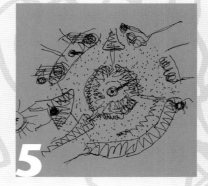

3

4

5

PHILOSOPHY, INSPIRATION, PROCESS

This afternoon, I am going to meet with the builder who is putting an addition on my house. We are not building out; we are building up, adding two storeys to the central room of our hilltop place to create a tower. The tower will be just three rooms, stacked one upon the other, my wife, Anne, graciously allowing my study to occupy the uppermost level with hers lodged below. The tower is this summer's project; previous years have seen the original core of the castle expand incrementally in successive single-room constructions. In the past season, my grandson planted a tiny entry garden beneath the enveloping birch and cherry outside the kitchen. My bed looks over an elevated boardwalk that extends outwards from the living-room into the forest's dance of trunks and foliage. The walk terminates in a ten-by-ten-foot railed

BELOW AND OPPOSITE Camp David

Snowstorm at Wings Point

8

Egypt

platform: a hovering stage for our alfresco lunches and evening cocktails in the foothills of Vermont's Green Mountains.

PHILOSOPHY

The process of addition and expansion, renovation and reinvention is never done. To build is to keep imagining fresh possibilities; if we stopped, the place would be static. Then, we would move out to new, unexplored quarters, like a butterfly emerging from its chrysalis – not because the insect has grown too large for its larval envelope, but because to stay in that envelope would be to seal off new experiences. I am always searching for the purest connection to that which holds us all together – we can call it spirit or mystery; it can be embodied by descriptions of the universe or of religion; it takes the form of sacred geometries and infinitesimal ecologies. There is an evolving, ever-changing, many-faceted order that binds everything into harmonious parts of the greater whole.

Sometimes, the pervading order is violated. Often, it is unseen, unknown, disguised or ignored. Anne and I live as simply as possible on the land, within the forest and farmland of northern New England. We chose to live here, in this way, to keep our minds open and our senses attuned to the organizations and evolutions of nature's order. The challenge is to preserve and feed an open mind, so that nothing is shut out by walls of preconception. The purpose is to see with the clear eyes of a child, so that all is new, so that the intrinsic solution to each problem is apparent. When people do not allow themselves to perceive and intuit the harmonies of form and proportion that surround them, and instead arbitrarily invent and inject disjunctive ideas, they stray from pure design (which is integral with the universal orders) and end up imitating or decorating. The greatest contribution a designer can make is to link the human and the natural in such a way as to recall our fundamental place in the scheme of things.

What is design? It is not something that sits on a shelf, waiting to be taken down. Neither is nature. Both are ever-present manifestations of a greater unity. Design is the same, basically, in all fields, although the tools and language are different. Whether it's music, writing, architecture or dance, the most important aspect is the energy of life itself. The thing that's important is not something called design; it's how you live, it's life itself. Design really comes from that. You cannnot separate what you do from your life.

This truth can be seen in the work of primitive cultures. They did not set out to 'design'; rather, the shelters they built, the crops they planted, the tools they crafted and the modes of communication they employed were direct responses to the climate, topography and resources that defined their communities. Today, we put their pottery in museums and call it art; we study their strategies of protection and call it architecture; we find inspiration in their agricultural practices for form and pattern in landscape design. The intimate assimilation of given conditions produced works of balance, rhythm and scale that please our contemporary senses because they reveal the governing efficiency and orders of nature. The reliance on functionality produced the purity perceived as art – beauty is the result, not a preconception. Today's technology can also be brought into the production of powerful experiences if one can see the determining factors clearly and respond with unadorned honesty.

Yet it is dangerous to be a slave to rationality. Life is fun and should be celebrated. One has to be open to the unexpected and the unserious. Although it seems obvious, many ignore the inspirational fortitude of love – love of family, love of place. When you are passionate, something is bound to happen. If you do something simply for money or to make a big splash, that's no basis from which to move forwards. I am motivated by the adventure inherent in seeking out the possibilities of life, and that includes a sense of lightness and spontaneity that frees one from sterile rules and procedures. The strongest artists and designers, such as the great poet Rilke, search for the mystery of who we are; they call it being. The best work comes from that search. The mystical dimension joins with our faculties to prepare us for further growth.

INSPIRATION

I was fortunate to be brought up poor. Which is to say that I was rich in freedom of experience and thought. My family lived in the Roxbury Highlands of Boston, Massachusetts, a once-elegant area abandoned by the affluent (unwisely, I believe, as it commands a glorious piece of land overlooking Dorchester Bay, Boston and Beacon Hill). I grew up running around the tight alleyways and labyrinthine fenced yards that surrounded my house; the dense layering of these architectural spaces – all connected, each leading to another and another – formed the foundation of my later understanding of structural interplay and spatial relationships. One of my earliest memories is of a picnic on a little patch of lawn in our neighbourhood; the vividness of that single green carpet, set within the urban encasement, still enchants me. Similarly, memories of my mother's habits infuse my perception of detail: she scrubbed the floor with lye until its white opacity was pristine; the polished brass piping and neatly arranged utensils in the kitchen had their particular allure.

Grandmother Baxter lived in an upland-pasture farm near the White Mountains of New Hampshire. As a child, I spent many summers exploring the piney woods, chasing my sisters across open fields, clambouring over old stone walls to find fern-filled shade by cold brooks. I was drawn to the richness of the rural landscape and fascinated by the force of its purity: one thousand sugar-maple trunks on a leaf-strewn slope; a rippling twenty-acre blanket of ripe, golden hay that reversed in winter to reveal a brilliant snow-field with just two ski tracks breaking its still surface; a burst of fragrant apple blossom frothing above the crab grass of the local orchard. It was at my grandmother's that I first felt infinity. I discovered, like Thoreau, that one need not travel to the ends of the earth or concoct some complexity to find the truest measurement of human existence; it is here all around us. And human intervention, if performed with sensitivity and knowledge, can reveal the structure of the land. In fact, our intervention is the most natural act of all – when we shape the land to live and eat and build communities, we are nature, too. But we must be attuned to the orders and systems of nature or risk destroying them with our work.

My father was the head of a construction business and an excellent boxer. We called him 'the Champ', and he kept us all on our toes. Especially me – I had to stand on my tip toes at the age of four in his favourite bar to drink the gin laced with sugar and hot water that he ordered for me (I have enjoyed gin ever since). The Champ taught me to dance and dodge and move as one. I learned that the body is fluid and balanced, and that our greatest strength comes from trusting the unity that flows from centred movement. It is so easy to fight against one's own natural instinct; once you let loose and allow your senses to perceive fully, you can move and respond with the highest efficiency. Like an animal. The exact same principles hold true for any activity, from skiing to golf to dancing. And these underlaying attributes of balance, counterpoint and intuitive tension and release are what drive the best designs. The body's lyric movement says something to you; it says something about space.

In secondary school, I caddied at the Charles River Country Club and fell in love with the vast sculptural quality of the fairways, with the morning mists rising off their smooth, green

View to Green Mountains

9

Snow-fields outside the office

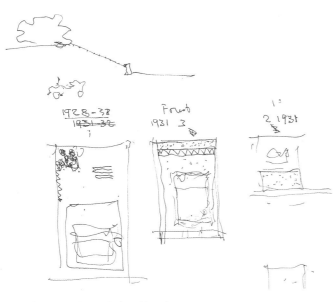

Three projects in West Roxbury, Massachusetts

10

Mrs Kuhnhardt's forsythia tunnel

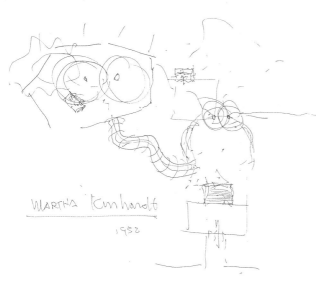

expanses. I began to research golf-course design and then plants. I think it was the variety and possible combinations of green structures that challenged me. I always enjoyed walking home from school through the Arnold Arboretum and reading the tags on the different tree species. My very first design job was for my parents. I dug a shallow reflecting pool in the backyard and placed two hemlocks behind it – this was the beginning of my romantic stage (which was quite tenacious; vestiges can be seen in the Collier and Stokes residences and other projects up through the mid-1950s). I also did a yard plan for my best friend's family; I cleared off an overgrown bank in front of their house and planted grass seed. I still wonder what happened, because nothing ever came up. Every day, my friend, his mother and I got down on our knees to check on progress, and every day we were puzzled to see a mordant dirt patch. Fortunately, my negotiating skills enabled me to secure a second job with the family of another friend despite this failure.

In 1932, I wrote to all of the landscape architects and planners in Boston, finally landing an apprenticeship with Warren Manning, who despite the Depression had a burgeoning landscape practice. 'My dear young man,' his job offer began, 'I would consider giving you a place in the office without salary, you to be here when others are out ... I could probably give you some outside work under my personal supervision that would test your knowledge with plants and planting and give you experience.' Manning was the top plantsman in the country at the time; he had worked for Frederick Law Olmsted, Sr (architect of Central Park in New York City) and then built his own firm. I joined eagerly, spent five years as Manning's assistant and was made an associate in my sixth year. Eventually, I was sent into the field, frequently on my own, to conduct site analyses, discuss designs with clients and install. One of my favourite jobs was at the Skowhegan summer theatre in Maine, where I spent several weeks rearranging the cottage-garden grounds with a bulldozer. Another solo adventure was the estate of Mrs Kuhnhardt, a lovely elderly woman with whom Manning thought I would work well. I designed a forsythia-arbour tunnel that connected her house, garden and paddock. From Manning, I gained extensive first-hand knowledge of plants (not spatial composition); it was the technical expertise that subsequently allowed me to develop an apt design sense. Without complete familiarity of a plant's growth characteristics, its visual effect, hardiness and nutritional needs, a landscape architect works blindly.

Warren Manning gave me two pieces of advice: not to join the American Society of Landscape Architects (he was a founding member) and not to attend Harvard University. I partially heeded this advice (only joining the American Institute of Architecture, briefly, for the insurance), but I did enroll at the Harvard Graduate School of Design as a Special Student in 1936. Throughout my attendance there, I continued to work up to thirty hours a week for Manning's office. This led to my personal approach to studio work: while classmates bent assiduously over their 'board's for days (we were required to use Whatmans #12 paper and watercolour for our presentation drawings), I would arrive the day before the deadline and paint the design directly from my head onto the presentation board. I signed my name 'Ki-lee', as the intrigue of Chinese gardens that I had seen in publications had heightened my vision of the romantic landscape. After a time at Harvard, I became fascinated by the logic and beauty of Japanese houses. Their composition of planes and shifting, ephemeral spatial order opened my eyes to a new diverse design discipline. At the same time, I struggled against the dry teachings of the Beaux-Arts-weaned faculty, finding the stiff symmetries and insistence on design rules set forth in their collection of dusty lantern slides unappealing.

Two classmates shared my distaste for the conservative, historicist tone of the department: Garrett Eckbo and Jim Rose. Garrett, an energized intellectual, was the one who introduced us to the growing tide of modern architecture and the new explorations in landscape design put forth at the *Art Deco Exhibition* in France in 1925. Following Garrett's lead, I too adopted compositional techniques from Guevrekian, Legrain and Vera, including ideas of graphically delineated plants beds and zig-zag edging. We also responded passionately to Mies van der Rohe's 1929 Barcelona Pavilion with its new paradigm of spatial volume, and to Fletcher Steele's capacity to invest his designs with international influences (Steele had been employed by Manning before my tenure there). Garrett, Jim and I strove to incorporate a contemporary language of materials into our designs – aluminium, plastic, steel-reinforced concrete – and were soundly rejected by both the landscape and the architecture departments, under the chairmanship of Bremer Pond and Walter Gropius, respectively. Neither was willing to accept the currency of fluid spatial dialogue between building and land. In retrospect, our fascination with the modern movement was fuelled equally by artistic and social inspirations – the people, cities and multi-cultural society envisioned for the future were tantalizing.

I left Harvard in 1938 and took a job with the Planning Commission and with Arthur Sylvester at the National Park Service in Concord, New Hampshire. I liked the big-picture approach to land planning, but was quickly put off by the bureaucracy and statistics that are inherent to the field. It seemed that design always fell by the wayside. To this day, I still have little patience with nay-sayers and obstructionists; there is always a way to get something done if it is the right thing to do. Nothing is impossible. Never say never; say, why not? The way in which you finally solve a difficult problem many times becomes the most significant thing about the design.

After a short stint in New Hampshire, I moved to Washington, D.C., and worked in the drafting barracks of the Public Housing Authority as associate to W. H. Planning, Architect. In addition to the many benefits of city living for a young man, my salary went up, to $3,600 a year. The PBA was running at full steam with orders generated by the New Deal; I first worked on post-office designs for small towns and then was transferred to the landscape division. I made friends with several colleagues who not only showed me a wonderful time in the social whirl of the Capitol but also introduced me to potential clients and collaborators. I then worked under Elbert Peets at the United States Housing Authority, where my attempts to integrate modernist touches into low-income housing projects were frowned upon. Although the modern movement had by that time saturated the architectural scene in the U.S. and Europe, it was still a hard sell in terms of site design. In the early 1940s, I was one of just two or three landscape

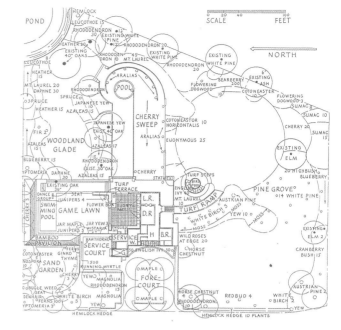

Schematic plan for Dumbarton Oaks

11

Schematic plan for integrated development of tract housing

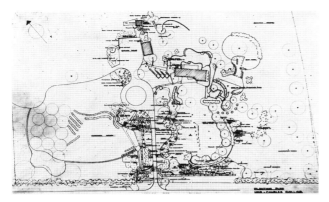

Collier Residence (1941)

12

Herrenhausen, Germany

architects who were crusading for the cause on the East Coast. Although this circumstance probably hurt me in some instances, it also opened many doors with architects who emerged in the following years, thereby enabling my professional development.

While at the USHA, I met Louis Kahn, the first truly inspired, talented modern architect with whom I had the opportunity to work. As I consulted on site plans for several of his housing projects, he taught me about the concise and eloquent use of materials; his devotion to clarity of design structure is a cornerstone of my design philosophy. I believe that we shared the search for magic, the latent poetry within a site or building that seeks simple, elegant expression. I left the USHA to live with Charles and Nina Collier while I developed and installed a landscape plan for their residence in Virginia. In fervid pursuit of the Modern on the land, my design for the Colliers included a series of terraces that expanded the indoor living space outdoors. While some might see these terraced platforms as precursors of the Miller House plinth, they have less to do with a sophisticated response to the house's geometry than with a devotion to the tenets of emerging landscape architecture as spelled out in Margaret Goldsmith's 1942 *Designs for Outdoor Living*: to extend 'house living areas into outdoor rooms'; to encourage 'the value of living close to out-of-doors'; to promote the concept of the 'whole terrain as a single unit of three-dimensional space made up of smaller units of design, some under roofs and some not, but all related, as our legs, arms and organs are related – actual connected parts of the whole living organism, capable of many necessary human activities simultaneously'.

The Colliers hosted a gathering of prominent geographers, ecologists, philosophers and planners, which, under the moniker 'The Land', provided a forum for the discussion of broad-ranging land-use issues. Pleased to participate, and the youngest in the group by far, I was impressed by the scope of knowledge and curiosity that united the well-read group. I had been ruminating over the role of landscape design in the larger environment just a short time before, when I had joined with old classmates Eckbo and Rose to produce a series of articles for the *Architectural Record* on 'Landscape Design in the Urban Environment', 'Landscape Design in the Rural Environment', and 'Landscape Design in the Primeval Environment' [see page 220]. Editor James Marston Fitch had invited us to respond to such queries posed by 'Modern life' as: 'How can man most constructively use his free time? What physical accommodations are essential to his recreation? How shall they be designed?'

In 1942, I married Anne Lothrop Sturges and opened an office near the ski slopes of Franconia, New Hampshire. For lack of other work, the majority of my projects in those years were architectural. With recommendations from Louis Kahn and Eero Saarinen (with both of whom I made acquaintance while in Washington), I received my New Hampshire architect's license. Several houses that I designed at this time received awards, and the practice helped formulate a later architectural approach to landscape design. When the United States entered World War II, I was sent to the Corps of Engineers in Texas, then was named Chief of the Design Section for the Presentations Branch of the Office of Strategic Services (on Saarinen's recommendation) at Fort Belvoir, Virginia. In this position, I travelled to Germany in 1945 to rebuild the bombed-out Palace of Justice in Nuremberg into a courtroom for the trial of war criminals. We reopened factories, extracted the remains of ruined public buildings and purchased materials on the black market to construct a venue for the most profound human judgements and newest media technologies.

The Nuremberg Courtroom effort left an indelible mark on my design expression. It was not the project itself, but rather the opportunity to travel around Western Europe and, for the first time in my life, to experience formal, spatial built landscapes (as championed in France by

André Le Nôtre at its grandest, most rarefied level, yet found on every street of tiny towns and cities). THIS was what I had been searching for – a language with which to vocalize the dynamic hand of human order on the land – a way to reveal nature's power and create spaces of structural integrity. I suddenly saw that lines, *allées* and orchards/bosques of trees, *tapis verts* and clipped hedges, canals, pools and fountains could be tools to build landscapes of clarity and infinity, just like a walk in the woods. I did not see then, and to this day do not see, a problem with using classic elements in modern compositions, for this is not about style of decoration but about articulation of space. The thing that is modern is space. You can't touch it; it is elusive but felt. I realized that the goal was to produce the art of necessity, to avoid caprice and ambiguity. To this end, as Goethe put it, '. . . Classic is the sound and Romantic is the sick. The Classic unfolds, the Romantic adds.'

Upon my return to Franconia, I began to employ the structural elements that I had seen in Europe, along with daily revelations of living within nature, in projects of all scales, from small residences to campuses to institutions. In 1946, Eero Saarinen invited me to join his team for the Jefferson Memorial National Arch Competition. Our team won the competition, and although my site design was not installed in its entirety, the exposure pushed me into the national consciousness. In the following decades, I travelled abroad extensively and found many places that seemed to get everything right, from scale to form to the life within it. For example, the Moorish gardens in Spain; the dignified remnants of Roman culture in Greece; the châteaux of France; the hillside farms of Italy; the stunning monuments of Egypt – these and many other landscapes have germinated in my thoughts over the years. Inspired by them, I have sought to create landscapes of resonance and response within the unity of life and design practice.

PROCESS

Each time you walk in nature, it is a fresh and original experience. Whether you squeeze through a small opening amongst maple trees, or pick your way across a rushing stream, or climb a hill to discover an open meadow, everything is always moving and changing spatially – towards the infinite. It's a continuing kind of pull. Instead of copying the end-result of an underlaying process, I try to tap into the essence of Nature: the process is evolution; things are moving and growing in a related, organic way; that's what is exciting, this sense of space and release and movement. As Ralph Waldo Emerson put it, 'Nature who abhors mannerisms has set her heart on breaking up all style and tricks.' Instead, one must go right to the heart and source: the interplay of forms and volumes that, when arranged dynamically, release a continuum that connects outwards. Should not the role of design be to reconnect human beings with their space on their land?

The design we're looking for is always in the nature of the problem itself; it's something to be revealed and discovered. You might say that you are searching for the design latent in all conditions. That's how it all starts, really: I am excited first to get a diagram. If the diagram isn't right, no matter how much you 'design', you can never solve the problem. The diagram has to be correct in its relationships, just like the human body. You must find out how it unfolds organically, from the overall structure down to the fingernails; don't start with the fingernails. It is intrinsic; it's all there, waiting for you to release it. A site is almost never a big, blank slate waiting for your creative genius; it is a set of conditions and problems for which one seeks the highest solution. I always start from a functional base. I want to protect from the elements, like a farmer or a caveman. For example, the first day at our farmhouse, which is laid out north–south,

Greece

13

The Office of Dan Kiley (1995)

Finding the spatial magic

14

we planted a row of sugar-maples along the west side to provide shade. That's landscape design: putting that row of trees in is a master stroke of design, it's the start of the structure for the site. Then arriving at and moving in and out of the house, then needing certain things that get planted in relation to the existing environment – it all adds up to compose the diagram. It doesn't come out of the air or your head; it comes straight from what the site tells you. But you must see it with an eye for balance and proportion – that part is intuitive.

One must begin with the site itself and take in all of its attributes with an open mind. When I go onto a site, often I have an immediate understanding of, and reaction to, it. It speaks to me right away. Once you see the physical aspects, the second consideration is the programme. How will the land be used? When? By whom? The programme is an outgrowth of the third, all-important ingredient in the design process: the client. A designer never works alone. Whether the client is a person or a city or a museum, there is immediately a kind of dynamic interchange going on. There is input, counter-input, explanation, encouragement. A wonderful client can make a wonderful project; a bad client should be dropped immediately.

I feel that my current work is reaching a new level of integration and fluid order. We are reaching for a reduction and amplification of elements, relationships and materials to achieve the purest connection to outer orders. My intent is to achieve the efficiency of form that leads to harmonic balance, the result of tapping into the source of life out of which Nature operates. Emerson knew this truth when he wrote, 'It is the very elegance, integration, and proportioned harmony between opposing tensions that make our world a manifestation of ordered beauty. Nature is economical and embodies its organic harmonies in the fit and graceful patterns. Nature takes the shortest route and is a fertile balance of tensions.'

When one of my sons was young, he would tag along behind the older generation and ask, 'When are things going to be real?' This question stirs me even today, as it grasps at the core of life: there is never a point when one can stop and say, 'Now I am done; this is the way it is and will be.' To maintain a connection to the ever-changing, growing network that is life, we must always be moving, ready to see and respond and evolve. Design is truly a process of discovery. It is an exciting dialogue that draws upon all of one's knowledge, intuitions, values and inspirations. Luis Barragán once said that '... beauty speaks like an oracle, and man has always heeded its message in an infinite number of ways ... a garden must combine the poetic and the mysterious with serenity and joy.' It is the mystic and the beautiful that we seek to attain through revealing our place in the order of Nature.

TRIBUTES

ON COLLABORATION WITH DAN KILEY

Dan's 'bald cypress swamp' at Fountain Place, Dallas: 444 trees planted amidst a congruent grid of trembling, sparkling granite-lined waterways spread out around and beneath two elevated office towers designed by Harry Cobb . . . A competition design at Omija, Japan: a large, elevated urban plaza planted with a wide array of shade trees surrounded by flowering cherry trees on all sides – an oasis in the midst of the new government centre! . . . An inspiring presentation: 'Architecture in the Land' at my retirement reception at the Arts Club of Chicago.

Stan Allan, architect, Chicago, Illinois

Dan Kiley has the rare ability to work with architects, not as a decorator who comes in to add frills, but as a true partner. He supports the architecture, and, more importantly, he adds whole new dimensions. His work has structure. He never thinks small. He always sees the big picture. There is no one like him.

Edward Larrabee Barnes, architect, Cambridge, Massachusetts

Dan Kiley caresses the landscape with his visionary pencil and the landscape smiles gratefully with satisfaction.

Santiago Calatrava, architect, Paris, France

Dan Kiley is one the giants of American landscape architecture. His residencies at the American Academy in Rome have proven to be high points in the education and enhancement of our Rome Prize Fellows. We will always be grateful to Dan, such a great artist, for his contributions to so many: be they architects, landscape architects, painters, poets or scholars.

Adele Chatfield-Taylor, President, American Academy in Rome

Many years ago, when we were working on the Mall and Pennsylvania Avenue, Dan taught me two important and architecturally humbling lessons about the public realm. On the Mall he made me realize that the buildings were merely the biggest objects in the landscape; on Pennsylvania Avenue, they were only there to frame the most important volume, the space in-between.

David M. Childs, architect, New York, New York

My collaboration with Dan Kiley in the design of Fountain Place during the early 1980s was notably successful on several levels. First and foremost, it produced a built work

that each of us counts amongst his best. On a more personal level, this collaboration was one of the most deeply satisfying experiences of my professional life. The sensibilities we brought to the project were entirely complementary, and this – combined with our respect for each other's work and our enjoyment of each other's company – made for an altogether pleasant and mutually supportive association. The joy we had in making Fountain Place (I, the building, and he, the garden) is, in my view, one of the main reasons it has given so much joy to others.

Henry N. Cobb, architect, New York, New York

Having worked with Dan on a few projects now and having learned so much from him in the process, I am no longer sure where architecture ends and landscape begins. At Woodend, the distinction does not exist at all. The house is best thought of as a series of linked rooms in the garden, and to achieve this, the level of understanding of both subjects by both designers needs to be of a very high order. The fact that it has all been huge fun is a bonus.

Kevin Dash, architect, London, England

Dan Kiley's contributions to landscape architecture in this century have been exceptional, and this potential was apparent during his student days at Harvard. We remember that pleasant and productive period when the symmetrical axial design became just another option, rather than mandatory, as it had been in the Beaux-Arts system.

Garrett Eckbo, landscape architect, Oakland, California

'Man is nature,' Dan responded to our mutual client who asked why the trees were to be planted in straight rows, 'and it is in the nature of man to build in straight lines. When you are flying over a desert or a jungle and you see a straight line down there – you know one of us has been fooling around down there.' Daniel Urban Kiley is without question the most important and most gifted in the world today.

Hugh Newell Jacobsen, architect, Washington, D.C.

I first met Dan when he came to my office in 1989 to begin work together on additions to two schools in Columbus, Indiana. I had seen Dan's gardens and landscapes in Columbus and in Dallas and was moved by their architectural rigour, their boldness and their pure delight. I was certain that his vision of the continuity of architecture

16

and landscape would enlarge our thinking as well. He arrived and entered our conference room with a burst of energy and hearty greetings. Our first series of model studies for the additions covered the large conference table, and after a moment's pause he pointed to one and said, 'That's it, that's the best scheme; trust me ...' He was right, of course, and we sat down to work.

Andrea Leers, architect, Boston, Massachusetts

The relationship of the buildings to the landscape and of the landscape to the buildings at the Getty Center was from the very beginning integral to the project's success. Dan Kiley was able to work with us to bring a sense of order and coherence to the landscape design that had not been possible to accomplish up to that point. The planting of the slopes with over three thousand California live oaks in a regular pattern that related to the grid of the complex was his brilliant idea.

Richard Meier, architect, New York, New York

Having worked with Dan for more than forty years, Mrs Miller and I still greatly admire his fresh and innovative genius, which is coupled with a sensitive understanding of the needs and legitimate desires of his client.

Irwin Miller, client, Columbus, Indiana

Dan is very creative and I enjoy working with him ... He brings a fresh idea, fresh solution ... I would say he is truly one of those few landscape architects we have today that came directly down from Le Nôtre ... The work demands that you think about land in the big scale ... It seems that the professional aspect of space is something that I find Dan and I are in tune about . Space is not something you stand at one point and take a picture of. It is something that you move through, you feel it.

I. M. Pei, architect, New York, New York

I first met Dan Kiley in the mid-1950s when I was working in the offices of Eero Saarinen. Dan was already a legendary figure. His landscape design for St Louis's Jefferson Memorial competition was much admired by all of us at Saarinen's office, and so were his later landscapes.

I was fortunate to work personally with Dan on the Stiles and Morse Colleges that Eero Saarinen designed for Yale University. Dan Kiley's landscape design was sensitive and fully complementary to Saarinen's architectural intentions. It is what Saarinen himself would have liked to do if he also been a great landscape architect.

Perhaps equally important, Dan is one of the most gracious and charming persons I have known. It was truly a pleasure to have worked with him and I count him amongst my most esteemed friends.

Cesar Pelli, architect, New Haven, Connecticut

For me, working with Dan is like taking a holiday with many of the people I like most – all rolled into one. You know the trip will be rewarding and 'fun' in the most frivolous and most serious sense; no matter what becomes of the project, you concentrate as much on the trip as on its outcome. Since Dan was trained as and thinks like an architect, he understands, as too few do, what an 'architecture of the landscape' is all about. So it's different from the usual interdisciplinary 'collaboration'. From the start, there is no necessity for a separation of roles, because there are no different agendas; no worry about what is his and yours, and no difference of focus between the natural and the built world.

Jaquelin T. Robertson, architect, New York, New York

Dan Kiley is the pre-eminent landscape architect of our time. He did a brilliant job of relating the Miller House to an existing river-bank environment and in the process created an entirely original and classical landscape. He is a joy to work with.

Kevin Roche, architect, New Haven, Connecticut

His prodigious talent, knowledge of history and instinct for the conceptually elegant not withstanding, Dan's most important contribution is the presence of his spirit. Of course he works very hard and very seriously as do we all, but when he's there it is as if we have shared a special elixir. There are always those ideas, half of which cause us to step back and see the grand opportunities and the other half, marvelous details to delight all the senses ... '*and for the path between the house and the sauna we'll plant mint so that as your legs brush by the scent is released.*'

That, of course, is the source for my idea of scented gardens for the weary travellers at the Kansai Airport. At Tampa, with the single stroke of the north–south canal, he unified the garden, then brought it into human scale with the understorey of white crape myrtle weaving in and out of my sable-palm grid. And on and on. Best of all, he is my dear friend.

Harry Wolf, architect, Malibu, California

17

A TANGIBLE ORDER: LINE, GRID, CIRCLE AND SQUARE

Speeding by train through Baden, Bavaria, Alsace and Burgundy in 1945, I had an epiphany. Or rather, a resounding confirmation of instinct, which until that point had had no means of cogent expression. What I saw in the fields and forests, town plazas and streets, was a language of form used to conduct the movement of daily life. We passed lines of clipped horse chestnuts along tracks and avenues, bristling double and triple rows of Lombardy poplars used as wind-breaks, endlessly expanding webs of orchards and vineyards thrown over undulating contours, miles of irrigation channels. In these orders and organizations of planting, productive both in the agricultural sense and in the generation of a collective identity, were landscapes of sustenance and of ego. What opened my eyes and changed my approach to the act of design was the spatial and compositional power of these simplest of elements – this was no less than living architecture. Not ornament or artifice or art. By means of a strong, direct response to existing conditions, the built landscapes of the farms, cities and industries that I saw immediately and forever displaced arbitrary formulas from my mind.

I wondered – I may have shouted – 'Why didn't anyone ever tell me?' I was eager to apply this rich vocabulary of *allée*, bosque, boulevard and *tapis vert* and to explore its potential within the modern environment. After completing the design and construction of the Nuremberg Courtroom (a project that I managed as director of the OSS Presentations Branch), I returned to practise in the United States and began to assimilate and translate the language of landscape elements that I had encountered in Europe into America's post-war suburban, corporate and industrial development.

Several projects from the late 1940s/early 1950s show signs of that synthesis of a strong classical language with the spatial play that I had been seeking. One can locate evidence of new thinking in the Baker House, the Osborn House and the Jefferson National Expansion Monument (done in collaboration with Eero Saarinen) of that period. At the Hollin Hills veterans' housing community in Alexandria, Virginia, I had the propitious opportunity to do a number of small lot designs very quickly – close to one hundred residences at the rate of one a day – an experience that pushed me to the discovery of a compositional technique, which, while loose and open, established a consistent set of elements. What I feel provide the critical foundations of site design – sensitivity to scale, resolution of relationships (including programme issues such as entry, screening and functional areas), the discovery of site structure and the selection of the most appropriate plant materials – began to coalesce into a discernible, highly flexible process.

18

OPPOSITE The redbud grove at Miller House

MILLER HOUSE

COLUMBUS, INDIANA, 1955

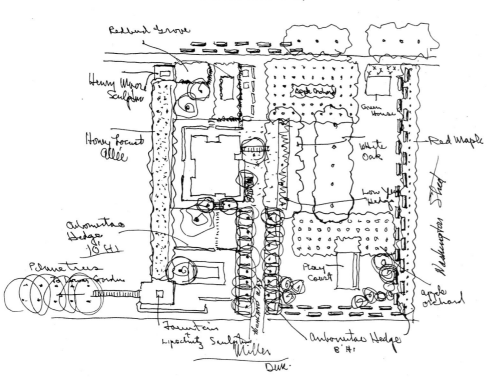

The architect, the client, the site and my vision were ripe to produce a fully integrated modern work of coherent scale.

Although the Miller House is often cited as my 'first truly modern design', it is more accurate to say that this project was the first opportunity I had to fully explore ideas that had been percolating for more than a decade. It is clear that my design language had been profoundly affected by a new understanding of the power of classic landscape elements that I encountered for the first time when I travelled to Europe

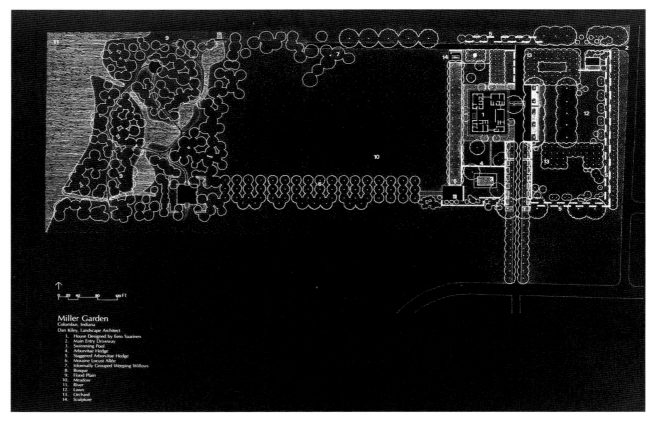

RIGHT Site plan of the Miller House garden which illustrates the ordered, geometric interplay of spaces emanating from the house versus the free-form, wooded river garden to the west.

Miller Garden
Columbus, Indiana
Dan Kiley, Landscape Architect
1. House Designed by Eero Saarinen
2. Main Entry Driveway
3. Swimming Pool
4. Arborvitae Hedge
5. Staggered Arborvitae Hedge
6. Moraine Locust Allée
7. Informally Grouped Weeping Willows
8. Bosque
9. Flood Plain
10. Meadow
11. River
12. Lawn
13. Orchard
14. Sculpture

as a member of the OSS in 1945. From that point onward, I experimented with the translation of various classic elements into a modern spatial sensibility, with the intention of creating landscape sequences to meet the daily needs of American families. I found that structural clarity and dynamism applied to corporate and public settings as well with powerful results. Yet it was not until Eero Saarinen, a gifted architect and warm friend who had invited me to collaborate on the Jefferson Memorial Competition six years earlier, called and said, 'Dan, this project is for you', that the pieces were all in place: the architect, the client, the site and my vision were ripe to produce a fully integrated modern work of coherent scale.

When I first visited the site of the Miller House in 1953, the residence was under construction. The house sat on a low bluff at the eastern end of a ten-acre rectangular parcel. The site descended westwards, towards the tree-lined banks of a creek. Between bluff and creek, a flood-plain of native meadow grasses and clumps of trees stretched uninterrupted to the north and south. At the time the Millers decided to build, this site was on the outskirts of Columbus' residential zoning; the property is now incorporated into a neighbourhood, although its western exposure is still open to the creek. In the post-war decades, the Miller family was central to the industrial, corporate and cultural environment of the city; under their patronage, Columbus engaged a number of modern architects to design a series of civic institutions. Irwin Miller wished to continue the promotion of modernism in the design of his own home.

Thus, it was understood from the beginning that although a private residence, this project operated within the standards of the public realm, and that our work would not be an isolated incident, but would travel through posterity as an element of the greater assemblage of Columbus' modern architecture. The knowledge that the work would receive museum-like care certainly affected the design, as many of the planting details required consistent attention to achieve full effect. The Millers were wonderful clients; if you could explain your idea clearly, they would agree. After reviewing the plans and the site with Eero, I built a quick concept model and presented it. Aside from minor changes, that design was fully approved and did not change much over the course of the project.

The house itself was quite simple and grand; it offered potential geometries that I chose to extend outwards into the landscape. Four blocks – Eero's interpretation of the

21

TOP Henry Moore's *Seated Woman* sits at the north end of the honey-locust *allée*.

MIDDLE Just outside the living-room, a pair of mature beech trees are drapes that filter the hot western sun.

BOTTOM The Moore piece can be seen through the ascending, dancing red-bud grove.

ABOVE View south down the length of the *allée*, with the western slope cut smoothly for maximum architectonic effect.

RIGHT At the northern terminus of the *allée*, the sculptural focal point is framed by a low marble wall against an arbor-vitae-hedge backdrop.

traditional wings of a residence – anchor corners of the rectangular footprint, each housing its own programme: master suite; children's suite; kitchen and service; garage, guest suite and anterooms. The four wings, or figures, revolve around an open core, or ground, which contains a sunken living-room. The sense that the house reaches from its centre out to the land is facilitated by Eero's use of devices such as glass walls and skylights, which allow phenomena of nature (light, shadow, breeze) and the qualities of interior space (volumetric definition) to co-mingle. I seized upon this transparency between interior and exterior space as a starting-point.

The house/landscape construct is more about a flow of articulated spaces than about reaching a static destination. One of our first moves was to pull the floor plane into the landscape. I worked closely with Saarinen's associate, Kevin Roche, to configure a nine-inch plinth that extends twenty-five feet out from the house. Along the east side of the house, a double row of white oak edges a central grass lawn bracketed between blocks of apple orchard. In the south-west corner of the grounds, a high evergreen hedge forms a swimming-pool enclosure. Much like Eero's concept for the house, each area, or 'room', has its own programme (orchard, children's lawn, recreation), yet all are bound together in a loose, dynamic order of spatial flow.

The Miller project was somewhat unusual in that topography and existing vegetation were negligible in the area directly around the house. That is one reason why the geometry is so legible – there were no contours or rebel trees to dilute the purity of formal expression. However, there were

LEFT A shallow pool with bubblers and perennial parterre animates the southern end of the *allée*.

BELOW Honey-locust trees are set closely together so that they effectively screen the western face of the house, yet also establish an axial rhythm which is resolved by a Lipschitz bas-relief to the south.

23

RIGHT The original planting scheme had arbor-vitae 'wing' hedge segments along the entry drive to syncopate side views as one entered.

BELOW The 'wings' were later changed to low, clipped yew panels. They are seen here at the base of mature horse-chestnut trees with the ten-foot-high yew walls of the swimming-pool enclosure in the distance.

a number of functional concerns that we addressed within the site plan.

For example, the *allée* of eighteen moraine honey-locusts was planted along the west side of the house to protect the living areas from sun and wind. The *allée* became a primary axis within the site diagram. Spatially, the *allée* is a permeable perimeter to the house proper; its rhythm of vertical trunks filters the view from the cultivated realm above down to the greater wilds. The *allée* is a private boulevard that connects two intimate plazas. As one walks between the parallel lines of trunks, there is a perception of dilation of the human scale that accesses the more spiritual aspects of the design.

The selection of plant materials is innately linked to the dimensions, proportion and rhythm of the planting plan in such a way that it is difficult to imagine another species in the

allée or in place of the clipped horse chestnuts, which make the entry drive into a tight, dark green tunnel from which one emerges into the open parking court. Or to imagine a columnar tree in place of the pendulous weeping beeches that drape the west doors. Along this line, in the midst of the project I received a letter from our supplier, Maschmeyer's Nursery of Indianapolis, in which they relayed the following query: 'Mr Miller liked the locust very much, but Mrs Miller did not like the seed pods; perhaps *Acer rubrum* might be considered for the thirty-six-tree *allée* to the west of the house?' Today, the suggestion seems nearly sacrilegious, as we have the benefit of forty years of hindsight to see how splendidly the unique characteristics of the honey-locust bring forth qualities of colour, texture and light that no other tree would do.

LEFT Soon after installation, the perimeter arbor-vitae segments appeared to be set far apart.

BELOW As the staggered segments matured, they began to read as a single, undulating line set in a bed of vinca. The twenty-foot-long segments allow visual privacy but avoid solid enclosures.

25

BOTTOM An outdoor dining terrace occupies a ten-foot extension of the interior's terrazzo flooring. The outer fifteen feet of the podium are planted with English ivy, blue squill and snowdrops.

RIGHT In the north sector of the garden, vents are integrated with ground-cover panels beneath the grove.

BELOW Alexander Girard's striking gate punctuates the approach to the swimming-pool room.

UNITED STATES AIR FORCE ACADEMY

COLORADO SPRINGS, COLORADO, 1968

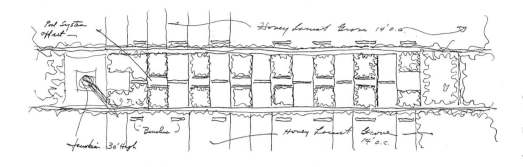

We pushed to reveal a sense of movement on the land, as well as to connect outwards to the essence and spirit of the site.

ABOVE The seven-hundred-foot-long Air Garden's arrangement of pools and walks forces cadets to deviate from their usual straight march.

In the midst of our collaboration on the Miller House garden, Eero Saarinen recommended that I join the team for the new Air Force Academy in Colorado Springs. As an adviser to the air force (along with Pietro Belluschi, Welton Beckett and Roy Larson), Eero had participated in the selection of S.O.M., led by chief designer Walter Netsch, to design an institution that would, in the words of K. Schaffer, 'inculcate into embryonic officers love of country, proper conception of duty, and highest regard for honour'. I was chosen because it was felt that my approach would produce the most appropriate extension of the building complex into the landscape of Colorado's eastern slope.

The commission was a very exciting project at the time, and it was no accident that my office was selected to consult. The air force had given the architects a mandate to create a modern opus of sleek technological beauty, a composition of rational discipline that would give form to the strictures of the cadets' daily regimen; I was at that point establishing a reputation as a landscape architect who rejected traditional compositional methods, instead seeking organic order and balance in concert with architectural elements. We pushed to reveal a sense of movement on the land, as well as to connect outwards to the essence and spirit of the site.

The Academy is spread across more than twenty-seven square miles of dry, mountainous forest land. Typical species include ponderosa pine, Douglas fir, juniper, spruce, aspen, scrub oak, sage and grasses. The preliminary plan was laid out by S.O.M. prior to my involvement, and I agreed with the majority of their decisions about siting, circulation and extension of building lines out into the landscape. The latter's majesty and intense vastness were unavoidable – caught between the ferocious uplift of the Rocky Mountains and the dry plateaus that stretch eastwards until they meet the fertile watershed of the Missouri River, it seemed that the proposed campus would be swallowed up by geological forces or blown away by the wind. I wondered, as Netsch did, how we could compete with infinity.

My work focused on the Cadet Area and the Community Centre, two nuclei set within the larger campus. The Cadet Area was to be the Academy's public face. Imbued with the lofty symbolism of the armed forces, yet unlike more cenotaphic national monuments, this figurehead had to be programmed as a space in which the cadets could perform their daily routines with the utmost efficiency. It sits on more than twenty-five acres of earthen terrace and is shored up with extensive retaining walls. Fully cognizant of the power created by a harmonizing of built form and land form, the architects placed the classrooms, dining and administrative offices into an L-shaped configuration that opens up to the existing landscape, an aspect of the design that I found to be crucial. This move allowed a small hillock beside the terrace – with slopes a good deal steeper than code allowed – to play an integral role in the spatial definition of the complex. In this way, nature's erosive forces, slowly subtracting and transposing the earth's surface over millennia, would intersect with a comparatively instantaneous human transformative act of construction. We all felt somehow that reference to this juxtaposition was an essential principle of the scheme. To me, the presence of that hill was so essential that I fought the Air Force Construction Agency who were attempting to shave it down to the regulation profile of 2.5:1.

We found inspiration in decoding the physical dimensions of ceremonial activities such as the breadth of a marching cadre (eighty-one feet) and the official path widths (four feet for one cadet, six feet for two abreast). These military choreographies translated into articulation

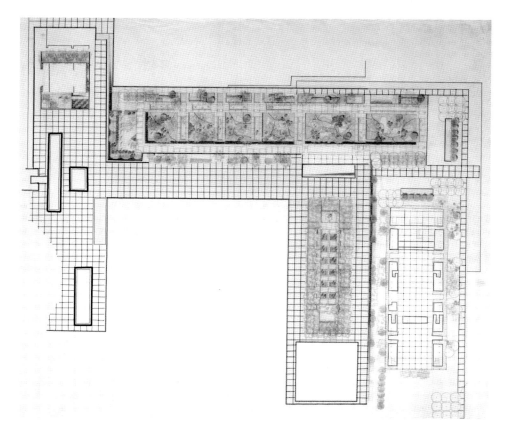

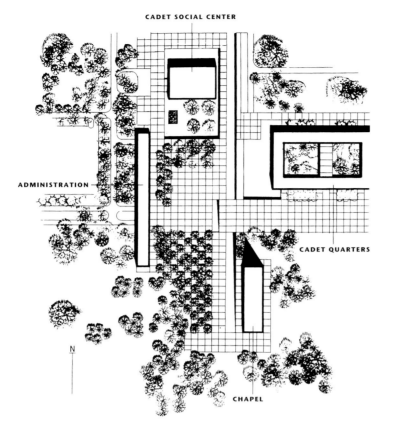

CADET SOCIAL CENTER

ADMINISTRATION

CADET QUARTERS

N

CHAPEL

30

of the ground plane; this is most apparent in the modular pattern of the parade-ground and Air Garden. Secondary boundaries, intersections and axes were derived from adjacent building orientation. Within this stringent order, I felt it was necessary – and only fair to the cadets! – to inject lightness and room for manoeuvring outside the bounds of military discipline. With this in mind, we designed the Cadet Gardens, housed within courtyards of the Cadet Quarters, as loose arrangements of plants and small pools. A variety of materials were used for lushness of foliage, bloom and texture, not only to contrast with the dry Eastern Slope ecosystem but also to be quite different from the unadorned clarity and eminent scale of the rest of the compound. Some of the species used include Washington hawthorn, Japanese tree lilac, magnolia, cherry, willow and maple, as well as natives such as spruce and juniper.

In contrast, plantings in the central Air Gardens are highly structured, with overt geometric rhythms and modular proportions that present intuitive links to nearby buildings. Yet the Air Gardens subvert the overarching uniformity and introduce intricacy and playfulness into the heart of the campus. The Garden is a seven-hundred-foot-long series of shallow pools, staggered so that it is impossible to

ABOVE Detail plan which shows the site's existing Douglas fir trees moving into the grid of the academic area (at lower left).

RIGHT The Academy is well sited on the balcony of the Rocky Mountains' east slope.

walk in a straight line from one end to the other. While the architects suggested one long pool, I felt that the scale needed to be broken up, yet still adhere to the serenity of overall unity. The central axis of the pools is raised out of two dimensions by hedge segments of clipped American holly. These call out a corridor that terminates ceremoniously at five high, thin water jets in front of the chapel. Behind the hedge, four parallel lines of honey-locusts, fourteen feet on centre, further increase the volumetric dimensionality of the garden, yet they do so delicately as an overlay second in visual importance to the graphic field

below. It is not clear if the pools are recessed or if the walkways that partition the water plane are extruded; somehow in this spot, one loses one's certain knowledge of where solid earth is.

At night, the pools glow warmly in a network of light that stands out from the dark solidity of the stone walkways above. Together, they weave a tapestry that stretches across the core of the cadet complex. The water jets, anchored by a central flag pole, reach up into the night sky of Colorado, to grab at the same stars that the cadets fly beneath but cannot see in daylight.

ABOVE While the walkway system objectifies the Air Garden's ground plane, bracketing groves of honey-locusts and centrally placed hedge segments raise the composition into three dimensions.

ROCKEFELLER UNIVERSITY

NEW YORK, NEW YORK, 1958

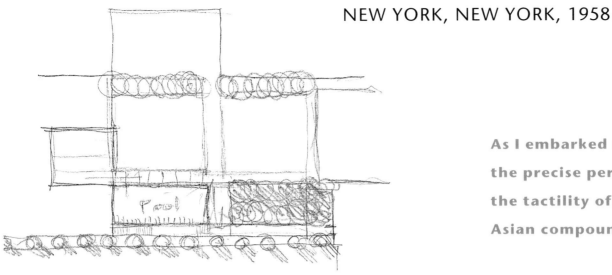

As I embarked on the project, it was the precise peristyles of Oxford and the tactility of the gardens within Asian compounds that inspired me.

In the spring of 1956, the trustees of the Rockefeller Institute invited scholars from around the world to its first academic convocation, signalling the institution's new role as a university. To prepare for its curricular expansion, the university worked with the architect Wallace K. Harrison on the design of three new buildings. At the same time, my office was commissioned to create a master plan and detailed planting schemes that would reinvigorate the fourteen-acre campus on the east side of midtown Manhattan. We chose to use the Beaux-Arts lay-out of the original campus as the starting-point and proceeded to revamp this core into a smooth, broad rectangle of clipped grass, bordered by a

RIGHT In the Philosopher's Garden, on the lower level adjacent to York Avenue, I planted ginkgoes amongst the existing plane trees.

four-foot-wide marble-slab walk on a bed of marble chips. Smaller satellite areas evolved, each according to specific conditions and programmes, and were then integrated within the overall scheme via lines of trees, hedges and stone walks that converge upon the central lawn.

The calibre of this project was equal to that of the Jefferson National Expansion Memorial and the Air Force Academy, yet it was a truly cloistered space that embraced, protected and soothed its inhabitants, as opposed to the other designs, which reached outwards as vocal public symbols, attempting to connect to the macro structure of the land or to induce a sense of cultural values. As I embarked on the Rockefeller project, it was the precise peristyles of Oxford and the tactility of the gardens within Asian compounds that inspired me. We strove to reinforce the idea of an urban oasis, and as in ancient walled gardens founded upon the notion of paradise on earth, to provide a sensory experience effective enough to envelope visitors.

The campus is on two levels. The upper one consists of small courtyards and walkways that link into the central mall; the lower one contains the entrances, parking and additional courtyards. A pre-existing line of mature London plane trees marches down one edge of the upper level; this is an appropriately erudite species with mottled bark and a high, open branching habit. These trees anchor the landscape structure and act both as a wall – a vertical plane that gives volume – and a meting out of the site rhythm with the repetition of individual trunks. Corridors of shade and sun are found between the building faces and the parallel lines of trees or evergreen shrubs. We used groups of ginkgo trees as punctuation; their thrusting branches and stark habit are almost sculptural in maturity.

Owing to the site's frequent changes in level within a limited area, it was best to address the grade variations succinctly: stairs instead of ramps; retaining walls and steeply angled cuts instead of gentle slopes that would require more square footage. In some cases, we chose to use these mediations of level to create a strong edge effect with linear massings of uniform plant palettes, while in other situations we saw an opportunity for design detail. For example, at the extreme north end of the campus the upper level cantilevers out onto a seventy-by-two-hundred-foot black slate terrace with white marble inset in a pulsating pattern. A web of stainless-steel cables in tension hangs through a cut in the terrace and supports marble treads, which

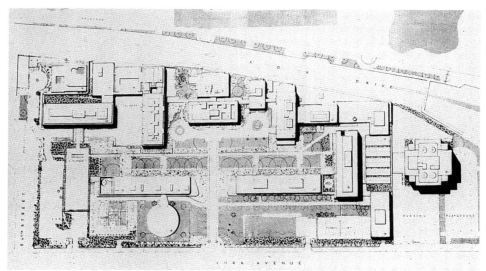

descend to the lower parking level. From below, the stair appears to float in a pool of light cast down through the hole in the overhead decking.

This lower level also houses the Philosopher's Garden, a sunken court that embraces a shallow pool. Just feet away from hectic York Avenue, the garden exudes a sense of calm seclusion with its splashing water (from small jets along one side of the pool), rustling leaves (a double line of European hornbeams rising out of an intimately scaled marble terrace) and – surprising to some in the depth of this urban environment – the daily activities of birds, chipmunks and others who occupy the English ivy beds and mats of Boston ivy that grow upon the eight-foot wall separating the garden from city streets.

TOP The academic promenade is flanked by an existing row of glorious plane trees on the left and a bank of flowering crab trees, with pieris, holly and azalea below, on the right.

ABOVE Master plan with academic promenade, at centre, the East River at top, York Avenue at bottom, the Philosopher's Garden at lower left and the most recent tower site on the far right.

33

The success of the Rockefeller University campus design is due in large part to the dedicated support of David Rockefeller and the then president Dr Detlev Bronk. These individuals promoted a vision that art and science can feed each other. At that first academic convocation, architect Wally Harrison summarized the spirit that guided us all throughout the project:

> This home for scientists . . . will always be an example of how the arts may aid the sciences by providing an atmosphere for easier and more effective communication of ideas . . . every scientist must be a creative artist. He must create an image in order to find reality. It was Leonardo, an artist, who gave science the artist's sense of the significance of nature's detail.

These words lingered in my mind thirty years later, when I was approached to work on another expansion of the

34

OPPOSITE ABOVE At the north end of the campus, an elevated plaza is pierced by a specially designed stair of marble treads in steel angles suspended by tension cables.

OPPOSITE BELOW A view from within the European hornbeam grove in the Philosopher's Garden. A stone-edged promontory on the right holds an existing tree.

LEFT Layered plantings reinforce the campus circulation plan and signal grade changes.

BELOW One of many schemes for the new tower site on the south end of campus.

campus. We examined the best way to integrate a new high-rise tower, and the resulting concrete box at ground level, into the 1958 master plan. Our site studies produced a tripartite strategy. First, transform the walls that dominate the space from stark concrete to a living curtain of green vines on cable armatures. Second, define the spatial boundaries and sequences with bosque, pergolas and hedges and outline a central gathering area (lawn) with a patterned pathway. Third, ameliorate negative qualities of the site, such as wind sweeping in from the East River and city noise, by the addition of etched-glass screens, splashing fountains and a water wall. Although not built, the current design strives to expand the university's potential symbiosis of art and science.

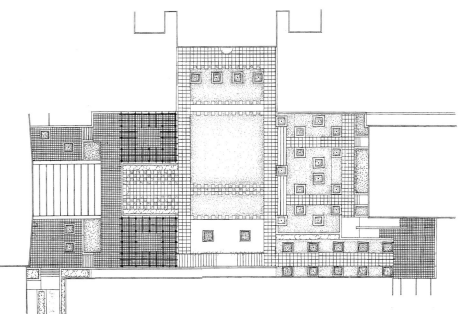

CHICAGO FILTRATION PLANT
CHICAGO, ILLINOIS, 1965

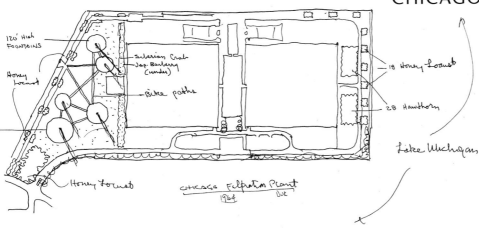

120' High FOUNTAINS

Honey Locust

Siberian Crab
Jap. Barberry
(under)

Bike paths

18 Honey Locust

28 Hawthorn

Lake Michigan

Honey Locust

CHICAGO Filtration Plant
1964   DUK

The dimension of the pools is so beyond human scale that a subliminal connection transpires with the city and the lake.

Chicago is known as the Windy City, a toponym bestowed upon the industrial and financial metropolis by virtue of its proximity to Lake Michigan and that vast water body's gusty effects. Several of the old piers originally built to accommodate a now-obsolete water-freight industry have been renovated to serve today's purposes. Just north of the Navy Pier (now a commercial complex), an immense protrusion reaches into the choppy lake waters. At first

glance, this pier is like the others – a relic of past industry remade into a cultural attraction. Yet in truth, this is not an abandoned structure with a new identity but a (relatively) recent constructed land form that performs an age-old function: supplying water for the citizens of Chicago. It is the city's filtration plant, and it is a working synthesis of urban infrastructure and public park.

The filtration mechanisms are housed in a sixty-eight-

RIGHT The filtration plant parcel juts off the eastern shoreline of Chicago into Lake Michigan (the Navy Pier can be seen beyond); the site design was awarded a *Progressive Architecture* award in 1964.

LEFT Each of the five crater pools contains a single, soaring fountain jet.

BELOW LEFT Site plan of the park with the five pools at centre, blocks of honey-locust at top, bottom and left boundary, and a triple band of hardy flowering trees at right along the building's west face.

37

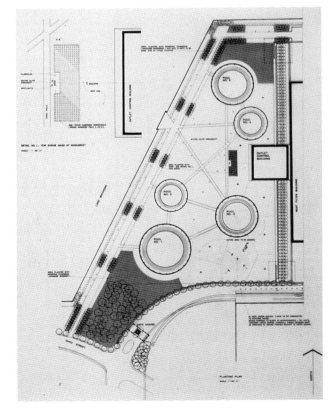

million-gallon subterranean reservoir. Above, the plant's administration offices, laboratories and pump-rooms are grouped midway along the sixty-one-acre promontory. A ten-acre parcel adjacent to Shoreline Drive was designated as open green space, both a destination of its own and a continuation of the linear park that follows the lake.

My first thought when I visited the site was of moon craters – huge, shallow pockmarks in the ground that would seem to fill up with water from below, as if the reservoir was seeping up to the surface. Tall fountains would erupt from each crater, like geysers from the roiling depths. Working with Stan Gladych of the architecture firm C. E. Murphy, we proposed that two entry points be cut out of a tree mass (one for the employees with direct access to the plant, one for the general public). We then extended the linear park as a bike path that traces the perimeter of the promontory; it is a balustrade between earth and water. But the body of the park is the five pools, placed not according to any circulation or structural concerns but in an intuitive balance of poetic forms (similarly, I like to think, to the rocks at Ryoan-ji in Japan).

The conceptual design and lay-out were easy to devise. The difficult aspect of the project was the selection of plant

RIGHT Honey-locusts crown the sea wall along the park's west embankment.

BELOW RIGHT The grading scheme creates a gentle upwelling at the perimeter of each crater, with concrete steps cut into the inner rim.

honey-locust in most of my designs; it is a canopy tree with delicate qualities that work well in precise formations such as *allées* and bosques. Yet the honey-locust is not an overly postured tree such as the Lombardy poplar or the pin oak; it also plays well in loose groupings. At the Filtration Plant, we used honey-locusts in both modes: informally massed trunks of the moraine variety at the point where constructed ground juts out from the shoreline, to create a curtain between park and city; in a double line to flank and give volumetric dimension to the bike path. The line of trees is segmented for a systolic framing of the view and a play between protection and exposure. The formal lines of trees evolve out of the unkempt forest; the shared material unifies two elements into one continuous composition.

At the end of the promontory, blocks of *Crusgalli* hawthorn front the honey-locusts and define seating areas with their lower stature and bright fruit. The brief slope down to water level is covered with barberry, a low, tough shrub with rich foliage and fruit. A triple line of another hardy hawthorn (*phaenopyrum*) forms a dense bar along the east border of the park, restricting access and sight-lines into the giant filter buildings on the other side.

species. Unprotected by topography or neighbouring buildings, anything that we planted would undoubtedly experience the harshest conditions the country's largest lake had to offer. Honey-locusts, which withstand extremes of temperature and wind, were our first choice and not a difficult decision, as this is one of my favourite species. I use the

39

Each pool is ringed with a twenty-foot-wide band of concrete that steps down to the water. The pools range in diameter from ninety to two hundred feet. When filled, their shallow sculptural depressions reflect fragments of sky like perfectly round jewels stolen from the lake and cast into concrete settings for the city to admire. A jet spouts upwards out of the heart of each pool when the system is turned on. Although the fountains were engineered to reach a hundred feet or more, they were restricted to just eight feet during past energy crises and have been kept low since. In the past two decades, the area has become very popular with cyclists who appreciate the paved paths that connect the consular water bodies. Some bikers particularly enjoy the lipped banks of the pools – our grading scheme has the ground swelling up towards each rim, as a crust around a crater. This sets up a splendid jump.

The craters' super-sizing indicates that this park was not built for the sole purpose of human interaction, but as urban infrastructure. The dimension of the pools is so beyond human scale that a subliminal connection transpires with both the intense anonymity of the city and the lake's limitless horizon of waves. The design is intentionally spare; we did not want to compete with the drama of the existing surroundings. But at night, when other sights are obscured, the fountains are illuminated with multi-coloured lights. The 1965 public relations brochure of the Department of Public Works proclaimed that the plant 'symbolizes the city's motto, *Urbs in Horto* – City in a Garden – the ideal that a great metropolis can live and grow in harmony with nature'. When seen against the backdrop of downtown Chicago, the Filtration Plant is not eclipsed; it operates on a grand scale and imparts a civic nobility beyond its utilitarian purpose.

DULLES AIRPORT
CHANTILLY, VIRGINIA, 1963

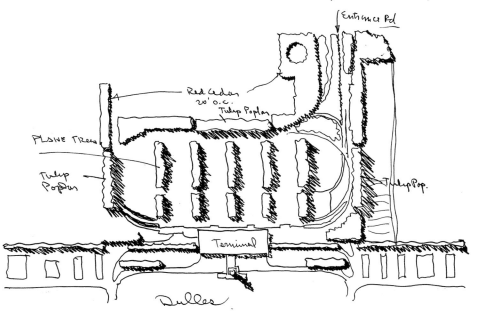

OPPOSITE ABOVE Red oaks were planted in three blocks to relate to the terminal's scale.

OPPOSITE BELOW The roadside bank was intended to be a solid blanket of firethorn.

BELOW The original site plan with ovate parking plain and approach road within a grid of aspen.

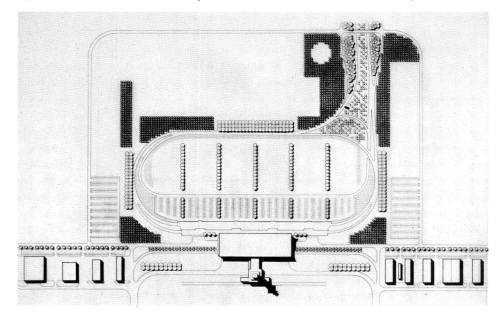

Dulles Airport stands out in my mind as one of Eero Saarinen's most elegant works. His terminal represents a manipulation of then-emerging technologies in both building systems and passenger ground transport that resulted in a public monument of sublime and inspirational innovation.

The airport is located twenty miles outside Washington, D.C. At the time it was built, the transportation complex grew as a solitaire in the Virginia fields that stretch west from the Capitol. As was his custom, Eero called one day to tell me of

> **We discussed that one cannot mix people, automobiles and airplanes without overcoming differences in scale, schedule and access.**

a 'small' project for the Federal Aviation Administration and inquired, 'Do you have any time for this?' And as was my custom, I seized the opportunity to work on a project of that magnitude with a good friend and architect of great skill. Over the preceding decade, in the course of working on many projects together, Eero and his wife had visited my office many times. By the time we came together to discuss the Dulles air terminal, we understood each other well. Dulles Airport was Eero Saarinen's last project before his untimely death.

Just prior to the Dulles project, I had been consulting on O'Hare airport in Chicago. I was discouraged by the lack of insight that was manifested there – specifically, the unwieldy lay-out of the terminals. It seemed obvious that no passenger would want to walk an entire mile between gates. The perplexing question of how to design a building that could simultaneously accommodate huge aircraft on the outside and efficiently process masses of people on the inside was on my mind; Eero and I discussed the idea that one cannot mix people, automobiles and airplanes together without cogent mediating factors to overcome differences in scale, schedule and access. Taking clues from European airport bus systems, Saarinen's office came up with the Mobile Lounge, a modified bus that alleviated the need for airplanes to attach directly to the terminal by meeting passengers planeside. Better yet, it carried them in comfort and style. It was the 1950s in America, and this was cutting-edge luxury. Chrysler built a prototype, and Charles Eames directed a short publicity clip – contrasting hundreds of stampeding feet with a man relaxing *con martini* in the Mobile Lounge – to sell the idea. I applauded and set about extending this paradigm of linked technologies, this studied integration of transportation systems cloaked in corporate finery and suburban ease, to the arrival and parking lots – the locus I understood to be the initiation of the passenger sequence.

The Virginia countryside, with its vernacular of red cedar, hawthorn, tulip-poplar and other vegetation, lies at the periphery of the terminal parking (which is all above ground and therefore requires significant acreage). I chose to use local materials, but in a structural, spatial way that would link to Eero's building and recede into the local hedgerows. The lot was seen as a vast entry plaza, its rectangular expanse distributed into the maximum number of minute parking units, its rounded ends providing ample turning radii for high-volume traffic. This ellipse was bracketed on three sides by long blocks of tulip-poplar, a tree that matures quickly and reaches giant proportions. The towering grace of the tulip-poplars was intended to correlate with the soaring concrete blanket roof and splayed section of the terminal; it was to be a dance of cambium and cement. Unfortunately, the tulip-poplar was later changed to a stiffer species, red oak, thus eroding the effect.

The simple plant palette was used in varying associations for programmatic emphasis. For example, groves of red cedars at twenty feet on centre (to allow mowing in both directions) are *poche* between the circulation routes and parking lots. London plane trees anchor the parking rows; the gently sloped edge of the lot is platted out with grids of firethorn. A ground cover of vinca and Wicherian rose paints swaths along the road and walkways. Banks of Japanese holly line the approach ramp to the departure drop-off. No trees are planted along the ramp, to avoid interfering with the building's sculptural presence.

Beneath the tulip-poplars-turned-red oaks at the arrival/parking area, we planted creeping juniper as a dark evergreen mat that brings forth a visual unity by putting the many trunks into relief. Our original plan also detailed a two-hundred-by-four-hundred checkerboard of azaleas and yews in this area. We selected both red and white varieties of azalea, so that the checkerboard would change over time – from green and white, to green and red, to green and green. Never planted, it was to be a horizontal mural beyond human scale, to be viewed from airplanes passing overhead. From that vantage-point, we wanted the Dulles design to stand out from natural patterns in its details, yet work within the larger landscape.

41

THE THIRD BLOCK OF INDEPENDENCE MALL

PHILADELPHIA, PENNSYLVANIA, 1963

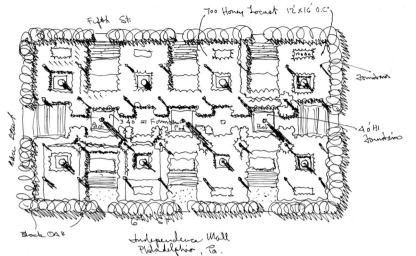

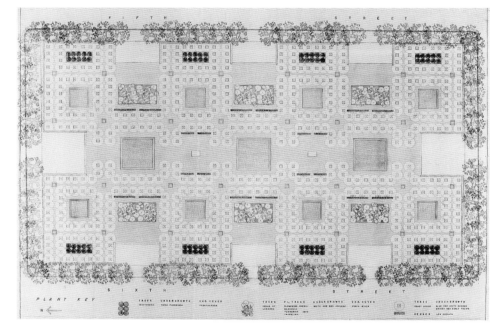

The block's construct of many individuals comprising an integrated body is a nested reflection of its context.

of the whole into smaller, equal parts – much like the grid of streets and blocks that comprise an urban plan. The Third Block's construct of many individuals comprising an integrated body is a nested reflection of its context; it is the nature of the city.

In the initial design-review presentations, I specified that the honey-locusts were to be twelve by sixteen feet on centre. The Planning Commission responded with a recommendation of a twenty-foot minimum, a distance that I was convinced would preclude spatial coherence. The following excerpts of several 1959 letters from our office to HHL&L, associated architects on the project, indicate the level of my concern and conviction:

> [The honey-locust] should be closely planted for compositional effect (void to solid) which automatically increases the feeling of scale and space... This is one of the salient design features in the contemporary landscape and reflects nature much more than wide spacing...
>
> Treated as specimens these trees would be costly to maintain. However, we are using them as a mass so that small deficiencies will not even show up as the trees will be mutually supporting and fill each other's weak growths up... There are countless groves or 'Bosques' in Europe where one can find spacings similar to the proposed Mall. In nature, the rule is close spacing – anywhere from one or two feet up.

In the end, the honey-locust trees were planted 12½ by 18 feet on centre (rising directly out of brick pavement for the most clean, tectonic effect); this was a compromise that lacked the strength of the original intent, but held potential. Other species were considered for the architectural forest: American beech (wonderfully expressive en masse, yet too sensitive to compression), European hornbeam (not large enough in stature), London plane tree (too large), littleleaf

ABOVE The site plan's geometry recalls the five squares of the historic city grid.

OPPOSITE TOP Along the block's axis, three forty-foot-high fountains burst out of forty-foot-square basins.

OPPOSITE MIDDLE The brick surface beneath honey-locusts is like an outdoor ballroom.

OPPOSITE BOTTOM In the original plan, four 'shell' fountains anchored each of the three primary geysers.

With geometric elements, closely spaced monoculture plantings and maintenance plans that specify strict clipping and pleaching of trees, my designs might not be the first that spring to mind to receive accolades from the American National Forestry Board. Yet our scheme for the Third Block of Independence Mall, with its seven hundred honey-locusts, did just that. The intent was to create an architectural forest within the heart of the city. The difficult selling point, and undoubtedly the most crucial, was to place the trees closely enough to achieve a tangible unity across the entire block. The continuous homogeneity of trunks forms a spatial mass out of which fountain squares are cut, resulting in the division linden (too tight in the canopy), ginkgo and red maple 'Schwendlerii'. But honey-locusts, with their lacy foliage, graceful branching and hardiness in urban conditions, were the most appropriate. Park entrances were called out with low-canopied accent plantings, each with a slightly different palette: autumn-blooming cherry at one entrance, stewartia at another, sourwood at a third. Blocks of evergreen shrubs and cedars of Lebanon were to ring the honey-locust mass at the street edges and were integral to the year-round site structure, but were never planted.

The forest is bisected by a wide corridor, on axis with the Liberty Bell and Independence Hall. I feel that it was wrong to extend the central axis out so far from the Hall – it should have been just one block, keeping in scale with the historic building – but to respect the design of the first and second blocks, both bilaterally symmetrical, we used the axis as a starting-point. From there, the design was a decision about the most effective modular scheme. Three square basins with tall jets of water sit on the central-corridor axis. A satellite pool with low fountains is set at the corner of each basin to form a quincunx. These pools, in turn, were to have a single jet at each of their corners (not included in the final scheme). This recurring composition symbolizes the five squares in William Penn's plan for Philadelphia (laid out by surveyor Thomas Holme). With it, we attempted to evoke a collective memory of the park's historical context, not by emulation of period materials or patterns, but via reference to the original intent of the city's founders. At the same time, we were playing with the idea of unending dilation and contraction: that from one point of reference, one can move outwards into the cosmos or just as easily inwards, into increasingly intimate models of physical or spiritual experience.

Unfortunately, the Third Block project is an excellent case study in the importance of site conditions. Because the subsurface fill was low-grade urban debris, extremely porous and possibly containing toxins, we developed a clay lens to rest on top of the fill to prevent excess drainage. Although it was engineered to prevent compaction, the clay did in fact compact and we were faced with the opposite problem: water could not drain through and thus, within a year of installation, symptoms of leaf wilt, discolouration and root disintegration were reported.

43

CURRIER FARM
DANBY, VERMONT, 1959

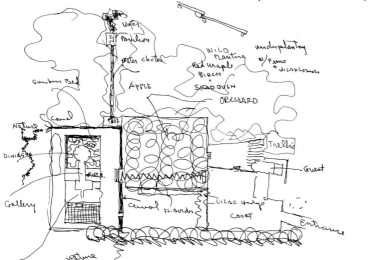

Here, as with the majority of my schemes, the classic structure has been used to reveal a modern spatial sensibility. The two operate simultaneously.

BELOW The site plan's three levels: arrival at right, orchard at centre, house on the left. The origin of the water channel is seen in the hillside forest at upper left.

Direct expressions of function and site are the most potent. At Currier Farm, these aspects are couched in the language of rural Vermont: mossy mountain streams and stands of maple, birch, beech and pine; old farm walls and abandoned marble foundations from the local quarry; overgrown lilac and blackberry bushes.

The approach to Currier Farm winds up the foothills of the Green Mountain range, with views southwards, out over cow pasture and rolling fields. As the road emerges from a second- or third-generation mixed forest, a line of sugar-maples, the traditional mark of byways in New England,

begins. As the drive curves sharply to enter the parking court, the line of maples extends past the court to run along the southern edge of the site. The maples tend to carry the visitor's eye from the point of arrival towards the interior, but this connection is broken by a thick hedge of common lilac that runs perpendicular to the maples and encloses the parking court.

The north side of the parking court is defined by a garage and a low fieldstone wall. The guest cottage adjacent to the garage sits above the court by several feet to distinguish it from the arrival area. This slight raising of the grade above surrounding surfaces produces a distinct guest area, one that is a bit removed yet maintains visual connection with the rest of the site.

From the arrival court, one proceeds towards the house along a path of local marble pieces set with grass joints. The path passes between the first and second row of a small orchard, just twenty trees, which is the heart of the site. The apple trees are gridded eight feet on centre and form a diaphanous vestibule that marks the transition towards the main house. In terms of formal effect, the orchard and other elements of the Currier design certainly can be traced to classical roots. But here, as with the majority of my schemes, the classic structure and local materials have been employed to reveal a modern spatial sensibility. The two operate simultaneously. The spatial volume activated by the proximity and seriality of the trunks is a formal instrument that envelops one in an experience of tension and release. In the spring, tiny sweet blossoms spill over the branches and, like the blazing fall foliage of the maples along the drive or the

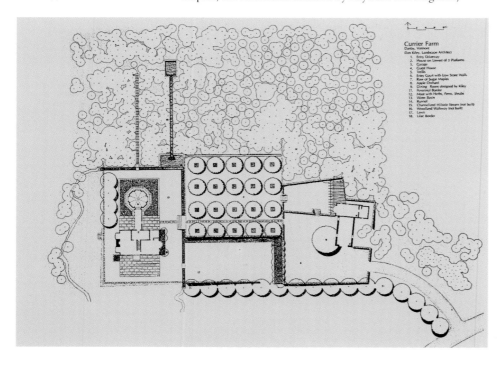

Currier Farm
Danby, Vermont
Dan Kiley, Landscape Architect
1. Entry Driveway
2. House on Lowest of 3 Platforms
3. Garage
4. Guest House
5. Trellis
6. Entry Court with Low Stone Walls
7. Row of Sugar Maples
8. Apple Orchard
9. Dining Room designed by Kiley
10. Perennial Border
11. Moat with Herbs, Ferns, Shrubs
12. Water Basin
13. Runnel
14. Channelized Hillside Stream (not built)
15. Woodland Walkway (not built)
16. Lawn
17. Lilac Border

vernal scent from the lilac hedge, are reminders
that these structural elements, integral to the site diagram,
are not only purposeful translations from the local idiom,
but are in a sense appropriations of nature's cycles into
the built realm.

At the edge of the orchard, the ground plane breaks and
descends two feet to the house level. Here again, a change in
grade indicates transition from one programme to another.
Unlike steps at other parts of the site, the marble pieces
appear to hover in the air, releasing visitors for just a moment
from the solid earth as they pass from one terrain to another.
The steps cross over a narrow channel of water that flows
from an elevated basin on the north side of the house. The
cold, clear water is collected from a mountain brook, held
briefly in reserve, then let slowly into a narrow channel
that traverses the width of the site, passing along the base
of the retaining wall. At the opposite side of the plateau, the
channel ends abruptly and the water is released. For a short
distance, a portion of the mountain's essence – the flowing
water that springs from its veins and traces its topography –
has been civilized, tamed and then let go as a feral agent on
the weathering hillside.

ABOVE We added a gallery and
octagonal dining-room to the existing
farmhouse. The interior is lined with
cherry; the exterior rises out of a
sunken garden.

LEFT The entry orchard incorporates
seasonal cycles into the arrival
sequence.

CURRIER FARM

RIGHT In several aspects, the farm is reminiscent of a hillside villa in Tuscany. It is in the heart of Vermont's marble-quarry region; thus, any stonework on site is locally harvested, either from quarry or from field. Here, suspended marble treads hover over the water channel.

BELOW RIGHT The outer edge of the arrival court is defined by a low, dry-laid slate wall, with lilacs along the far side.

BOTTOM RIGHT Marble pieces set with thyme joints (lemon thyme for martinis, woolly thyme for the feet) form a small terrace at the edge of the site plateau.

FAR RIGHT The channel issues from the stone-lined tank and cuts through the site. Water is a human imprint on the land, but it starts and ends in nature.

CHICAGO ART INSTITUTE SOUTH GARDEN

CHICAGO, ILLINOIS, 1962

I found myself evaluating the garden scheme repeatedly, until it was pared down to its simplest and most eloquent expression.

Bounded on one side by busy Michigan Avenue and on another by East Jackson Boulevard, the Chicago Art Institute's South Garden fits adroitly into the right angle formed by the Morton Wing addition to the original Art Institute. In this project, our intent was to create an intimately scaled garden in which individuals could find respite alongside larger groups of museum visitors. Further, I hoped to devise a scheme that respected the grand, classic

physicality of the Institute yet merged effectively with its dense urban context. Equal to the rigour of the physical and stylistic parameters of the project, the keen aesthetic sensibilities of the generous patron, Mrs Stanley McCormick, and board director William Blair required that my office continually review our design strategy. From paving detail to plant material to spatial structure and the relationships between specific elements, we were challenged to prove our

RIGHT Aerial view of the garden in autumn.

design against exacting standards. I found myself evaluating the garden scheme repeatedly, until it was pared down to its simplest and most eloquent expression.

While designing the garden, we tried to draw together all of the complex and conflicting demands of the context in such a way that their significance to the site would be clearly stated. There is little in the design that is arbitrary; it is a direct answer to specific conditions. For example, the intersection of the Institute to the Morton Wing at a ninety-degree angle was a major determinate in the organization of the space. And although a parking garage below restricted soil depth, the adjacent four-storey façades suggested tree masses and other vertical elements to mitigate the looming quality of the buildings. Thus, we used plant boxes to gain an additional thirty to forty-eight inches of planting depth. Additionally, the shady, highly articulated loggia of the Institute, emphasized by the unadorned walls that frame it, seemed to me to be a weaving of austerity and richness that I took as a clue for the garden's character.

The garden itself is eighteen inches below street-level, a small but crucial change in grade that does everything to define the site as an open – not protected by walls – yet distinct place. Along East Jackson Boulevard, a bosque of

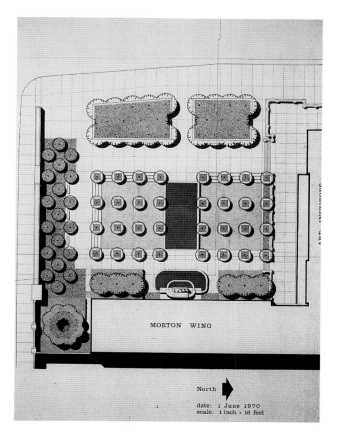

MORTON WING

North

date: 1 June 1970
scale: 1 inch = 16 feet

LEFT Site plan with the hawthorn bosque and pool at centre, honey-locusts along Michigan Avenue at top. The original scheme involved more intricate modules of plant boxes and pool.

BELOW LEFT The pool's jets echo the grid lay-out of the hawthorns. In the foreground, red granite slabs appear more as a fine flooring than as a city pavement.

49

52

hawthorn trees creates a screened edge. This element is echoed by a raised planting bed with three staggered rows of honey-locust trees, underplanted with Regels privet. I selected honey-locusts not only for their size and delicate foliage but also for their high tolerance to the stress of urban pollutants. The honey-locust bar is broken into three segments for access into the sunken garden. Upon entering, the garden's classical composition is readily apparent: it is a simple plane of crushed rock on which marble-capped planting boxes, twenty feet across and thirty inches high, parse the flow of space into a grid of hallways that straddle, not quite symmetrically, a central pool. The Platonic forms and serial rhythm of figures produce an anonymity of location that allows privacy within this public park.

Each plant box holds one *Crusgalli* hawthorn tree, a species whose branches arch gracefully to touch each other until they form a contiguous roof over the garden. Dense with foliage in warm months, when they provide protective shade from Chicago's heat, the hawthorns appear in the winter as a lacy skeleton, their branches occasionally highlighted with snow. In response to comments that the large planters were too angular and severe, I suggested that seasonal flowers be added to bring colour and perhaps some degree of softness to the site's structure. Thus, red geraniums for summer bloom, bronze chrysanthemums for accent in autumn, and grape hyacinth to celebrate spring sprout beneath the hawthorns. Additional bulbs enliven the ground below the honey-locusts.

RIGHT The merging vision of reflective pool and mature hawthorne meld into an elevated expression of the garden.

BELOW Water elevates any site to a higher experience of design and nature.

BELOW RIGHT From Michigan Avenue, the bosque and pool deftly frame the Laredo-Taft Fountain.

A rectangular pool bisects the central bosque. Its dimensions and centralized relationship within the site's spatial organization relate the existing fountain on the Morton Wing to the street. My intent here was to create a drama: to substantiate the act of passing by a grove of trees within the city, to suddenly find oneself before a long vista over a pool, to have one's eyes arrested by a beautiful sculpture. The effect is carefully crafted: any removal of trees or increase in the distance between plant boxes would have weakened the framework. Thus, the relationship between façade and garden would be hard to distinguish, and subsequent confusion would develop as to which feature was more important, the pool or the bracketing spaces.

The garden espouses steadfast formality, yet revels in the transience of daily and seasonal changes. The solid elements of the site magnify the little garden's vital permutations. The pool and plant boxes are a stage upon which ephemeral hues of foliage and bloom, the textures of stone and bark, the play of light and shadow, and the exposure to rain and snow all interact. Strict orthogonal order speaks to multiple scales – museum to city, garden to street, singular tree to enveloping grove – and justifies each as a constituent part within an ordered whole.

53

THE NATURE OF CONTEXT: CONNECTION AND TRANSITION

Frederick Law Olmsted posited that above all else, a design must be apt. Appropriate. It must respond to the orientation, the topography, the plant materials, the hydrology and the built elements of a site, as well as to the locational codes, budget and needs of the client. In the most basic sense, these aspects are interrelated, and their cumulative influences result in the notion of context. This is one of the few points on which I agree heartily with Olmsted, and it is one that guides my work every day. A designer must study and understand the idiosyncracies of a given project, for that is where initial inspirations and indications come from. Design is not about preconceived ideas, and it does not spring from the air – it is a studied reaction to a set of given conditions. Then, intuition kicks in and brings fluidity and magic to the scheme.

Along the same line, one's response to contextual concerns is never the same twice. Every project is different – yet there may be similarities in terms of specific qualities that over time allow the designer to develop certain strategies (all of which evolve and change) to common circumstances. For example, I find that selection of the best access route and primary circulation is often the first thing drawn on a concept sketch. I tend to call out that axis with lines of trees, blocks of planting or special paving. Sometimes, connection is about linking two similar elements; at other times, it requires integration of heterogeneous components. In the latter case, the method and material of transition from one entity to another is what fuels connectivity. The creation of a lucid transition between the outer contextual shell and the inner realm brings attention to the nature of the design itself.

The Tenth Street Overlook uses paving texture and an unfettered axiality to connect with its context (the heart of the Capitol district). In contrast, a scheme like that of the Oakland Museum relates to its surroundings by proclaiming the polarity between urban density and inner oasis via a high perimeter wall; interestingly, it is the clarity of the dichotomy that allows one to rest within the other and therefore ensures the integrity of the whole. The Ford Foundation and London Standard Chartered Bank atriums were founded upon a similarly striking duality between city and garden that serves to unite the two.

Without the revelation of transition, in a way the work is invisible. Which is not to say that one should create abrupt, disjunctive spaces – rather, in noting and gracefully articulating a change from one thing to another, a designer is actually promoting a sense of continuity. The goal: to build a universe of rich experience within which individual acts relate as parts of an encompassing, harmonious whole.

OPPOSITE The Oakland Museum's roof-top garden.

2

LINCOLN CENTER FOR THE PERFORMING ARTS

NEW YORK, NEW YORK, 1960

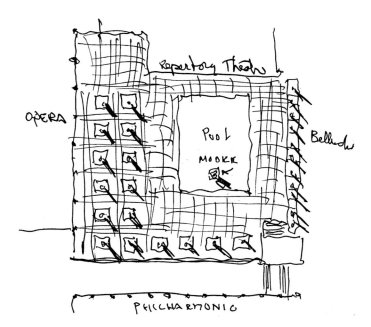

The living elements of the landscape became wholly integrated and spatially related to the surrounding buildings.

Developed under the leadership of John D. Rockefeller II, the fourteen-acre Lincoln Center site is just north of midtown on Columbus Avenue. A product of mid-century urban renewal, the conglomeration of performance venue and educational resource is configured as a civic plaza, its central volume broken into three parts (rather than the traditional open core) by six halls. Each was commissioned to a different prominent architect of the day, and accordingly each reflects the independent vision of its maker. I began to attend meetings when the buildings were in design development; it was fascinating to hear the architects critique each other's work (and worrying, too, as I knew my turn would come). The landscape had to be a unifying force between the contrasting proportions and details of Eero Saarinen's Vivian Beaumont Repertory Theater, Wally Harrison's Metropolitan Opera House, Philip Johnson's New York State Theater, Max Abramovitz's Avery Fisher Hall, Gordon Bunshaft's (of S.O.M.) Library and Pietro Belluschi's Julliard School of Music.

Visitors enter Lincoln Center via a broad rectangular arrival plaza bounded by the Philharmonic Hall to the north and the State Theater to the south. A giant fountain dominates the open space; once past it, one crosses the plaza's inner threshold: a set of low steps that extend across the width of the complex and lead up to the entrance of the Opera House. The Opera bisects the west end of the plaza, effectively wedging itself between Damrosch Park on one side and the North Court on the other side. My firm was primarily responsible for the design of the North Court, but for the sake of continuity of spatial order our thoughts extended into the other two areas, which were commissioned to others.

The North Court is a well-proportioned space that relates directly to Saarinen's theatre. The 80-by-120-foot pool that occupies a significant percentage of the one-acre court was proposed as a smaller, central element, and our earliest scheme called for paved panels to be set in a geometric pattern across the water. When the Henry Moore piece was acquired, we decided that the water element would be most effective as an uninterrupted expanse of calm, from which the two-part *Reclining Figure* would emerge.

The court's inner corner is held by an L of twenty-by-twenty-foot plant boxes in a double row along the south and a single row along the east side. The plant boxes add needed soil depth (there is parking below grade) and are an outgrowth of the plaza's paving module. Cove strips along the base allow the boxes' vertical sides to curve into the travertine ground plane. Originally, each box held a quartet of London plane trees closely spaced at ten to twelve feet on centre and clipped for the utmost architectural clarity. The living elements of the landscape became wholly integrated and spatially related to the surrounding buildings. Thick beds of red and white azalea below the trees codified the unified effect. A third line of quartets defines the court's north side atop the wall and steps that lead up to the Julliard School bridge.

Eventually, the plane trees were replaced with a single Bradford pear tree in each four-hundred-square-foot box. Sadly, this action emasculated the volumetric power of the original planting plan and severed the link between the architecture of plantings and buildings that together form a civic space of integrity.

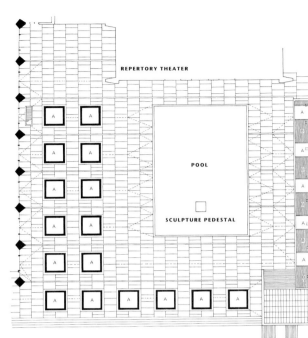

REPERTORY THEATER

POOL

SCULPTURE PEDESTAL

FAR LEFT Even at just thirty inches high, the ordered placement of plant boxes (which double as benches) activates a spatial flow.

LEFT Plan view of the north court with a Henry Moore sculpture in pool at centre, plane-tree quartets at left and bottom, steps up to the Julliard School on right.

BELOW The pool provides a wide, calm base for Moore's piece on an intimate scale, and for the surrounding high-profile buildings on the macro urban scale.

OPPOSITE BELOW In each plant box, the quartet of plane trees is tightly spaced for a strong spatial effect.

57

ROCHESTER INSTITUTE OF TECHNOLOGY

ROCHESTER, NEW YORK, 1965

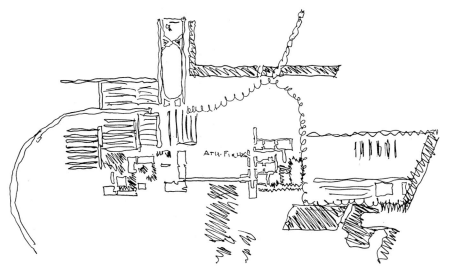

These studies were meant to coalesce into a coherent master plan but also work towards a prototype of campus planning for the late twentieth century.

As a school of ten thousand students, a significant percentage of whom commute to campus by car, the Rochester Institute of Technology is an effective showcase for the necessity of expert master planning. In 1963, early in the planning process of a new campus, I was asked by the institute's directors to conduct a site evaluation, suggest building location and lay-outs and propose detailed planting plans. These studies were meant to coalesce into a coherent master plan that would not just offer logistical solutions but could also work towards a prototype of campus planning for the late twentieth century. While engaged in our master-plan work, I participated in the selection of architects to design the campus buildings. We were fortunate to bring together a skilled group with high collaborative potential: Kevin Roche, Harry Weese, Edward Larabee Barnes, Hugh Stubbins, and Anderson, Beckwith and Haible.

RIGHT The planting plan illustrates a consistent palette which calls out vehicle circulation and parking across the extensive campus.

OPPOSITE TOP A broad pedestrian avenue links the two primary hubs of the campus.

OPPOSITE MIDDLE Roadside plane trees are an important component of the visual landscape.

OPPOSITE BOTTOM Gathering areas are well shaded.

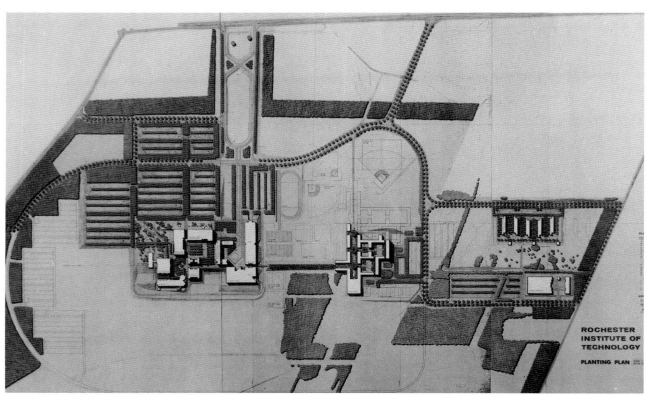

ROCHESTER
INSTITUTE OF
TECHNOLOGY

PLANTING PLAN

The R.I.T. site occupies more than thirteen hundred acres of rolling Upstate New York farmland, forests and several small stream systems. It is a striking setting, and one that was particularly vulnerable to future development. My first suggestion was for the school to purchase additional acreage beyond its peripheral road, as a protection and measure of control against unwanted suburban growth. Bracketed by double rows of London plane trees, the raised drive is a raised inscription across the fields, a stroke of green structure cutting through the waving meadow grasses.

We proposed that the buildings be grouped into two nuclei – one for academics, a second for dormitories. The two are separated by the athletic fields, an efficient arrangement that offers more privacy for the residences. In the tradition of grand lawns and manicured gardens that provide context for villas of past centuries, the mowed, lined fields of the athletes, heralded by uprights, nets and backstops, are the zone of interaction and recreation that insulate *domus* from *rus* at R.I.T.

The academic and residential compounds are connected by a ten-foot-wide pedestrian avenue that is elevated above the athletic fields by a gentle slope. We planted a double line of evergreens on both sides to protect from icy winds. Once mature, the trees enclosed the thoroughfare in a green tunnel, thus emphasizing the idea of passage between and arrival at each terminus. Small courts open off the pedestrian avenue. The original plan called for alternating materials – smooth grass panels, brick terraces and gridded groves of flowering trees – to create a rhythm of massings that operate within (yet relieve) the strictness of the building clusters.

Rather than distribute parking areas throughout the central campus, we chose to concentrate the cars and heavy traffic at one primary lot adjacent to the academic core. Secondary parking is available near the dormitories, but our aim was to keep the number of cars around the living quarters to a minimum. Parking aisles are defined by long lilac hedges, an arrangement ironically reminiscent of agricultural plantings (the most efficient lay-out for crop-tending machinery), or, more accurately, a protective system of hedgerows. While the wind-breaks of the surrounding countryside protect fields from northern winds and indicate property lines, the parking-lot hedgerows at R.I.T. defend our eyes from quantities of cars and disguise the outcome of our proclivity for individual transportation.

OAKLAND MUSEUM

OAKLAND, CALIFORNIA, 1969

The visitor is very much enveloped within a total system of art, culture and flora: documents of the human condition and specimens of evolution.

At the Oakland Museum, architecture and landscape are integral and inextricable. This regional museum is not only home to collections of art, science and natural history but also provides valuable public parkland and a horticultural resource at the heart of downtown. In a presentation to the City of Oakland, architects Kevin Roche and John Dinkeloo proposed that what the city really needed on the site was not another building but open green space. Accordingly, the two designed a structure set into the ground, its stepped roof becoming a multi-level civic garden. I was pleased to join the design team, which also included Geraldine Knight Scott, renowned landscape architect and California plantswoman.

The challenge of the project was two-fold: to establish enough plantings to create a park-like setting without overloading the roof-top structure, and to select a breadth of species suited to the unusual conditions of shallow plant beds and dry climate that could serve as an extension of the museum's exhibits. In essence, our job was in equal parts that of engineer (to devise optimum planting profiles, including intricate irrigation and drainage issues) and that of curator (to research appropriate species and arrange them in a meaningful manner). The lay-out had already been done by the architects – we were given an armature of concrete planting troughs, steps, balconies, walls, banks, gutters and shelves to fill with living material.

Almost all of the built surfaces are concrete or glass: precast units for walkways and terrace surfaces, sand-blasted reinforced concrete for walls, steps and other structural elements. Plantings fill and spill over everywhere; thus, there is little distinction between building and garden; it is all one continuous construction. The building meets the street with high concrete walls – one cannot see directly into the interior park, yet profluent foliage and flowers peer over the walls at some points, and vigorous ground covers pop up above the roof line at other points, giving away the nature within. Upon entering through thick walls and arriving at the interior court, the visitor is very much enveloped within a total system of art, culture and flora: documents of the human condition and specimens of biological evolution.

OAKLAND MUSEUM

RIGHT, BELOW RIGHT and **BOTTOM RIGHT** Plant forms, concrete retainers, and steel-tube handrails become a multi-faceted, inhabited exhibit.

FAR RIGHT Part building, part landform, precisely constructed yet growing and changing daily, the garden is a curated event which functions as a fortified park.

64

OPPOSITE A George Rickey piece sits on the entry lawn, the only level of the garden not over structure (and which can accommodate full-scale trees such as the cedar of Lebanon in the foreground).

RIGHT Visitors to the garden's plant collection see thousands of local and exotic species.

FAR RIGHT Rosemary cascades over concrete.

BELOW RIGHT The fish pool is an extension of the museum's classroom level. It hosts aquatic plants from three continents.

Mainstays of the botanical collection include clinging, climbing vines such as honeysuckle, bougainvillea, wisteria and roses; creeping ground covers such as strawberry and jasmine; cascading species such as rosemary; dense shrub masses such as azalea; small trees that could be accommodated in raised plant beds such as Japanese pear, olive, lemon, hawthorn and pine. Species are grouped by common soil, light and moisture requirements. This strategy also simplifies feeding and maintenance. We let not-so-subtle changes in leaf texture, fruit/flower growth and habit contrast within each bed – typically, the visual impact of each planter or group of planters is irregular. At entrances and primary circulation paths, specimen plants with unusual characteristics are placed to attract passers-by.

In addition to the roof-top garden, the museum is surrounded by arboretum grounds. In its entirety, the Oakland Museum's seven-acre collection includes over thirty-five thousand native and exotic species. Ten years after its construction, the critic Allan Temko commented that the Oakland Museum was 'less a conventional building than a new kind of park-like fabric'.

FORD FOUNDATION

NEW YORK, NEW YORK, 1964

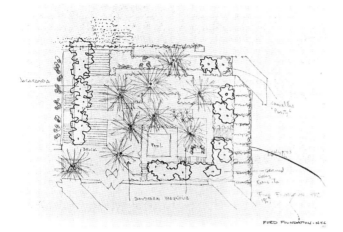

I never did get to see my best inspiration materialize: a glistening, noisy thunderstorm inside the atrium each afternoon.

As the first major interior atrium in the United States, the Ford Foundation project embodied both risk and fun. Although it may not have been what the clients expected to hear, I told them frankly that the project was an experiment. Faced with a dearth of technical information regarding ornamental interior plantings – Fritz Wendt's book on commercial crops such as tomatoes was one of the few pertinent texts I had – we embarked upon intense research that expanded the studies Eero Saarinen and I had made the previous year for the Bell Labs project in New Jersey. We consulted with regional nurseries and interior plant experts to develop installation and maintenance guidelines tactical in

BELOW View of the atrium from upper floors.

detail (the research was eventually published in a small booklet used in future atrium jobs such as the London Standard Chartered Bank, Pierpont Morgan Library in New York and National Gallery of Art in Washington, D.C.).

At the corner of 42nd Street and Second Avenue in downtown Manhattan, the atrium garden comprises a third of an acre. It is nested within ten-storey-high glass window walls, separated from interior office space by a balcony and window system. Overall a strong design, the Ford Foundation was one of Kevin Roche and John Dinkeloo's first following Saarinen's death. Unlike the typical urban tower rising out of an exterior plaza, the Ford Foundation presents a well-defined built edge to the street. I strove to compose a spatial statement that would fill the loftiness of the hundred-foot-high glass room.

The atrium is intended to establish an intermediate experience between outside and inside, as well as to obviate strict connotations of public versus private space. The ground plane is a series of terraces that negotiate a thirteen-foot change from street level to the first-floor offices. The garden's main structure is provided by eight, eight-inch-caliper Southern magnolias, transplanted directly from a field in Virginia. This was the first time that magnolias were used in an important interior planting – I was encouraged to use them after great success with a magnolia court for a private client in Columbus, Indiana. The trees rise up over an architectural topography of steps, terraces and walkways that connect 42nd and 43rd streets. A shallow, square pool sits at the front centre of the floor, its still water brightened

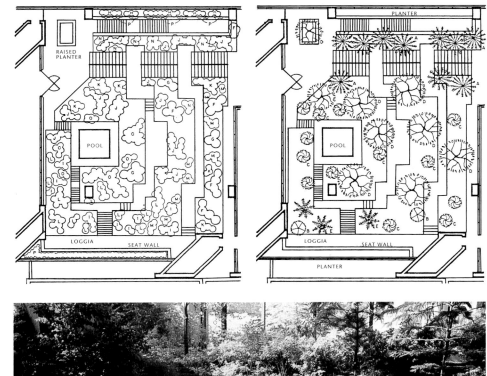

RIGHT Planting plans: shrub layer [left], canopy layer [right].

BELOW RIGHT From within the atrium, the proximity of 42nd Street is disguised.

by Oriental waterlilies whose blossoms are mirrored on the water's surface.

The original planting plan included a rich variety of species, some of which failed while others survived in this then-experimental microclimate. We installed jacaranda, evergreen pear, eucalyptus and Japanese cryptomeria; an understorey layer of camellia, fuchsia, andromeda, azalea varieties and star jasmine; and baby's tears, mondo and Korean grasses, roundleaf and tassel ferns and spleenwort. Red bougainvillia, creeping fig and blood trumpet vine reached up walls. In choosing the plant palette, we purposefully avoided species that are always found, dust-covered, in offices and hallways (such as rubber plants).

The critical factor affecting the health of interior plantings is light level – once this is satisfied, other factors such as soil are less determinant. The more light available, the greater variety of species the designer has to choose from. Testing determined that while the building's southern exposure and skylight admitted prodigious sunlight, they were not sufficient to ensure a minimum light level of two hundred foot-candles at the atrium floor. Thus, downlights were attached beneath the tenth-floor overhang for the balcony plantings as well as uplights at ground level. The many lights not only feed the vegetation but also provide a theatrical effect at night when viewed from outside on the avenue.

Environmental inputs such as irrigation, drainage, humidity, cooling and ventilation systems are carefully reglated; pop-up heads distribute liquid plant food; foliage is cleaned by overhead sprinklers; a special soil mix of sand, peat moss and fertilizer provides stability and efficient nutrients per pound.

I took a Darwinian attitude towards the installation's survival. Warren Manning, whom I worked for early in my career, delighted in letting plants fight it out – he would purposefully overplant in some cases, then evaluate which species dominated. To my knowledge, the magnolia trees grew well for over eighteen years. I believe that our innovation at the Ford Foundation produced positive results. In the end, however, I never did get to see my best inspiration materialize: a glistening, noisy thunderstorm inside the atrium each afternoon to greet workers as they left the office.

TENTH STREET OVERLOOK
WASHINGTON, D.C., 1967

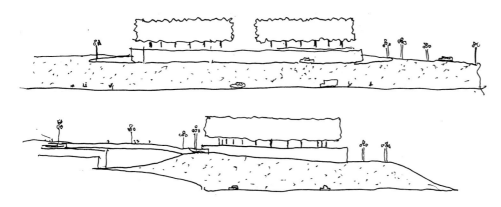

OPPOSITE TOP The Overlook is an island rising above the urban river corridor.

OPPOSITE MIDDLE An axial approach connects the site to downtown.

OPPOSITE BOTTOM The fountains generate energy and animation.

68

BELOW Site plan with the Overlook at centre.

Occasionally a designer is presented with a *tabula rasa* – a site relatively free of limiting conditions or relationships that preclude a new site structure – such as I encountered at Collier House, Independence Mall or Fountain Place, to name a few. In these situations, I take great pleasure in discovering relationships on the site that will create the most appropriate design diagram. In other projects, upon arrival I find that the site is already so well defined that our role as designers is to reveal the existing infrastructure; to amplify, interpret and provide architectural clarity. Such was the case at the Tenth Street Overlook.

The Overlook differs from my other projects at the time in that it lacks layers of organizational devices as well as the interplay of varying scales, two methods used to elicit a sense of open-ended spatial flow. The design is simply a point at the end of a line, a succinct response to its location and programme. The site is the terminus of the Tenth Street Mall, a pedestrian aisle that begins at the courtyard of the Smithsonian Institution, passes beneath the Forrestal Building on Independence Avenue, then runs due south towards the Potomac River. Along its course the mall cuts through L'Enfant Plaza, a complex of offices, restaurants and commercial operations that, when we constructed the Overlook, were expected to fill the site with visitors. However, adjacent development lagged behind our schedule, and thus when first installed the Tenth Street Overlook was physically isolated to the degree that it sustained vandalism and other symptoms of underuse for several years. Broken light fixtures were replaced repeatedly, until L'Enfant Plaza and its populace began to inhabit the place and appreciate its broad views.

Although essentially a Beaux-Arts composition, the Overlook is very modern in its conception. Its elevated, elliptical form results from the geometrics of the road lay-out that surrounds it: the divided lanes of Tenth Street swing around the ellipse, then descend from its east side to meet the roadway at river level. It is unclear which came first, the oval promontory jutting out from the density of the federal city, or the artful curve of the roadway, necessitated by the intersecting path of the Potomac. In truth, and as a respectable attempt to retain pedestrian integrity in the face of urban renewal of the 1950s and '60s – the age of automobile

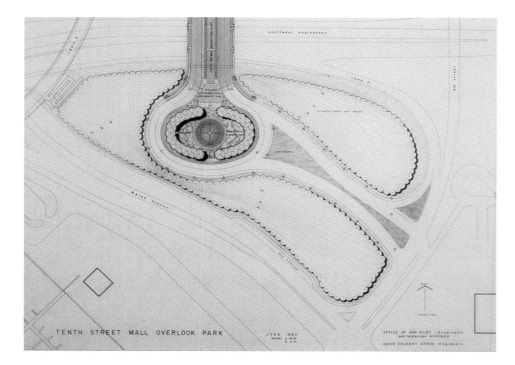

TENTH STREET MALL OVERLOOK PARK   JUNE 1967   OFFICE OF DAN KILEY · Architects

supremacy in America, particularly along the waterfront fringes of our cities – the design evolved as a conjugation of the two factors.

Initial plans showed the ellipse as a level plane, extending the grade of Tenth Street out as a belvedere above the river's flood plain. Then studies revealed to us that this would actually appear as a bulging up of the ground at the end of the mall, and thus we depressed the entire plaza, so that it took on a slight concavity – we called it a parabolesque section. Similarly to *il palio* in Siena, the concave ground plane increases the perception of a unified space.

The two-hundred-foot-diameter plaza is paved with granite squares, the same material used on the four-block mall (designed by others before we were brought in). At its centre, a fountain reaches up forty feet, its glistening, ephemeral columns a beacon against Washington's monuments and solid building blocks. The design of the water feature evolved from those we did at Independence Mall in Philadelphia, although here it is circular instead of square. Water wells up out of a shallow, quartered cone of honed green granite, rises into the air, then splashes back down with gravitational alacrity, glides over green granite and is collected in a perimeter moat. The fountain is illuminated at night, to maintain a strong terminal presence even after dark.

69

A double row of London Plane trees, 'Bloodgood' variety, rings the elliptical plaza to provide shade and vertical definition. The spatial volume created by the trees, the fountain, and the concave ground plane relieve the strict simplicity of the site plan. They are the release mechanism that every design needs. Uplights are set flush with the pavement beneath the trees to highlight their branching. The ring form is reiterated by benches set between the plane trees and the fountain, and again by a low concrete wall outside the trees. The wall begins as a low lip, creating a subtle gateway into the plaza, then becomes a retaining wall that holds the Overlook above the Potomac River.

The Tenth Street Overlook is not whimsical; it is an honest response to site and programme, an ode to the physics of traffic flow and to L'Enfant's original plan for the District of Columbia (as interpreted by the Redevelopment Land Agency). The potentially prosaic plan belies a duality that the project successfully negotiates: the Overlook is at once integral infrastructure of the capital city – at a monumental scale – and a space of humanized detail, fit for an individual to find a bench of one's own.

GREGORY HOUSE

WAYZATA, MINNESOTA, 1963

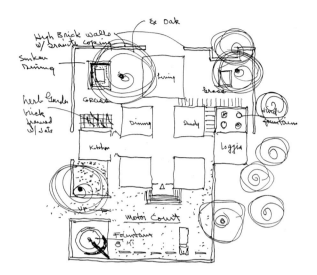

The hilltop location and intimidating climate directed my thoughts away from composing the site's spatial structure with plantings.

As a visiting critic at the University of Minnesota, I was introduced to several members of a tight-knit community of families who frequently entertained to benefit the arts in Minneapolis, several of whom later became clients. Thus, for several decades my firm carried out a number of projects in the upper Midwest – in addition to our work in Columbus,

BELOW Master plan with the new site entrance at left, house and terraces on right.

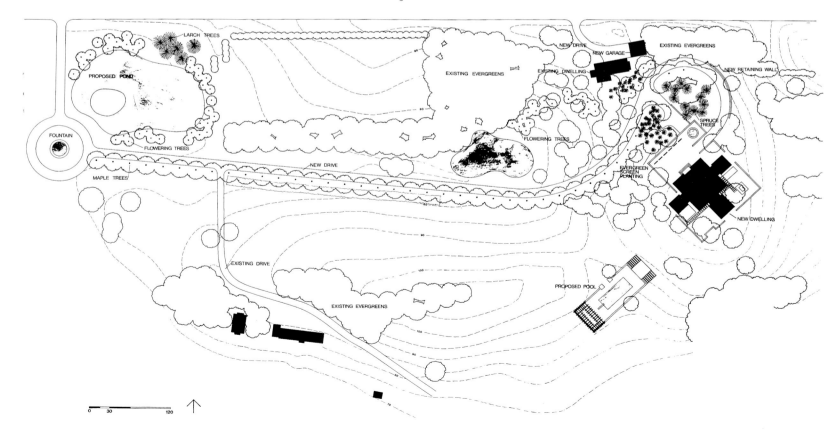

Indiana – including campus plans for the University of Minnesota (with Laurence Anderson and Pietro Belluschi) and St John's and Carleton College, as well as residential designs. At the time, I liked to say that jobs were chosen according to the client's wine cellar – a most delicious and inspiring method. At one supper, I met Bill and Stanley Gregory, a congenial couple who were in the process of constructing a striking modern fortress with the architect Ike Coburn. I was pleased to join their project early in the design process as it allowed my firm to have input regarding the configuration of the house and thus capitalize on the interplay of outdoor and indoor spaces.

The Gregory property overlooks a network of marshes that collect runoff from the Lake Minnetonka watershed. The entry drive turns off the town road as an unassuming narrow lane, then leads directly to a circular turnaround that swings visitors ninety degrees to the east and puts them in line with the long axial approach to the house. A fountain at the centre of the turnaround announces the beginning of the formal arrival sequence, which is further manifested by a single line of red maples that parallels the length of the drive. The original driveway entered the property just below the house; the new one is pulled away to incorporate the site's topography and pastoral richness into the overall design and to set up a long view of the hilltop structure. We made a duck-pond in a low spot at the new entrance, complete with a tiny island and ringed with Wisconsin weeping willows. Throughout the property, existing trees were protected and woven into the site plan.

The architect's design is four cubes balanced on either side of a central corridor. The living-room extends off the east façade; it protrudes into the lawn panel and divides the space into two outdoor rooms. On the north and south façades, the kitchen and a loggia volume are similarly extruded, thereby enclosing the terraces further. The initial floor plan called for these two rooms to abut the core volume; I suggested that we pull them away just enough to allow passage, to imply continuous spatial flow between front and back areas and between indoor and outdoor volumes.

A brick retaining wall wraps around the entire house and defines an edge for outdoor living spaces. The wall is topped by granite posts with a five-inch-thick lintel. This stone lintel acts as a balustrade and doubles as a bench. It is also an immutable datum above which shifting scenes of the countryside and seasonal cycles are staged. The wall breaks briefly at each wing of the house and allows the meadow grass to sweep right up to the domestic palisade.

The client's active schedule inspired us to design not just passive lawns but integrated features for outdoor entertainment (much like the gardens of eighteenth-century châteaux). For example, we custom-crafted a twelve-foot-

TOP Brick frames a petite water-and-herb parterre.

ABOVE Set against the house foundation at the base of picture windows, tiny umbrella jets draw the eye and aerate the pool.

LEFT The granite set floor and slab table rest within the grass terrace like remnants unearthed from long-ago festivities.

OPPOSITE TOP The sunken dining cove becomes a snow form in the long Minnesota winters.

OPPOSITE MIDDLE A brick-and-granite balustrade defines the terrace perimeter and incorporates existing trees.

OPPOSITE BOTTOM Vines soften the brick palisade.

square sunken dining area set into the grass beneath an existing, magnificent white oak. Up to twenty guests can dine and fill their glasses from the jet that bubbles up into a shallow, square basin as the granite table's aqueous centrepiece. In a miniature parterre just off the kitchen, function and art are entwined: tiny water jets twinkle and draw the eye to the textured tapestry of herbs within a twelve-by-twelve-inch brick grid; the Lilliputian pools also provide a quick rinse for herbs fresh plucked from the dirt.

Our design scheme for the Gregory House is an expression of architectural landform. Two factors – the hilltop location and the intimidating climate – directed my thoughts away from composing the site's spatial structure with plantings. I think that the retaining-wall system gives the house not just a base but a true presence (and reiterates the architect's evocation of fortress imagery). Once communication between the house and the land had been established, we carefully tuned the scale of the balustrade and other critical features to human dimensions. Selected as the 1968 Hallmark House of the year, the Gregory residence is a study of unified indoor/outdoor spatial sequences in a land of long winters, where just the knowledge of such a possibility is essential.

73

DALLE CENTRALE
LA DEFENSE, PARIS, FRANCE, 1978

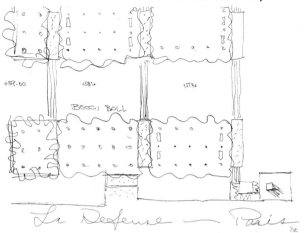

Our role was to design a central, wide pedestrian concourse. The half-mile-long element operates as both a corridor and a linear park.

Dalle Centrale is one of the esteemed 'grands projets' of Paris's ongoing revitalization programme of urban and park design. Located two miles out on the Arc de Triomphe axis and part of the revival of the La Défense segment of the Champs-Elysées, Dalle Centrale has an important role in the visualization of late twentieth-century civic monumentalism. The development is one phase of a much larger scheme that began centuries ago with Haussmann's clearing of broad boulevards through the dense urban hives of Paris to establish open sight-lines and channels of transportation able to accommodate high volumes. Long ago, the implementation of boulevards encouraged the concept of a united city that instilled loyalty beyond localized neighbourhoods; today, the project strives for similar results on a regional scale. When it is complete, the axis from the Tuileries garden at the Louvre will pierce the Arc at L'Etoile and cross the Seine to La Défense in the Nanterre sector; from there, the line to the heart of Paris will continue west to St-Germain-en-Laye.

Primarily a business district with some residential mid-rises, Nanterre was in need of public open space as well as efficient pedestrian circulation routes. Considering the scale of development involved, La Défense is essentially a new city within the city of Paris – it is a large mixed-use nucleus of office blocks, commercial and residential units, hotels and restaurants. Our role was to design a central, wide pedestrian concourse to provide a spine for the district. The half-mile-long element operates as both a corridor for through movement and a linear park for congregation and recreation. It is filled with large pools of water animated by jets and waterfalls, shaded seating areas, earthen *bocce* courts and open-

OPPOSITE BELOW Aerial view of La Défense axis.

RIGHT Parallel rows of London plane trees form the pedestrian mall and establish a scale against the engulfing blocks of office and retail units.

BELOW RIGHT A consistent palette of planting, paving, lighting and other elements along the length of Dalle Centrale contributes to its identity.

LEFT Within the continuous rows of trees, intimate courts and cafés are carved out.

BELOW LEFT The unifying power of monocultural plantings is evident.

OPPOSITE ABOVE The unchecked growth of vines and ivys links building and nature into one experience.

OPPOSITE BELOW Numerous cafés along the mall offer views of fountains and passers-by; the prevalence of foliage is a pleasant *vêtement* for the typical city 'hardscape'.

air cafés. The metro, commuter rail lines and parking lie below grade.

Given the artificial ground plane – much of the site is decking over transportation nodes – the planting plan was in part determined by which areas had sufficient soil depth and weight tolerance. We used a pedestal paving system of aggregate concrete with open joints, which allowed water to drain through the joints into a plenum. Thus, the entire width (over three hundred feet) and length of the corridor are level. Above ground, we planted long, linear bosques of pollarded London plane trees on either side of the corridor. The bosques, composed of four rows of trees set twelve feet on centre, frame the view of L'Etoile and provide enclosure, shade and spatial activation. The majestic species, some segments set at grade in stone dust and others underplanted

with cotoneaster, constitute the structural framework of the design. The selection of London plane is a reference to the elegant Parisian avenues and unifies visually disjointed areas.

At the mid-point of the corridor, a seventy-by-two-hundred-foot pool occupies the centre of the axis. The sculptor Agam created a mosaic of brightly coloured tiles to line the pool's bottom. Computer-controlled jets shoot up to sixty feet in the air and provide lively plays of light and water that are a focal point of the spatial expanse. A waterfall, which we suggested, spills over the pool's western edge; water drops twenty feet to a drain basin next to the roadways and parking access that pass beneath the invented/constructed plane of civil interaction. The waterfall stitches the two levels together (those on foot elevated above and those in vehicles set below) with a vertical screen of water; the glistening curtain also acts as a sort of billboard advertising the amenities at its source.

Our office (at the time of this project, Kiley/Tyndall/Walker) was required to establish a satellite studio in Paris for the duration of the work. The most difficult hurdle was to convince those in charge that all four rows of London plane

trees were essential to the design. It was clear that to bring integrity to the *nouvelle urbanisme* and, crucially, to reinforce its axial relationship to the Arc de Triomphe and the Champs-Elysées, the trees were needed as vertical elements.

OPPOSITE ABOVE The tile pool created by the sculptor Agam is a brilliant centrepiece.

OPPOSITE BELOW Perspective sketches of the site scheme.

RIGHT The Arc de Triomphe is visible through the dance of jets.

BELOW RIGHT The new, massive icon of La Défense framed by London planes and water sculpture: it is a progressive mix of art, nature and commerce as urban infrastructure.

NATIONAL GALLERY OF ART
WASHINGTON, D.C., 1977, 1989

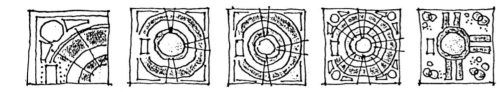

Both sites, located just off the Washington Mall, are imbued with profound cultural, historical and social qualities.

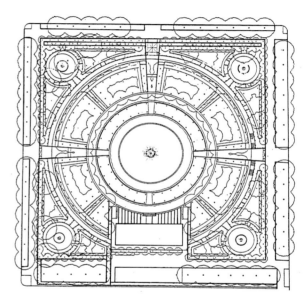

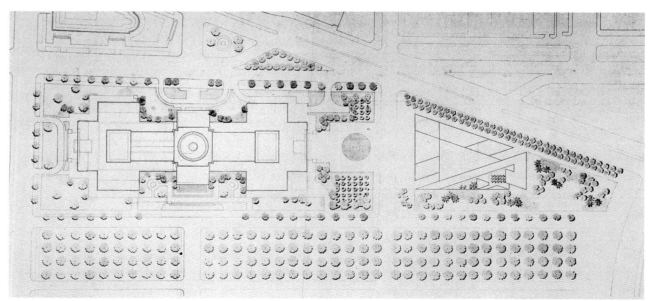

ABOVE Partial site model of the final scheme for the National Sculpture Garden.

ABOVE RIGHT Plan view of the final garden scheme (not implemented), with circular pool at the centre as generative form.

RIGHT Master plan of the National Gallery of Art, with gallery entrance at centre, Pei's East Wing to the right (1977), and the Sculpture Garden far left (1989; not shown).

80

BELOW LEFT Groves of flowering cherries are used to bracket entrances in a definitive but delicate manner.

Our work at the National Gallery in Washington encompasses two projects: first, a pedestrian connection between the gallery and its new East Wing (designed by I. M. Pei), as well as a roof-top terrace; second, a proposal to revitalize the six-acre National Sculpture Garden on the west side of the gallery. Both sites, located just off the Washington Mall, are imbued with profound cultural, historical and social qualities.

There were several critical issues to resolve in the design of the East Wing pedestrian connection. Foremost was the need to develop an order and texture of landscape elements that could mediate between the historic National Gallery, a Greek Revival masterpiece, and Pei's powerful modern gallery on the other side of 4th Street. Although our first instinct was to place lines of large, grand shade-trees to effect an enclosed corridor between the two buildings, soil depth did not allow this. Thus, twin groves of a smaller species, saucer magnolia, were planted on either side of the gallery's east entrance. The magnolias shape the open-air place into an elongated court, extend the façade's symmetry and initiate an urban court as dialogue between the two monoliths. Boxwood borders continue from the new plantings along Constitution

82

Avenue and merge with existing landscape structure to the west. Banks of cherry trees form a curtain between the gallery and the Mall.

At the East Wing's recessed entrance, two massive points of the building's triangular form rise cleanly out of the paved plaza. There is a contrast between the branch-, blossom- and leaf-filled gallery court, painted with splashes of shadow and light, undergoing changes with each season, and the unadorned visage of the East Wing, with no organic movement other than the daily play of shadows falling from its own stone form. The landscape scheme underscores a respect for alternate modes within a city whose primary axis is a stretch of lawn. One is a palace in the park, at which visitors draw up to a green vestibule. The other asks visitors immediately and without pretension to enter within – that is where the richness and glory and content are found.

The East Wing roof-terrace flooring is a pattern of marble pieces cut to fit within the building's pervasive play of off-set triangles. White wisteria softens the neighbouring roof overhang. The terrace is unified by a bosque of tea crabs that rise out of white wooden octagons. Espaliered firethorn creates a sculptural bas-relief on walls that receive sun.

The six-acre Sculpture Garden is essentially an alcove off the Washington Mall directly across from the Hirschorn Museum. Our design, never built, was a classical balance of geometries infused with details of water movement, plantings and illumination to bring out the spirit and magic of potentially predictable structures.

The origin of the garden is a 120-foot-diameter reflecting pool that retains its function of a skating-rink in the winter. A radial-cut granite promenade encircles the water and is echoed by an arched double row of pleached littleleaf lindens that rise out of a crushed-stone bed. The littleleaf linden is the perfect tree for this application; its medium scale, thick, straight trunk, well-balanced branching and propensity for easily shaped foliage work well in formal landscapes. The circle is again expressed by a wider granite walkway, encompassed along its outer perimeter by a grove of honey-locust trees. Larger, looser and more delicate of foliage and branching than the linden, the honey-locust provides dancing shadows and bright foliage and casts lacy silhouettes onto a sidewalk, contrasting with the other trees' density and canopy clipped to eight feet above grade. The honey-locusts maintain a branching ceiling of fourteen feet.

Within the honey-locust groves, sculpture rooms are outlined with hedges and alternate with bosque infills. Pathways follow the pattern of various geometries within the overall composition. The outermost circle is a twelve-hundred-foot-long, six-foot-wide moat that overflows the outer rim to cascade over a green granite slab into a canal four feet below.

OPPOSITE, ABOVE LEFT The entry hall to the East Wing is dominated by a powerful Calder mobile.

OPPOSITE, ABOVE RIGHT A fusion of landscape and building.

OPPOSITE BELOW We placed low, circular planters in an open arrangement to complement Calder's work and Pei's soaring space.

ABOVE Magnolia blossoms carpet the ground outside the gallery entrance.

JOHN F. KENNEDY LIBRARY

BOSTON, MASSACHUSETTS, 1978

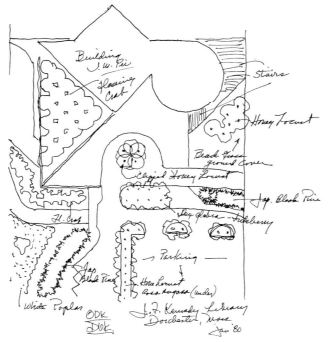

Unlike other projects, the starkness of the site called for a most direct experience of interior and exterior.

The approach to the Kennedy Library cuts through a swath of waving beach grass along the edge of Dorchester Bay, its progress noted by a parallel arc of short white cylinders. Bollards by definition, through competence of form these figures manage to evoke imagery of a receding line of columns that traces the crest of a dune. The drive's westward curve across the Columbia Point promontory is terminated by I. M.

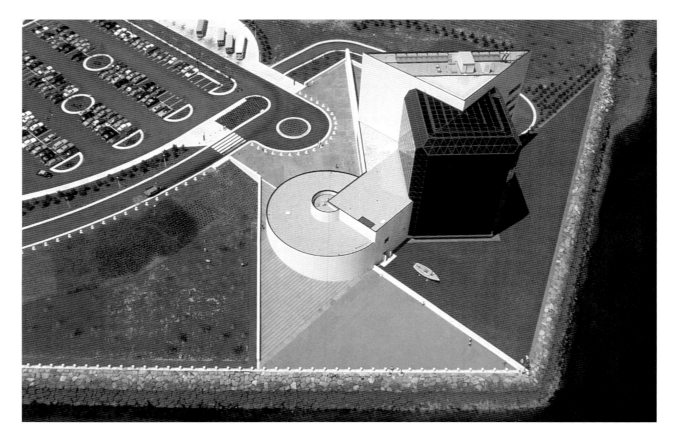

RIGHT Aerial view of Pei's library with arrival and parking on the left, Dorchester Bay (part of Boston Harbour) to the right.

LEFT Site plan which indicates parking at centre, museum at top, Rosa *rugosa* and beach-grass bank between entry drive and ocean on the right. Black pine is used as screening on all sides of the parking area.

BELOW LEFT As one approaches, the library's dark glass façade rises above a curtain of black pine.

85

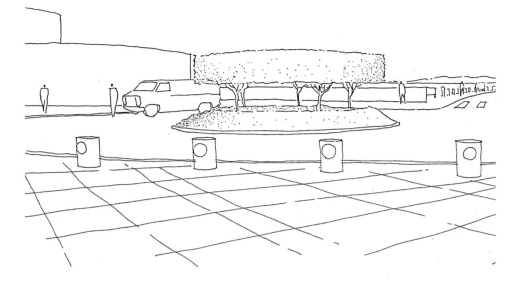

86

Pei's library building, a conjugation of triangle, cube and circle that houses a museum, an archival library and a research centre concerned with the Kennedy administration and contemporary issues. Unlike other projects in which we used interlocking spatial volumes to bring the play of tension and release from within the architecture outside, in this situation the starkness of the site called for a most direct experience of interior and exterior: there would be Pei's iconic forms, then the vast ocean and the Boston skyline, without the mediation of the middle ground usually provided by landscape constructs. Pei's beautiful building had to be revealed without screening its setting, without intrusion by irrelevant plantings. It had to be enhanced by the strength and structure of succinct plantings as they related spatially to the building, site and sea.

The site was a challenge. As a former landfill, below grade the earth seethed with methane gas that migrated horizontally from a nearby dump. An almost impervious clay lens on top of the fill caused severe drainage problems. (Because of prohibitive costs, only select areas of the site have drainage.) The conditions were so caustic that at one presentation to the Kennedy family, I suggested that we could lay a grid of pipes across the site, and at each intersection small valves would release a gas-fed flame to provide free night lighting. Senator Ted Kennedy jumped up and proclaimed, 'Magnificent!' Above grade, constant onshore and offshore winds presented an inhospitable planting situation of high exposure and potential salt damage. The site conditions were so harsh that the building foundation had to be wrapped in heavy plastic.

We realized soon into the project that our plant palette would be restricted to species that already existed on the site or that grew in similar situations – to specify anything outside that limited zone would be a waste of plant material and labour. Accordingly, we selected (and intensely researched) American beach grass to hold the thousand-foot-long, 3:1 slope that falls from the sweep of the entrance drive down to the ocean's edge. The beach-grass 'gallery' is an introduction to the unique character of the place. Some visitors will see it echoed in the oversized photo of President Kennedy, walking through dune grass at Hyannisport, that concludes the museum exhibit. Massings of Rosa *rugosa* line the entry drive as it nears the library. A circle of Sargeant's crab-apple – clipped to just six feet off grade – anchors the centre of the drop-off circle at the building's main entry. Black pines define the exit road and screen the parking area.

Away from the library, down at the water's edge, a paved walk follows the sea-wall. Waves roll in, brought by strong winds and shaped by the ocean's floor. John Kennedy's favourite sailboat, the *Victura*, is permanently secured on land, and tourists can find grassy areas to picnic a round it. We planted loose clumps of honey-locust in this area to provide light shade. Above the picnic areas, the beach-grass slope is accented with beach plum and bayberry shrub groups. Despite using the most rugged species, the plant material has had a tough time.

At the time of this project, I shared partnership of the firm with Ian Tyndall and Peter Ker Walker. We were invited to join the library design team by Mrs Paul Mellon, a landscape designer herself, noted for the rose garden at the White House. It was she who suggested that we use beach grass along the east bank of site. Our work was deeply inspired by the design of I. M. Pei, as well as by close work with the Kennedy family.

87

ABOVE The simple honey-locust grove and picnic ground which sit above the sea wall.

LEFT A view along the waterside walk.

OPPOSITE TOP Scheme for a ring of clipped Sargeant's crab at the drop-off area.

OPPOSITE MIDDLE Pei's striking creation and its wind-swept location were a challenge and an inspiration.

OPPOSITE BOTTOM *Rosa rugosa*, in the fore- and middle ground, is one of the hardy species we selected for tolerance to harsh conditions such as high wind, salt, exposure and poor soils.

LONDON STANDARD CHARTERED BANK

LONDON, ENGLAND, 1979

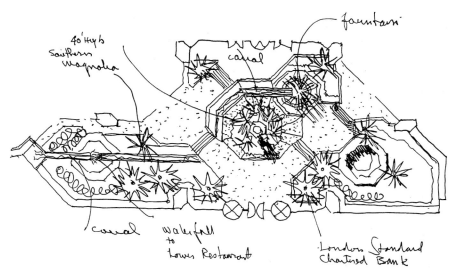

40' High
Southern
magnolia

fountain

canal

canal

waterfall
to
Lowes Restaurant

London Standard
Chartered Bank

The nine-storey atrium called for trees of significant stature or else the design would be a weak gesture, a floral carpet in the depths of the soaring space.

An intriguing aspect of the London Standard Chartered Bank atrium project was the search for plant materials. Inspired by the success of the Southern magnolia installation in the Ford Foundation atrium, we wanted the core of the bank's planting scheme to be these stately trees of rich, glossy foliage and creamy blossoms sybaritic in their generous dimensions.

My quest for appropriate magnolias began in Europe, for ease of transport to London. One afternoon in Milan, my wandering was interrupted by the sight of several fifty-foot-tall, precisely trimmed Southern magnolias set within a small courtyard. I knew immediately that these shaped trees – clipped and managed for years in a manner that I had never seen in the United States – were far more expressive in form for interior planting than the free-growing version I had used previously. I was informed that in Pistoia, outside Florence, many nurseries specialized in these pyramidal pruned magnolias. I immediately boarded a train, and as we tracked westwards, we passed field after flat field striped with long lines of tall magnolias, all clipped and shaped into strong postures.

After much appraisal and negotiation, the Baldacci and Matti nurseries agreed to provide us with sixteen *magnolia grandiflora*, stunning narrow specimens (eight-foot-diameter at the base of the canopy and tapered to a point). The next challenge was to transport the trees, which had flourished in the mild Italian climate, in a way that would not shock or retard their growth excessively. The nurseries built shade structures to acclimate the magnolias by subduing their voracious appetite for sunlight – cultivated in their youth in the fields of Tuscany – from approximately fifteen thousand

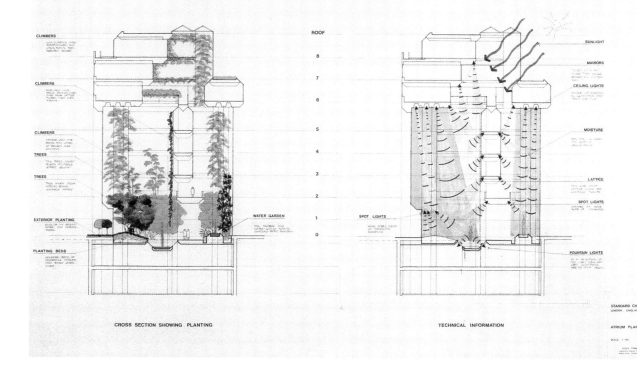

CLIMBERS

CLIMBERS

CLIMBERS

TREES

TREES

EXTERIOR PLANTING

PLANTING BEDS

ROOF

8

7

6

5

4

3

2

1

0

WATER GARDEN

CROSS SECTION SHOWING PLANTING

SPOT LIGHTS

SUNLIGHT

MIRRORS

CEILING LIGHTS

MOISTURE

LATTICE

SPOT LIGHTS

FOUNTAIN LIGHTS

TECHNICAL INFORMATION

STANDARD CHARTERED BANK
LONDON · ENGLAND

ATRIUM PLANTING

OPPOSITE BELOW The atrium entrance
as seen from the balcony of the upper
floor.

LEFT The study of light levels and plant
growth characteristics was a crucial
component of the project's
development.

BELOW LEFT An axonometric view of
the planting scheme.

89

foot-candles down to the twenty-five-hundred level that
would be the norm in the bank atrium. Lighting consultants
instructed us that once in place, the trees would need fourteen
hours of simulated sunlight per day between May and
September, less in winter months. Complex engineering,
lighting and irrigation plans were worked out by the
design team to accommodate these special needs.

Two years later, the trees were moved to south-west
England, heeled in the earth and encased in a plastic silo
system. During this period, Rochford Landscape Ltd acted as
caretaker, carrying out a meticulous maintenance programme.
In opportunistic retrospect, the silos were in the then-budding
tradition of environmental art: the installation was comprised
of sixteen three-storey translucent silos that marched down
a broad slope. One could just make out the magnolias'
branching and foliage beneath the heavy plastic sheets; they
resembled giant cocooned ghosts mired on the English moor.
While resting thus for three years, more than halfway into the
journey between Italy and London, the magnolias withstood
terrible winds and several harsh ice storms. Subsequently, we
felt confident about their resiliency and potential to survive.

In 1983, the magnolias were installed in their final
resting-place. Our design for the atrium of the London

Standard Chartered Bank was a studied response to its location, both within the financial district of London – more specifically, Bishopsgate redevelopment – and within the history of the bank itself. My partner at the time, Peter Ker Walker, was instrumental in devising a plan that accommodated the atrium's dual programme and double orientation.

Designed by the architecture firm of Fitzroy Robinson, the bank building is situated at the point where Threadneedle Street enters Bishopsgate at an angle. While our floor plan originally called for a regular grid to be laid across the atrium as the organizing framework, we soon altered this strategy to achieve equal orientation towards both entrances, thereby respecting the ancient pedestrian thoroughfare. Thus, the grid became a matrix of octagons, a frame that admits

significantly more angles, axes and points of reference with which to order space. The nine-storey atrium called for trees of significant stature or else the design would be a weak gesture, a floral carpet in the depths of the soaring space. Most interior plantings are too diverse for their limited area – in this project, we endeavoured to simplify and create a quiet but rich palette of materials.

At the bank's main entrance, a grove of four magnolias ushers in customers and passers-through. Set within the grove, peering through backlit branches, a statue of one of the bank's distinguished founders greets observant visitors. This statue was found at a branch of the bank in India and was at first deemed inappropriate for current use. But when I examined it, it seemed perfect for the atrium. Design is not about fancy drawings, but

90

RIGHT Water pours out of the channels and cascades to a café at lower levels.

91

about seeing and recognizing something that is unique, then using it correctly.

The spatial and programmatic relationships of the atrium are expressed in part with water. At the VIP entrances, water sources bubble up and flow into a free-standing granite-walled canal. As it traverses the floor, the waterway delineates various spatial compartments with its raised canal system. The water runs over river-washed stones and pebbles, falling alongside or flowing under stairs that mark grade changes. At one point, the water cascades down a cylindrical aperture in the floor plane, falling into a café on the lower level. A second source of water emanates from a pool at the Crosby Square entrance. Once inside the main doors of the atrium, visitors must literally cross over the canal in order to enter the inner bank offices.

Magnolia, crab-apple, ficus and bamboo, placed individually or grouped, are vertical members within the spatial structure of the atrium. The trees are underplanted with a variety of ground covers and low shrubs, including java fig, creeping fig, dwarf pittosporum, laurel, rhododendron, cotoneaster, herald trumpet, bougainvillea and ivy. The ground covers are meant to be low and flat to express the arched contour, which reaches into the base of the trees.

In a planting situation as contained as the atrium, lighting, humidity and irrigation must be rigorously monitored. In addition, the maintenance staff is vigilant to secure the bank's green investment from unsolicited interests, in particular the mealy-bug, red spider mite, greenfly, fungus and sooty mould.

Along the balconies of upper levels, we continued our strategy of dense massing of plant material – primarily Ficus *benjamina* or crab underplanted with English ivy – for texture and to heighten the contrast between built, static structure and dynamic spaces. Overall, I hoped the plantings would not only soften the architecture, but proactively create a quality of dispersed dimensionality throughout the atrium. We wanted to develop an elusive sense of space that could not be experienced all at once; it is revealed gradually, found amongst refulgent layers.

Due to the successful complexity of engineering, plant care and careful design, the bank atrium plantings thrived and became an important node in the urban fabric of the Bishopsgate redevelopment. Sadly, the atrium suffered extensive damage in a bombing incident in the early 1990s. Its current condition aside, however, the project is well documented and stands as a useful study for future interior design with living materials.

SPACE WITHIN PLACE: UNITY, MYSTERY AND INFINITY

In the fourth decade of my career, our designs began to exhibit a complexity that was unlike the unabashed Platonic geometries seen in earlier works. Always intent on solving problems rather than decorating, we adhered to the mode of drawing the strongest diagram from the site, the client and the context. In contrast with the clarity of order-follows-function that characterizes preceding projects, and building upon a definitive response to context, by the late 1970s designs emerging from our office were crafted landscape encounters, constructed with layers of pattern, volume and time woven together. The result: the essence of infinity, the perpetration of nature's mystery.

In this period, my partners and I became well versed in systems of order and scale, still using classic tools (lines or grids of trees, planes of grass and water, repetition and rhythm) to form newly organic geometries. The geometries are often irregular but always balanced. Above all, geometries – usually expressed first as a pavement pattern on the ground plane, then seen in the modulation of plant beds and water elements, and finally confirmed with tree placements – instill a unity that relates directly to building and context. Spatial volumes that accommodate programmatic elements – blocks of trees, rows of hedge or ground cover, water walls and fountains – are integrated into the underlaying, unifying order in a harmonic manner.

Unlike earlier projects that revel, but do not intercede, in the cycle of the seasons, several works from this era actually manipulate nature's behaviour to bring a more thoughtful meaning to the site design. The poetic system of blossom collection and distribution at NationsBank Plaza is one example of this. At Fountain Place, the Dallas Art Museum and the Henry Moore Sculpture Garden in Kansas City, one can find more evidence of our efforts to bring a sense of place alive with the activation of space and time unified by geometric continuity.

OPPOSITE Fountain Place Plaza

3

THE DALLAS MUSEUM OF ART

DALLAS, TEXAS, 1983

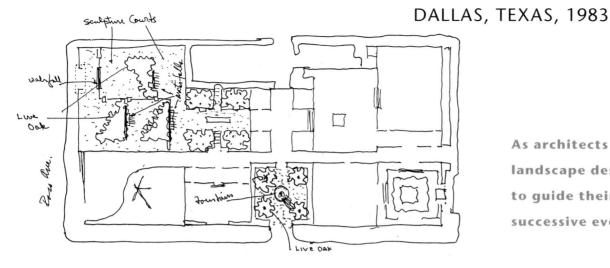

Sculpture Courts

waterfall

Live Oak

Ross Ave.

Fountains

LIVE OAK

As architects of a living medium, landscape designers have a mandate to guide their work through its successive evolutionary stages.

Just three blocks from Fountain Place, the City of Dallas commissioned a new museum to house its eclectic and growing international art collection. The museum was to play an important role as the terminus of the soon-to-be-announced Arts District's central spine. With it, the Dallas Arts District Consortium was championing a national trend by encouraging public and private investors to come together in the promotion of a 'lively pedestrian environment and distinctive urban setting'. For us, setting a stage for the art was as crucial as the pieces themselves. Edward Larrabee Barnes designed the museum, and its eight-foot-high exterior walls of Indiana limestone, to enclose a total of 193,000 square feet of exhibition space. Barnes's scheme included an outdoor sculpture garden, divided into

RIGHT Aerial view of the museum's sculpture garden and vaulted entrance. Triangular blocks of live oaks establish a strong geometric play against the building's mass and the steel Snelson sculpture behind.

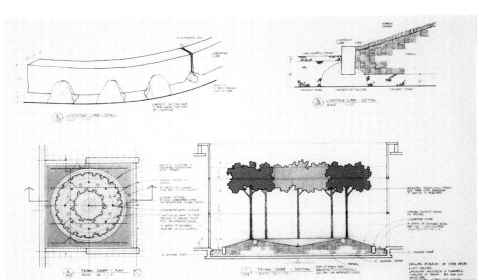

LEFT Plan view of musuem showing sculpture garden on the left, inner courtyards, parking on the right, and street trees. Strong plantings were used to create continuity of interior and exterior space as well as integrate the overall complex into the city.

BELOW Planting and wall details of the Tribal Court.

95

'rooms' by free-standing water walls, which we brought to fruition with planting plans.

The museum's main entrance is a recessed court that faces tree-lined Flora Street (the Arts District's central thoroughfare). At each corner of the cobblestone entry plaza, a live oak tree stands guard. With three-inch calipers, the trees were meekly undersized when installed, but in time they gained sufficient stature to participate in the building's proportions of massing and void. A circular fountain at the centre of the plaza swings circulation to the sides and prevents visitors from approaching head-on. This simple manoeuvre embellishes the arrival sequence. The fountain basin's curved perimeter and wide diameter balances the museum's barrel-vaulted entrance.

Once inside, visitors encounter a central gallery. Turning left, one enters an open-air sculpture court, protected from the city street by perimeter walls. Three freestanding water walls partition the court into individual 'rooms'. In each one, a stepped triangular plant bed holds a small grove of live oaks. Beneath the oaks, spring bulbs hover briefly inches from the ground, bright but temporary focal points above the evergreen vinca and Asian jasmine. These are quiet spaces. Muted colours and subtle textures permeate and materialize as cut planes of stone, water, crushed stone and framed views of the Texas sky above. Grasses, ground covers and climbing vines are used as architectural veneers: a delicate tracery of Boston

and English ivy clings to the stone walls, a foreground to their austere simplicity.

The essential element of the garden rooms are the water walls. Designed by Allistair Bevington of Ed Barnes's firm, these glistening structures are at once spatial divisions within an open floor plan, a background for plantings and seating areas, and a tripartite sculpture of liquid bas-relief. The fall of water is refreshing in the arid Dallas climate, and its murmur pulls visitors away from city sounds. A narrow canal at the base of each wall catches water and recycles it through the system. All three catchments turn ninety degrees at the

LEFT Japanese wisteria climbs cables set into the limestone wall and erupts in a green froth overhead.

end of the water walls, in effect creating a reason for their termination, and join each other to form a singular line of water that stretches towards the court's north wall. The ribbon of water acts with the water walls to define three compartments. Massive works of art stand in the gardens.

There are three interior garden rooms as well: the Tribal Court, the Dining Court and the Wisteria Court. In the small Tribal Court, we planted a ring of ficus trees in a raised planter with a dome of Zoysia grass below. The scheme is an uncomplicated response to a shaded alcove of limited dimensions. It is a design of minimal ingredients for maximum energy.

It is the bane, or perhaps the beauty, of many designed landscapes that significant and ongoing care is required not only to preserve day-to-day appearances, but to ensure that the design's structure evolves fully. This was true at the Dallas Museum, as project manager Chris Dunn pointed out, because 'the citizenry looks to the museum as a standard of culture and elegance, and the grounds conditions, if unkept, can easily detract from such an experience.' When crucial aspects of the maintenance schedule – the particular pruning regimen for the live oak and yaupon holly, or the dethatching and aeration needs of the planting beds, for instance – are ignored, the link between building and designed landscape is weakened, the synthesis between art and its context is muted. As architects of a living medium, landscape designers have a mandate to guide their work through its successive evolutionary stages – or relinquish its integrity.

LEFT A narrow water channel cuts through the sculpture garden as a glistening band which segments space and reflects light.

BELOW Spring bulbs and ground cover beneath live oaks bring colour and the cycling of seasons to the garden in contrast to the immutable sculpture.

FOUNTAIN PLACE

DALLAS, TEXAS, 1985

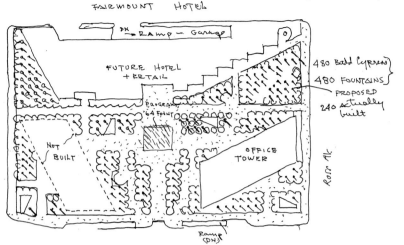

I love the plaza when all is still, and one can see the reflection of endless rows of trees in the clear pools.

I may have startled architect Harry Cobb of Pei, Cobb, Freed when I announced on my first visit to the Bank Tower site: 'You will walk on water!' Rarely before had I been struck so soundly and quickly by a vision for a project. My first impression was a reaction to everything the place was not. Yes, this arid urban plaza in the heart of Dallas could be transformed into acres of cascading, cooling water. It was just what the city needed: an urban swamp. Not a replication of nature, but a compacted experience of nature so intense that it would be almost super-natural. A place so unusual and so refreshing that it would draw visitors from outside the city to come in for picnics; office workers would venture out of air-conditioned hallways to be enveloped in the clamour of falling water and the particles of moisture carried on the breeze; people would stay downtown at night to attend parties amongst the illuminated cypress trees and glowing fountains.

Fortunately, the owners and architects agreed that their sixty-storey glass tower would benefit from such a surrounding. We knew what the end result should be – a weaving together of water, trees and pavement into an animated composition that could change by the hour and by the season, a place in direct contrast with the hard constancy of the city. We then had to work backwards and examine exactly how the concept would fit the site. The six-acre lot is bounded by busy Ross Avenue and Field Street and is adjacent to Dallas's growing Arts District. The grade drops twelve feet between the two streets; this had to be accommodated in a manner that would not disrupt heavy pedestrian traffic through the site. From this condition came the realization that not only would

the site be all water, but it would actually be a giant waterfall, or a series of smaller drops, to negotiate the grade change.

Under the direction of Peter Ker Walker, our design team worked for three years to develop a site diagram that included a network of wide slate-stepped walkways and ramps. The walkways meet in the middle of the site to form a central plaza for large gatherings. A computerized system of 160 jets is embedded in the pavement of the plaza. Engineered by WET Enterprises, the jets can be programmed to move in choreographed displays of various geometric shapes. The feature can be set to operate with accompanying music and is illuminated at night for spectacular effects. Since the jets are recessed, the central plaza can also be used with the water turned off.

The walkways, central plaza and tower itself are the only solid ground on site. The remaining seventy per cent of the acreage is a carefully constructed set of shallow pools, through which 650,000 gallons are pumped daily. Water bubbles up at regular intervals across the water's surface, maintaining a constant depth as it spills over descending levels in its journey from one end of the garden to the other. Debris is filtered from the water, and the system continually recycles. Walkways are edged with a weir-and-gutter system that allows the paved surface to be flush with the water – a play of solid and liquid, the mechanism by which one can indeed appear to walk on water.

A forest of 220 bald cypress trees rises out of the water. Each tree is set in an individual seven-foot-diameter concrete well that expands to ten-foot-diameter below the water's surface. The planters are fifteen feet on centre (it is critical to

RIGHT The interplay of water and glass reflection links plaza and tower and intensifies the depth of space.

BELOW RIGHT The grid of bald cypress and low water jets is a continuous, unifying element across the entire plaza.

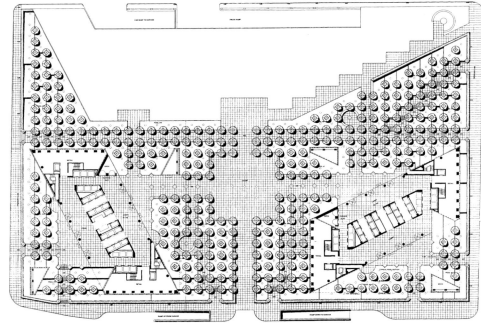

get the trees close together for the strongest spatial effect) and form a grid across the site. A separate irrigation system feeds the trees, as they cannot be exposed to the treated fountain water. In the early stages of the project, I was told by several people that it would be impossible to locate so many trees of one species, all at the same size and adapted to the same conditions. My response was, 'Well, have you tried?' We found the trees, all of excellent form and character, at a nursery in Georgia.

Honey-locust and London plane were briefly considered as alternate options for the trees. But we felt that the bald

TOP From above, the texture of cypress branching and roiling water create a rich tapestry.

ABOVE Plan view of plaza with footprint of towers.

LEFT Aerial view of plaza in winter, when the bare trees are ghostlike.

cypress was the most appropriate choice for several reasons. First, like the others it is a deciduous tree and thus emphasizes an awareness of seasonal change within downtown Dallas, yet its tiny needles are less likely than the leaves of a broad-leafed tree to clog the pool and cascade system when they drop; second, the cypress is native to Texas and a water-based environment; and finally, I felt that the height of the cypress would work successfully with the prismatic Bank Tower. The architects were very aware of these issues, and in fact discussions with them helped finalize some of our decisions. They were concerned that the trees beneath the tower's entrance would not receive enough daylight and installed grow-lights in the soffit. The trees are now seventy feet high.

There was concern initially that the cypresses would be stunted by the growing conditions. Although I reassured the owners that we merely needed to apply my special fertilizer, 'Up', it turned out that what we really needed was the other stuff, 'Down'. After twelve years of maturation, the trees have grown quickly, and we are now faced with a decision about how to tame their vigour. As it stands, the grid of cypresses is a splendour of living order. Although exciting with the

OPPOSITE LEFT Descending cascades articulate the drop in grade across the site. Concrete-block planting drums echo this movement yet maintain grade level alongside the tower.

OPPOSITE RIGHT From within the plaza, bubblers and tree trunks proceed in all directions, drawing visitors further into the oasis.

RIGHT Workers from nearby offices, passing shoppers and curious tourists are soothed by shade and the giant waterworks' cooling effect within the hot city.

BELOW RIGHT The magic of Fountain Place is that when one is there, one is soothed by the sensation of waterfalls, rivers and tree-filled swamps within the heart of Dallas.

RIGHT At night, each of the 263 bubblers is lit from within via encased wet lights.

BELOW The glowing eruptions flicker like stars on the pools' dark surfaces.

fountains turned on, I love the plaza when all is still, and one can see the reflection of endless rows of trees in the pools. There is a poetic starkness to the scene in the winter months.

At Fountain Place, we hoped to achieve a complete transformation of urban space. With the most basic materials – water, trees and concrete – and skilled engineers, a place of wonder was created. The plaza is outside the parameters of conventional urban design; in fact, it is said to be the most extensive water garden built since the Renaissance (this despite the fact that just half of the original plan has been implemented thus far). The architectural critic David Dillon described Fountain Place as 'a unique combination of precise geometry and luxuriant nature, reason and sensation intertwined'. I see it as a chance to connect people with the essential ingredients of life.

ABOVE LEFT With the overflows illuminated, it appears that light, not water, is the fluid element which falls from level to level.

ABOVE I love the idea that the fountains are used as a stage for festive gatherings – the plaza provides the type of place for activity and public celebration that all cities need.

LEFT Dramatic lighting unifies plaza and tower and reveals Fountain Place as a room within the encompassing urban theatre.

NATIONSBANK PLAZA
TAMPA, FLORIDA, 1988

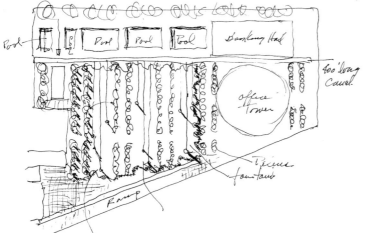

Our work was an attempt to release people into space, to provide an experience different from the city surround – like the ancient concept of Paradise.

In the mid-1980s, architect Harry Wolf asked me to join him in the transformation of a vacant riverside lot in downtown Tampa into a corporate headquarters with a garden open to the public. Harry had designed a powerful thirty-three-storey tower of simple form and delicate proportioning. He suggested that we extend the tower's fenestration pattern – based on the Fibonacci series – to the plaza as a way of linking building and park. Like the Golden Mean, the Fibonacci series represents a very simple set of true, harmonic relationships that occur in nature and that serve as the foundation of many cultures' architectural orders. In design, the concept is applied to proportional ratios of elements.

At NationsBank (formerly NCNB) Plaza, we translated the mathematical sequence, just as the architect had done to determine tower radius, floor heights, dimension and frequency of window punctures, into the dimensions of the walkways and the pattern of the paving stones. We then stepped back and considered how the site fitted into the urban context. Using this study, we laid out the primary circulation paths in the park as extensions of the city grid.

The site occupies a 4½-acre wedge along the Hillsborough River, with a parking garage underneath. Although public, the park is not directly accessible from the street. To enter it, visitors cross over a line of five large, square pools that parallel Ashley Street and are flush with the sidewalk. Throughout the park, water is revealed in various incarnations: a wide, luminous canal as portal; still, gleaming pools as cleansing transition from city to oasis; narrow runnels threading grass planes into a single whole; animated jets and bubblers as focal and gathering points; a fertile water garden for children's play and education. The placement and treatment of water elements, etched over the initial site diagram of walkways, became the park's infrastructure. Thus, a weaving of circulation – pedestrian and water – expresses an underlying order. A wide ramp and stair ascend the eight feet from entry level below the canal up to the interior park. Nine water channels issue from low

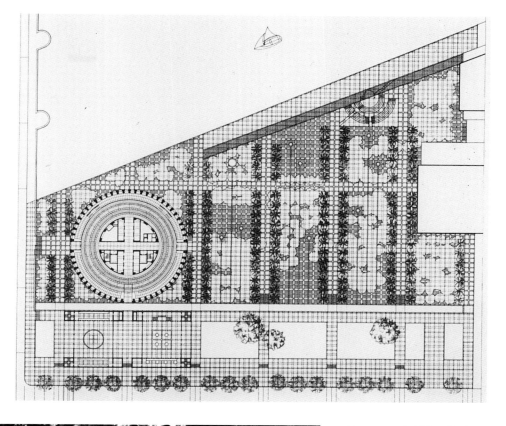

107

OPPOSITE LEFT Aerial view of bank tower and cube with canal and park at centre.

OPPOSITE RIGHT Loosely scattered crape myrtles spill over the ordered ground plane and create a play of tension and release.

ABOVE Plan view of the park with footprint of tower and adjacent office.

LEFT The geometrically ordered paving scheme covers the entire site, with thirteen-foot open modules for planted areas and solid bands for walkways.

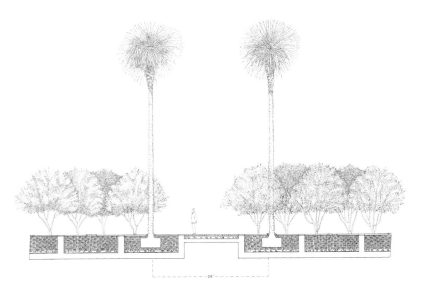

OPPOSITE LEFT To enter the park, visitors pass beneath a four-hundred-foot-long plexiglass-bottomed canal. This is also the access to the parking garage.

OPPOSITE RIGHT The canal strikes out from the bank buildings and announces the park structure. A single tree rises out of each pool at street level.

LEFT A sketch by Peter Shaudt shows in section the relationship between understorey flowering trees (parkland) and soaring palms (circulation).

BELOW Custom-designed stone furniture adds a solid, sculptural touch within the ephemerality of blossoms and foliage.

108

bubblers and cut across the site to join the canal on the
perpendicular.

The best designs begin with a clearly stated structure,
which I think of as the expression of human order on the land.
Yet the next step is equally critical, and without it a design is
diminished into a static exercise: to bring a sense of mystery,
loose rhythm and infinite expansiveness to a design. At
Tampa, once the structure and order had been established,
we sprinkled eight hundred crape myrtle trees randomly
over the bed of precision. Between the clarity and the spirit,
a reaction occurs that in turn produces what one might
understand as a third and final overlay of the site design.
This aspect cannot really be designed at all; it consists of the
phenomena that occur as a landscape evolves throughout
seasons and time. They are the true beauty of landscape
design; they reveal the soul of the site: early spring green buds
silhouetted against clear blue sky, ice drops caught on the
underside of a branch, a suddenly bursting fountain inciting
the screams and dances of children. Our work at Tampa
was an attempt to release people into space, to provide an
experience markedly different from that of the city surround
– much like the ancient Persian concept of Paradise.

ABOVE The patterned ground plane extends into the water garden near the Tampa Museum entrance.

RIGHT AND BELOW A low bubbler catches late sunlight in ripples which play against the integrated basins. Crape myrtle blossoms are caught in the water channels and flow into the main canal, where they drift overhead at the entrance.

FAR RIGHT In the children's garden, a checkerboard of five-foot-square beds is filled with dwarf yaupon holly, jasmine and parkinsonia trees.

NELSON-ATKINS MUSEUM OF ART: THE HENRY MOORE SCULPTURE GARDEN
KANSAS CITY, MISSOURI, 1988

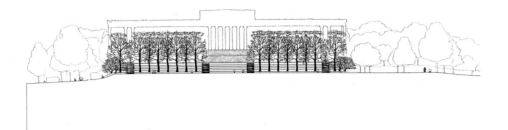

The project was an attempt to provide a space in which artworks could be displayed as the integral anatomy of a garden.

On the grounds of the Nelson-Atkins Museum of Art in Kansas City, the Henry Moore Sculpture Garden combines a setting that befits a superb collection of fourteen Moore sculptures with a valuable addition to the city's park system. The design evolved from intensive study of the site and its context within the city; the two cannot be isolated from one another. While the small-scale details of sculpture placement were critical, more challenging to us was the opportunity to produce a truly classic work in keeping with the museum's Beaux-Arts character (constructed in 1933). The design programme included a master plan for the adjacent property, which, when implemented, will add another seventeen acres to the garden to the west and south. My office collaborated on the project with the architect Jaquelin Robertson; together, we set out to build spatial links and shape the grounds into an ordered series of connected graceful volumes.

We strove to mould the land itself. Five earth shelves are cut into the slope that descends from a balustrade at the museum's south façade. Clipped grass provides a smooth, unmistakably well-tended surface on each tier. These long, level planes of grass, or *tapis vert*, are succinctly defined by bands of Japanese yew – the dense evergreen contrasts with the grass and sets up an isometric rhythm of alternating colour and texture. The effect of the yew is important: the change in plant material emphasizes the change in grade separating the stepped lawns, thereby encouraging a sense of serial spaces through which visitors move, much like the galleries within the museum. From above, one does not see the evergreen material, only lawn stretching away from the museum's balustrade. From

RIGHT Preliminary site plan of the museum grounds and sculpture garden (only the upper half has been realized).

Ginkgo trees planted on five ascending terraces read as one bosque from below the museum's south façade.

BELOW RIGHT Aerial view which reveals the final site design as an extension of the museum's classically composed façade. Meandering sculpture walks are seen on either side of the main lawn.

below, the surface of the tiers is barely visible, and the yew reads as a wall that forms a base beneath the museum.

In working out the site diagram, we found that the strongest solution was to express the park's complementary relationship to the building with the circulation system, then layer on top of that a planting plan that would give form to the programme. The grading scheme mediates between the two: it gives topographic impact to the green spatial structure, as well as enunciates pedestrians' experience of the place. A broad corridor extends out from the museum's central portico and descends the sculpture terraces via white concrete steps set flush with the grass. This corridor opens a grand axial vista, framed by ginkgo trees planted in a staggered double line on each terrace. These trees create a three-dimensionality within which Moore's *Reclining Figure* nestles. The ginkgo has a dramatic character; it is itself a dynamic sculpture that heightens the effect of human work and stands out against the plain surface of grass. The ginkgoes' thrusting branches and golden fall foliage bring levity and a graceful agility to the solidity of the artwork. And since they have an open habit and relatively sparse leafing, as the ginkgoes mature they will not put the bronze sculpture – which basks in the sunlight – in shadow.

The descending motion of the stepped tiers comes to rest at a stone crosswalk. From this point, the terrain becomes uniform in a wide grass mall that stretches to the south, bracketed by parallel *allées* of Redmond linden (a hardy species developed in Nebraska). Limestone 'zipper' paths edge both sides of the mall and are lined by five staggered rows of lindens planted in square yew panels. This simple, highly ordered space is articulated by the pattern of grass, stone and yew and is animated by shifting matrices of light and shadow. Views are maintained without interruption, but are metred by the fixed tree trunks as visitors walk through.

The formal organization of the main space contrasts with more intimately scaled parkland to the east and west. Vine-covered pavilions of trellised steel, standing at either end of

OPPOSITE ABOVE The wide walkways draw the visitor's eye from the building out into the distant landscape.

OPPOSITE BELOW Soon after installation, the grading and paving are the visually dominant site characteristics; over time the ginkgoes and lindens mature to provide a canopy layer and spatial volume.

LEFT Moore's *Reclining Figure* basks amongst the ginkgoes in its open-air gallery.

115

the transectional walkway at the base of the tiers, serve as gateways into irregular groves, gently sloped open spaces and meandering paths of red brick. In this informal sector of the museum grounds, sculpture is tucked into the trees and topography, to allow visitors a sense of discovery and to provide a variety of staging for the pieces. Moore's *Three Way Piece No. One: Points* and *Upright Motive No. 9* can be found amongst groupings of flowering trees, set on stone plinths above bases of evergreens and spring bulbs. At the end of one path, visitors are met by *Seated Woman. Sheep Piece* sits on a grassy shelf of the great lawn. The winding brick paths eventually connect to create a continuous, complete circuit through the sculpture glades.

Our original plans called for the lower seventeen acres of the museum grounds to be a continuation of the open mall, separated from the existing segment by an elevated belvedere (which does double duty as the paved pedestrian crosswalk for Brush Creek Boulevard). Circular groves 150 feet in diameter, of tulip-poplar, red oak or other statuesque species, were to join together to form an immense ring. This ceremonial gathering space is centred on the main axis of the museum, yet it begins to soften the rigour of the site structure by blending constructed space into and out of more natural forest.

Our original plans also called for a large rectangular pool as the southern terminus of the museum grounds where Brush Creek crosses the property. Existing trees were to be incorporated, their bodies pushing the pool edges into unexpected curves (I love the idea that the nature of trees intervenes in the controlled geometry of the pool). Works by the Swedish sculptor Carl Milles are displayed on a little island. We designed the pool not just as a compositional element, but primarily in response to the need for a retention pond for the development. In a way, this water feature connects the museum grounds to the region far more instrinsically than any road system: Brush Creek is fed by the regional watershed; its waters flow through the pool and imply a connection to the museum, to culture from nature.

Soon after the installation, Roger K. Lewis described the sculpture garden in *Museum News* as 'a peaceful refuge, civic destination, and urban landmark in which nature is in balance with construction'. While I hope this is true, the project was also an attempt to provide a space in which artworks could be displayed as the integral anatomy of a garden, a technique practised to good effect in Europe, Asia and other cultures. This type of exploration differs from the

ABOVE The sense of perspective condenses and expands from various points within the grounds, as one moves from the open meadow to the more enclosed lawn tiers.

idea of sculpture parks or environmental art that have sprung up in the past two or three decades. Here, we were constructing a garden to best display completed works of art, whereas the other solution usually supports art and landscape as simultaneous, symbiotic developments, viewing both as materials to be manipulated into one, codified expression. At the Nelson-Atkins, we sought a unity of two bodies – sculpture and garden – that does not blur the distinction between the two, but rather contrasts them in a complementary manner, resulting in a richer whole.

RIGHT Our signature 'zipper path' allows grass to flow through the walk and therefore does not interupt the continuity of the ground plane.

BELOW RIGHT Architecturally cut banks and tiers energize the land form and become part of the overall site order.

HALL HOUSE
MISSION HILLS, KANSAS, 1991

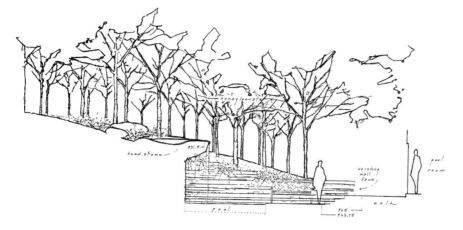

A dialogue between existing features and applied design brings forth the natural beauty of key predecessor elements.

In the pool room of the Hall House, we set out to create an environment rich in colour and light. Two robust Phoenix *roebelini* palm trees were placed in balance at one end. We planted creeping fig vines in pots against the mullions of floor-to-ceiling French doors, and in just a few years, the vines crept up the walls in a woody web that reaches across the ceiling. My office researched maps of the constellations before sketching out a night-sky scene for the bottom of the children's pool: *Ursa minor* and *major*, the Pleiades and other figures are spelled out in tiny gold tiles against a blue background. A custom-designed bronze cover allows kids to play around a central fountain. The larger pool is also lined with blue and gold glass tiles and scored with strips of black terrazzo at expanding and compressing intervals to induce a heightened experience of speed as swimmers pass over. Cut modules of earth-toned Chinese slate – a muted medley of warm beige, russets and rust – compose solid flooring around the pool.

The entire property is screened by an arbor-vitae hedge except for the street edge. Here, we planted a line of oaks to match the predominant species on site and to link with the greater suburban community. The dense evergreen perimeter is interrupted intermittently by existing trees. This immediately gives the screen a correspondence with the original site and its vegetation, as well as allowing occasional views over into the neighbour's garden. Along one side of the front acreage, a line of ginkgoes stands against the cedar backdrop, gesticulating with horizontal, thrusting branches and fan-shaped leaves. The entry drive meanders gently around existing clumps of mature oak. As with the broken perimeter hedge, this strategy elicits a dialogue between existing features and applied design – a condition that, while not desirable for many sites, in this situation brings forth the natural beauty and meaningful presence of key predecessor elements.

At the front of the house, the drive turns and widens into a granite pad with granite edging. The façade itself has a poised air that we thought would be best complemented by

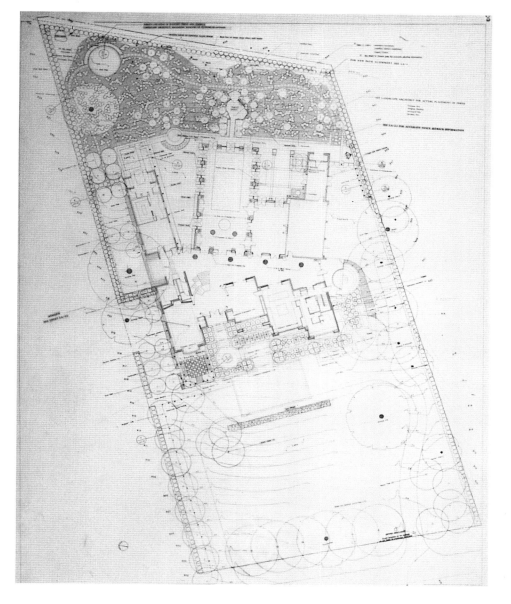

more of an outdoor vestibule than a simple drive court. Light steel-mesh bollards mark the edges and match the front gate, which we also designed. The court is further delineated by a low hedge of clipped yew. From this plateau, the grass lawn, riddled with oaks, falls away freely towards the property line. The front door of the house is flanked by stepped limestone planting beds designed by the architect. We filled the beds with flowering crab, magnolia, cotoneaster, vinca and English ivy. This gregarious arrangement welcomes visitors and contrasts with the more subdued tone elsewhere.

A private sauna and outdoor hot-tub complex is attached to the master suite. Here, we provided an intimate garden enclosed by evergreen hedges, concrete-block wall (painted

OPPOSITE The stone grotto offers a sense of mystery and a literal oasis within suburban Kansas.

ABOVE Site plan of the Hall House and grounds.

HALL HOUSE

RIGHT and **FAR RIGHT** Two palms contribute to the indoor pool's exotic appearance; the room's plush decoration contrasts with the general strong simplicity of the architecture.

BELOW RIGHT A concrete-block wall encloses the master-suite sauna and connects to a stone hot tub.

OPPOSITE Broad limestone columns demarcate the pool court on one side and a vinca-carpeted honey-locust grove on the other.

white) with steel-mesh gates (painted white) and a twelve-inch white aluminium grid extending overhead. I left a pattern of gaps in the block wall, primarily as wind slots but also for visual rhythm within the enclosure. From this little enclave, our original plans called for a water channel and cascades to descend on axis from the outer woodland into the indoor pool. I like this use of water to link indoor and outdoor space, although this element is not yet built. However, a grotto, at fifteen by ten feet just large enough to fit two people on its sunken deck, has been built. The grotto is cut into the hillside and faced with local stone. Water drips down its layered, mossy face into a carp pool. The multiple varieties of ferns, hollies and mosses that we planted around the moist edges have thrived and now spill over the dry-laid stones.

Above the grotto, above the house and its connected outdoor living spaces, we planted a forest of honey-locusts, rising above a shadbush and holly understorey. Stepping-stones set in vinca and bulbs wander loosely up the brief slope, then enter the grove. A circular seating area – the archetypal clearing within a forest, here neatly prepared and controlled – provides a destination for those who follow the path away from the house; a semi-circle of yew around the perimeter is a balustrade to gaze back over towards it.

LEFT Architect Harry Weese's modular façade and the entry court as seen from the tree-studded lawn.

BELOW LEFT Clipped yew gives form to an exedra of smooth grass tucked into the woods.

RIGHT A winding stone path, set into vinca and other forest ground covers, leads to the forest clearing.

FOX RESIDENCE
CLAYTON, MISSOURI, 1991

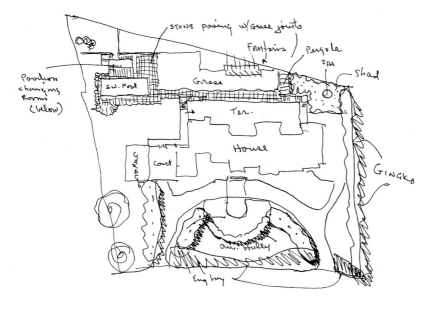

Our design was intended to give the family some measure of privacy, yet emphasize a visual connection out into the adjacent park.

At the Fox Residence, I set out to compose an entry sequence and a series of exterior living-rooms that could integrate logically with the existing house. Bounded on the north and south by neighbours and to the east by a town road, the property opens on its west side to the pastoral acres of Carrswold Park. Our design was intended to give the family some measure of privacy, yet emphasize a visual connection out into the adjacent green park.

To enter the property, one follows a semi-circular drive that loops from the town road to the front door. This arrangement extends the arrival sequence, literally in linear feet and the time required to gain access, but also in the perceived relationship of the house to the road and the public realm. In contrast, a perpendicular intersection of entry drive and house would have a foreshortening effect. The inner curve of the drive is lined with littleleaf lindens, set fourteen feet on centre.

At the apex of the drive, the tree line breaks and opens up to an ornamental planting: an arc of American holly that encircles a bed of cotoneaster. A horseshoe-shaped pool and concrete-block water wall are set into this green tableau on axis with the front door, providing a focal point as one enters and leaves the house. Statues of sleeping lions flank the pool and are echoed by matching specimen Japanese maples on either side of the door. I have recently suggested that the owners construct a tasting room for their wine cellar beneath the pool. Given a glass bottom, the pool would then act as a membrane casting shimmering, waving light down into the room below.

The back, or west, side of the house is subdivided into outdoor rooms. Extending out from the living-room, a

124

BELOW Site plan of the Fox Residence and grounds.

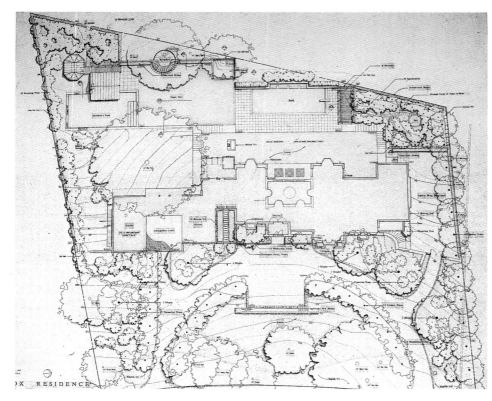

RIGHT From the house above, the pool
and pavilion appear as an extension of
outdoor living space.

BELOW RIGHT The stone-and-grass
joint surface knits together the
pavilion, pool and open-air dining
terrace into a continuous composition.

BOTTOM RIGHT Detail plan and
sections of interior atrium.

125

checkerboard terrace of twelve-by-twelve-inch stone pavers
set into grass carries the entertainment floor from within to
outside. The terrace is separated from the park margin by a
six-foot-high arbor-vitae hedge, a figural gesture that
parallels the house and plays an important role in the site
structure. Although the hedge provides clear definition
of the terrace volume, I feel that it is a somewhat static
arrangement that could be energized by placing a second,
taller hedge line behind the first. With a segment removed
at the centre of the front line, a sense of depth would be
created between the two rows, much like the sensation of
successive layers of curtain sweeping back from centre
stage in a theatre.

A wooden pergola anchors the north side of the living-
room terrace. Planted with vines, the pergola is an extension
of the house into the land and is used as a tool to moderate
spatial flow as well as an indication of programme change.
In the corner partitioned off by the pergola, a copse of
shadbush trees, ferns and mosses creates a micro-environment
that responds less to its context than to the client's request
for an intimately scaled garden. To the south, a smoothly
mown grass panel separates the living-room terrace from a
swimming pool, spa and pavilion. Acting as a headboard
at the far end of the pool, another wall of arbor vitae screens
the neighbour's yard. We detailed the pavilion with light,
black steel members and antique glass clerestory panels.
As the grade drops away from the pavilion's outer wall, we
planned a set of attached steps, additional plantings and a
covered viewing platform beside the park.

TRANSVERSE ELEVATION

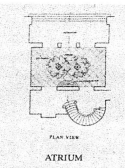

PLAN VIEW

ATRIUM

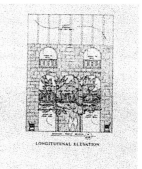

LONGITUDINAL ELEVATION

FOX RESIDENCE

RIGHT Secret garden adjacent to the house, partitioned off from 'public' areas by a pergola and enveloped in a shadbush grove.

FAR RIGHT Interior shot of the pool pavilion and fireplace.

BELOW Elevation, section and detail of a proposed viewing platform.

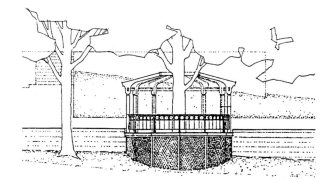

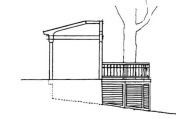

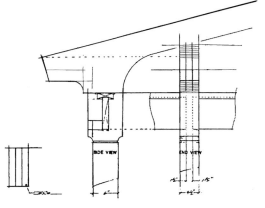

LEFT Schematic sketch of the pavilion and pool with a water wall at the far end.

BELOW The pavilion's light steel columns are designed for a delicate effect which does not impede awareness of the surrounding forest from within.

127

LEAR RESIDENCE

BRENTWOOD, CALIFORNIA 1990

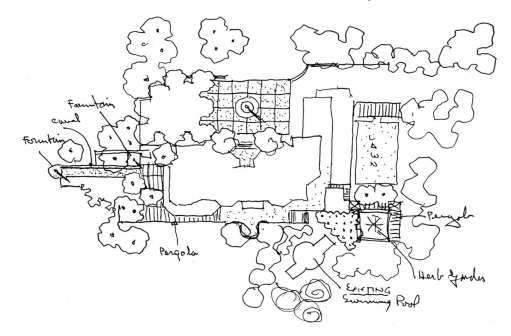

ABOVE An azure ribbon of water juts off the west lawn into the surrounding canyon heights.

Space is compartmentalized and elements are fully detailed, to draw attention inwards from approach to pool to intimate garden.

The hills that rise above Hollywood are filled with the grand villas and lavish estates of the American glitterati. Swimming pools, hot tubs, tennis courts, meticulously manicured lawns and ornamental plantings of exotic materials abound. The climate of Southern California is hot and dry, severe enough that those who have the resources try to escape, conceal and modify their living environment by artificial means. What is often missing in these residential compounds is acknowledgement of the rich natural conditions. Our intent for the Lear Residence was to construct a landscape of luxury that, rather than precluding perception of the context, would actually heighten the sense of place via an open-ended structure reaching out into the surrounding hillsides.

The large house sits at the end of a steep canyon road over which hover eroding brown slopes, tangled webs of vine and weed species. The driveway turn-off is between two solid stone retaining walls, a welcome intimation of stability on the shifting canyon face. Although the walls frame the entrance, they are low enough that the way appears more as a parting of the forest than as a grand ceremonial entrance that dominates all else. The house itself sits on top of the ridge line: it is truly perched. The original owners constructed a swimming pool and tennis terrace at an oblique angle from the house, elements that seem obtuse at first glance, but that do provide some balance to the sizable mass of the building. Instead of cutting into the steep site, the pool deck and court are raised on pilings high above the hillside, such that they are at almost the same elevation as the house. It was clear that our design would have to transform these unwieldy platforms into an arrangement of flowing order.

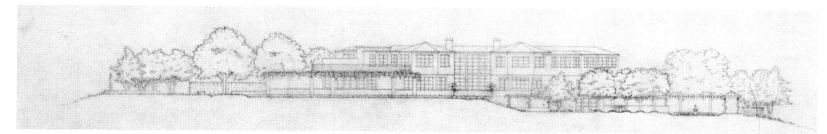

ABOVE South elevation of the Lear Residence.

RIGHT Roses spill over the checkerboard paving which edges the *tapis vert*.

129

The arrival court is a level plane of crushed stone. At this initial point, a grid of ficus trees puts visitors in direct contact with the site's integrated order and a sense of green structure. Parking spaces are found within the bosque of ficus trees, which rise out of the court surface at twelve foot on centre. Stone bands run across the court; they break the expanse into smaller modules and help contain the crushed stone. A circular pool, raised eighteen inches off the ground – just enough to read from a distance – sits on axis with the main entrance to the house. Two tall shade-trees flank the steps up to the front door. On the other side of the ficus grove, visitors can enter the garden via a gate.

To solve the problem of the oblique angle of the pool platform, we planted a wedge-shaped parkinsonia bosque that addresses the competing orientations. It successfully mediates the awkward junction and provides a smooth spatial transition from the open swimming pool into a neighbouring herb garden. This petite garden is a mandala of potent smells and flavours. A stripped-cedar pergola with sono-tube concrete columns frames two sides of the garden; it is webbed with bougainvillea and provides shaded seating around the herbs. In this arrangement, space is compartmentalized, elements are fully detailed, and attention is drawn inwards from approach to pool to intimate garden. The progression then emerges through a second, free-standing pergola at one end of the east lawn. An open *tapis vert* stretches low and uninterrupted from the pergola, a simulation of green velvet that is as far from suburban crabgrass lawn as snow is from the streets of Hollywood. White square-cut stone in a diagonal checkerboard pattern edges the clipped grass to form a rectangle. At first, we installed the stone in a solid line, but we

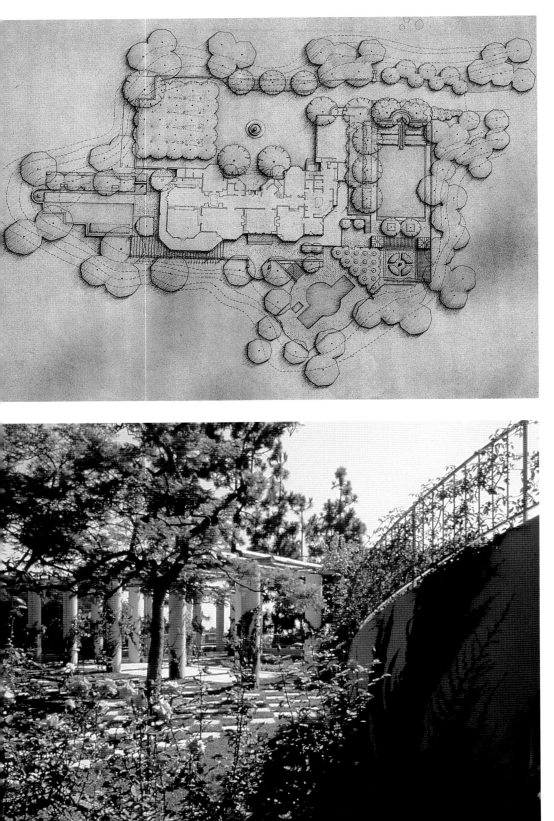

later determined that the edge needed to be less rigid. A rose garden and a Spanish-style wall with a gurgling water slot are two event points as one moves across the central lawn.

The site's spatial progression reaches its most expansive moment in the west lawn, a bi-level renovation of the old tennis platform. The perimeter retaining walls are low here, their poured concrete painted white with no further embellishment so as not to interfere with the views. A linear perennial bed (including galanthus, scilla, snowdrops, narcissus, white muscari, alium, coreopsis, delphiniums, Siberian and dwarf iris, veronica, rose varieties, ajuga, artemesia, helioctrichon, stachys byzantia, agapanthus, yucca and Natal plum) follows the base of one wall; its reach is paralleled and its soils contained by a long, narrow water channel. This water ribbon, cut into a deck of limestone, stretches away from the house on axis with the main hallway and ends at a semi-circle apended to the site platform. The protrusion is just big enough for a singular water jet. This garden is calm in content, but thrillingly precarious in context. It is here that one is thrust into the canyon, into the sky, into the sun. The wall around the garden is broken in several strategic spots, to let the scorched contours spill up into the tended green grass of the lawn. At other points, the solid wall alternates with a metal grill for a similar effect.

The Los Angeles firm of Rios/Pearson was an effective associate, as was the project's architect, Variations in Architecture. To assure the clients a successful plant palette, we consulted with local horticulturalists for the various gardens. The herb and perennial gardens, for instance, are carefully crafted for best texture and year-round colour.

OPPOSITE ABOVE Site plan of Lear Residence with, clockwise from top, arrival court, *tapis vert*, herb garden, swimming pool, pergola corridor, west lawn and water ribbon.

OPPOSITE BELOW A curved stair, the armature for climbing roses, descends from the upper living areas to the garden level.

RIGHT A concrete-and-wood loggia frames views to the south and connects to the site's perimeter wall.

AG GROUP HEADQUARTERS
BRUSSELS, BELGIUM, 1996

Our concept evolved from an ordering and embroidering of circulation patterns as they relate to the surrounding building.

In 1996, I had the pleasure of meeting H.R.H. Prince Charles of England at the opening of the AG Group Headquarters in Brussels. Six years of design development and extensive reworking of the programme – an enjoyable arbitration amongst the client, the local architecture firm of M. Polak (represented by Joanna Alemenstioni) and my office – had resulted in a corporate cloister of dense detail and sensitive articulation. Our design provides a variety of experiences condensed into a relatively small area, as if one were walking through a city or a whole park. Dressed in the *vêtements* of grid and hierarchy, plant materials are both

BELOW Site model which shows the dilation of spatial volume as one moves from north to south, with the roof-top vine grid to the west.

structure and infill. Trunks, low hedges, vine canopies and raised panels of ground cover segment the site into three distinct volumes.

For a roof-top development, the garden is extensive, covering almost an entire city block near the heart of Brussels (the Grand Place is a close neighbour). Our initial concept evolved from an ordering and embroidering of circulation patterns as they relate to the surrounding building. We first divided the space into three 'rooms', each composed of an ascending complexity of materials: the first of primary stone and water (it is an essentially open plane with one, central element); the second of gridded trees set in ground cover (a diaphanous volume of multiple, equal parts); the third, a simple built structure (placed in balanced plurality with dissimilar components). Bluestone paving patterns and clipped yew hedges provide secondary definition of spatial and visual compartments. Spatially, the design is a linear progression from exposure to enclosure.

The open space, or Grand Court as it was labelled, has the air of a miniature plaza. Its east side is adjacent to the main lobby; its west connects into the auditorium. The court is an extension of the pubic nature of these facilities. Granite cobblestones pave the floor, and at the centre of the square, a fountain surges out of an inclined black slate base. A broken ring of benches sits in concentric cooperation with the fountain's visual dominance. I first imagined the water half-encircled by a pergola for greater vertical impact, or set in a nine-square anchored at four corners by flowering trees. Early plans also called for the area to be bracketed on two sides by light glass structures (a conservatory and café).

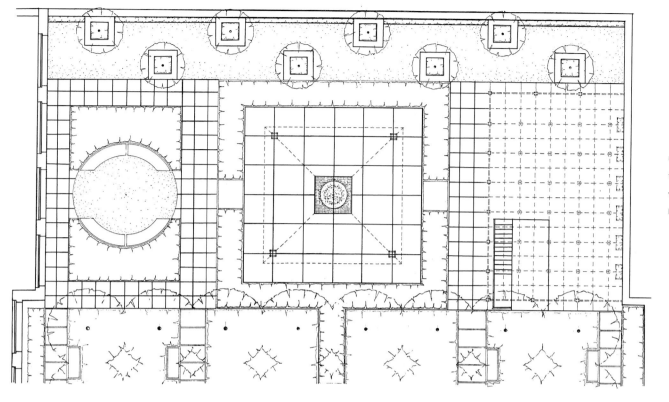

LEFT Detail plan of the bubbler pavilion flanked by yew court and exit court, with a line of ginkgoes above and the honey-locust bosque below.

133

But for now, the fountain is on its own, and the court is an empty box, waiting to be filled with people and conversation.

The second part of the AG Group garden is directly north of the Grand Court and signals a change of programme by means of an increased interplay of materials and vertical structure: a bosque of forty-eight honey-locusts is set on a grid at eight foot on centre; the trunks rise out of plant beds thick with vinca. Benches are set along gridded paths of bluestone. From May to October, the bipinnate foliage and open crown of the honey-locusts stipple the ground with shadow. When the leaves drop, for a brief time workers in the offices above look down onto thousands of bright golden nests strewn across the evergreen vinca. A low, clipped yew hedge slices through the bosque; on axis with the court fountain, it acts as a compositional link in the tripartite scheme.

As it emerges from the honey-locusts, the yew hedge becomes a low wall that encloses a wooden pavilion in the third portion of the garden. The pavilion houses a bubbler, also centred on the Grand Court's fountain axis. Access to the pavilion is from either side, thus bringing circulation along the edges while the site's main axis remains purely visual. Looking out from the pavilion towards the bosque and court fountain, on the left is a vine-covered trellis over the parking-garage exit, on the right a circular seating area is carved out of the yew mass. A line of tall sentry ginkgo trees marks the northern edge of this area.

An extension of the garden sits one floor above and is invisible from below (as well as inaccessible). We discovered

that from above, viewers would be confronted with a bland crushed-rock roof two-thirds the size of the garden itself. To mitigate this, we designed a system of vine supports – three-foot-square boxes set on a grid, with wires stretched between. It is a lacy green plan with no purpose other than visual effect. Although compared to the bare roof, the vines may have cooling properties.

Unhindered by factors of ecological context that often influence landscape design (topography, soils, exposure), our work at AG Brussels is essentially a scheme of spatial and textural compositions; the issues that guided our design were interpretation of programme and efficiency of circulation. Tight proximity and concise connections between elements, subtle contrasts of colour and texture, and narrowly defined proportional relationships all require that this garden be well maintained to sustain the desired effect.

OPPOSITE Within the newly installed honey-locust grove, sunlight is filtered and shade abounds.

ABOVE The roof-top vine boxes are connected by cables over which the vines will grow to form a green mesh.

RIGHT The pavilion bubbler is on axis with the plaza fountain, glimpsed here through the bosque.

THE MEASURE OF MAGIC: SUN, SHADOW, STONE AND WATER

All design is the same – whether for a small homestead in New England or a corporate campus in a major city. One should begin with an open mind: study the site, the client and the conditions; allow impressions and information to infiltrate the mind and instruct the site diagram. This is the way in which I approached a number of residential and small-scale commercial jobs in the early 1990s: diagram and spatial structure first, then details of plant selection, paving materials, lighting and so forth. These details are obviously essential to the finished product, yet they are like fingernails: although necessary to achieve the end result, one does not start with the fingernails. They come after the body of the design has been formed, and they are not selected randomly.

Yet it is the movement, textures, colours, smells and sounds of the details that engage people on a day-to-day basis and bring the design to life. It is almost as if the grander spatial composition is innately perceived while the substance of the materials that reflect the daily/seasonal cycles is the extrinsic medium within which one communicates with the site. And this communication, or perception and reaction to the built environment, is what we are trying to shape. As a landscape design matures, its qualities evolve, leading to a 'mature' state that is quite different from the same site at completion of installation (a phenomenon to which most of the other design arts are not subject).

For this reason, plants and other materials are chosen with current as well as future dimensions in mind, with awareness of summer as well as winter habit and so on. Specific effects are crafted to be vocal at various stages of development, and it is precisely these dynamic changes that measure the spirit of a place. For example, we designed a free-standing pergola for the Shapiro Residence, which by dint of its proportioning and construction (concrete and wood) became the anchoring element from Day One for the perennial garden lay-out. A year or two later, the vines that we had planted overtook the structure and transformed it into a very different element of drama and verdant depth. The intrigue of the design is being revealed over time in all the permutations of its physicality.

OPPOSITE The pergola at Kimmel
Residence

4

CORNING RIVERFRONT CENTENNIAL PARK

CORNING, NEW YORK, 1992

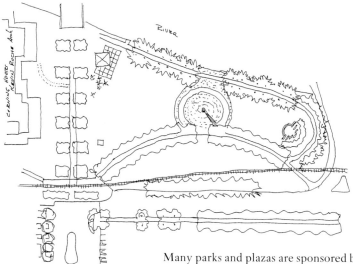

By no means a private industrial campus, the park is a gift to the public in a town where many of the citizens are employed by the corporation.

Many parks and plazas are sponsored by and are adjacent to corporate headquarters. Fountain Place, NationsBank Plaza, the Ford Foundation atrium and AG Group Headquarters are examples in this category; all of them are located at or near an urban core. Of this ilk, yet cast into a manufacturing village in rural Upstate New York, Corning Riverfront Centennial Park is an unusual hybrid of corporate plaza and more expansive

greenway park. By no means a private industrial campus, it is a gift to the public in a town where many of the citizens are employed by the corporation.

The three-acre site began as an asphalt parking lot on the banks of the Chemung River. Corning Incorporated Glassworks hired Kevin Roche to design their new headquarters, and he in turn called on me. The initial design

RIGHT The headquarters building presides over the pavilion and sixty-foot-high fountain of Riverfront Park.

OPPOSITE ABOVE Site plan of Riverfront Park.

OPPOSITE BELOW At night, the towering fountain is illuminated and is a beacon easily seen from the nearby bridges of the Chemung River.

stages progressed quickly, as the programme was relatively simple and the context indicated a logical site diagram. We worked out a circulation system and two focal points; the interstitial spaces provided ample dimensions for programmed features such as a garden amphitheatre, a children's play area and a recreation lawn.

Our first step was to move surface parking to one edge of the parcel, away from the river and up against a block of brick factory buildings. Centerway Plaza, a small terminus of the town's pedestrian mall, became the park entrance. We extended this axis as a broad walk to run parallel to the headquarters' façade and connect to a pedestrian bridge that links to the museum and offices across the river. The walk is lined with quartets of London plane trees, which confer a stronger effect in a short span than a line of single trees. The fire code required height limits on plantings close to the building and was an excellent excuse to specify a maintenance program of semi-annual clipping for the plane trees – a practice that soon created architectural character as the foliage grew together into a tight, controlled canopy.

As visitors first enter the park, they cross over a set of railroad tracks. Since the tracks are still used, we needed to keep them accessible yet prevent them from interrupting the park atmosphere. To achieve this, we planted grass right up to and between the iron rails. Where they intersect the walk, the tracks are flush with the brick surface. What might have been a negative element was turned into a playful trompe l'oeil: as the train passes along the tracks, it appears to be gliding over smooth lawn and serenely threading its way through the honey-locust grove.

One of two primary elements in the park is a pavilion set adjacent to the pedestrian bridgehead. A light, vine-covered aluminium trellis on concrete sono-tube columns angles obliquely from the roof line of the central enclosed core, creating a new orientation towards the greater body of the park. The ground slopes with architectural abruptness from the trellis down to a wide, open lawn. A brick walk curves out from the pavilion towards the site's heart, where it joins with a second walk leading from Centerway Plaza. At the intersection of the two, a sixty-foot fountain shoots up from a circular base of cobblestones. The fountain is a beacon for cars passing over the Brisco Bridge downriver.

The linden-lined walkway extends across the breadth of the park and divides the site into distinct programmatic quadrants: the children's play area is closest to the entrance; the open lawn stretches out from the pavilion; a loose grove of

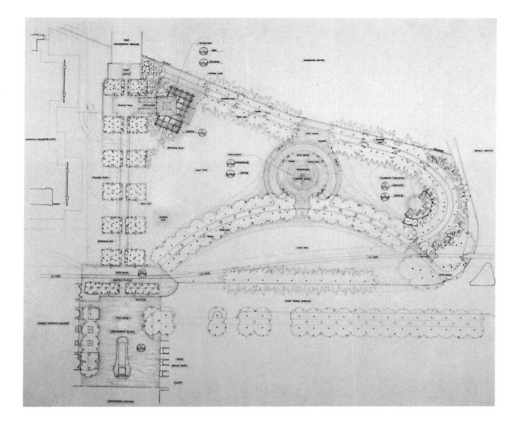

139

BELOW A night-time view of the pavilion with Corning in the distance.

RIGHT A play of depth and shadow veils the seating area within a framework of poured-concrete columns.

BOTTOM The pavilion's open-roof structure and vines cast shadows onto the plaza below.

140

RIGHT A detail of the pavilion ceiling.

BELOW At the height of summer, the dense linden foliage and spouting fountain are welcome sights.

honey-locusts borders the parking area and acts as a visual filter; the garden theatre is tucked at the far end of the park against a screen of evergreens. If all the plantings were removed, the grading scheme on its own would provide clues to the first-time visitor: all walkways trace gentle ridges that rise above the base elevation; the pavilion and fountain each rest on heights of land; a small earth stage pops up at the foot of the amphitheatre's incline. At the fountain, the earth is held in place by a low retaining seat-wall; from there, the grade ramps down towards the river. This slight retainage is a minor promontory of sorts and heightens a sense of place-specific prospect.

RIGHT The site's primary circulation and pedestrian link to the existing city mall is lined with quartets of plane trees clipped for architectural form.

TWIN FARMS INN

BARNARD, VERMONT, 1992

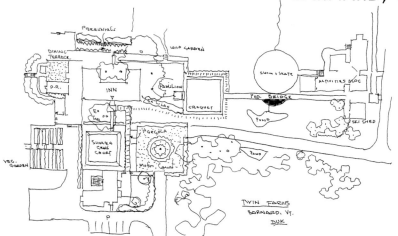

What struck me most clearly on my first visit to Twin Farms was a sense of the remembered human geometry on the land.

On the day they met, Sinclair Lewis promised Dorothy Thompson a quiet farmhouse in Vermont. She, a journalist, and he, a renowned author, were mainstays of the American literati of the 1930s. They found their retreat at Twin Farms, a 235-acre farm that includes open fields, forests, a small ski slope, streams, ponds and a lake just twelve miles north of the lovely village of Woodstock. In the early 1990s, the property was purchased by an entrepreneur with plans to transform it into one of the most luxurious inns in the world. Christy and David Garrett were brought in as project consultants, the architect Tom Cullins was asked to renovate the two existing farmhouses, and the late Jed Johnson designed the interiors. My office signed on to create a master plan and site design for the inn and its grounds.

144

RIGHT Below the dining terrace, a flagstone path winds through terraced perennial beds.

OPPOSITE An aerial view of the inn with the lodge at lower right and the entry road above.

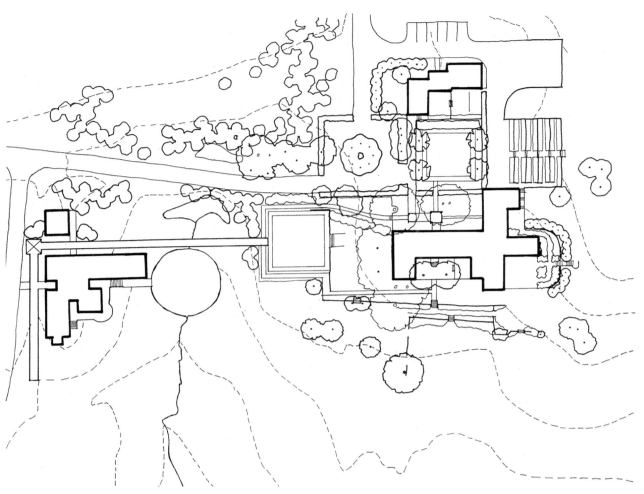

ABOVE Plan view of Twin Farms, with the game lawn at centre, arrival court above, inn on the right, pond and recreation lodge on the left.

LEFT Interior shot of the steel-truss bridge at night; its design was inspired by historic railroad structures of New England.

FAR LEFT A pedestrian bridge spans the stream (its flow held briefly in a perfect circle of water) between the inn and the recreation lodge.

What struck me most clearly on my first visit to Twin Farms was a sense of the remembered human geometry on the land. Orchard fragments; lines of ancient, arching sugar-maples along overgrown roads; low walls whose bits of lichen-coated fieldstone were migrating back to the beds from whence they came, like a school of lithoid fish along the field edge. I felt the character of an earlier time in New England imbued in the landscape – an operative rusticity that I first experienced at my grandmother's farm in New Hampshire, where I spent many summers as a child. With this in mind, our design strategy for Twin Farms was to bring subtle ordering and fine detail to the site without overriding the existing features.

The approach to Twin Farms ascends several miles through a mature forest of sugar- and red maple, white and yellow birch, beech and shadbush. The entry drive slips along waving pastures, then dips down into a tight, birch-filled gorge and continues towards the main lodge. Grass and gravel tracks branch off, leading to seven individual guest cottages (each with its own unique style, such as 'The Treehouse' and 'The Studio') that we helped to site.

At seventy-five by seventy-five feet, the inn's entry court is intimately scaled: we intended the entrance to be a courtyard, less of a passenger drop-off. Red maples mark one edge of the court and indicate parking spaces for six cars. A circle of flowering crab-trees is set in the centre of the crushed-stone surface. To draw the lodge out into the entry area and create depth against its unremarkable façade (as well as to embellish the act of arrival), we ran a wooden pergola about ten feet from the main door. A garden of ferns and bulbs fills the ground between the structures. Together, the flowering trees at the centre of the court, the maple line and the pergola create a frame that draws the visitor into successively defined spaces as they approach the lodge.

On the south side of the inn, a terrace extends off the living-room. A second, higher terrace offers outdoor dining. We specified large broken flagstones to be set with grass joints to create a soft informality (as opposed to crushed stone or cut pavers). Two ginkgo trees rise, straight-trunked and shade-giving, out of the level terrace. The grade drops sharply from the edge towards three tiers of perennial gardens that traverse the rolling meadow below. These gardens were laid out by Thompson when she and Lewis lived at Twin Farms; we only added a stepping-stone pathway and a third tier of planting beds to increase the effect of flower masses. From this upper slope, visitors can look out across open lawn to distant Mount Ascutney. If one wanders through the gardens into the lower reaches of the lawn, an abandoned road appears, lined with ancient maples now crowded with the new forest growth of recent decades. This is a segment of the old road to Woodstock. While others suggested clearing the road-bed to use it as the primary access route, I felt that this wonderful message of history and connection – much like Robert Frost's Old Marlborough Road – should be kept unpaved as a spiritually vital link in the inn's story.

On the west side of the inn, a croquet lawn stretches out from the building as a green carpet. From here, the grade drops steeply down to the ravine, through which a stream courses after release from a pond above the inn. On the other side of the ravine stands the second original farmhouse.

This has been renovated into a pub, game room and spa. Connecting the two foci of Twin Farms life – the main lodge and the recreation lodge – we designed a steel-truss pedestrian bridge of rural gentility. The bridge reaches across the deep fold in the land, its delicate strength reflected in a perfect circle of water below. I love that one, clean circle of cold water, caught in the primitive gorge. The bridge is painted black and seems to simultaneously contrast and blend easily with its sylvan surroundings throughout the seasons. The view is particularly emotive in the foliage season, when the fiery leaves and silhouetted trusses seem to be in a perpetual process of conflagration. At other times, it is the filtered sunlight, shadows stirred by mountain breezes and sounds of the stream that are most alluring at Twin Farms.

OPPOSITE ABOVE A viewing terrace adjacent to the inn is set beneath the shade of maples.

OPPOSITE BELOW The entry pergola and fern garden as seen from the side of the inn.

BELOW Guests are met at the arrival court and ushered in via the pergola , a mediating device which expands the entry sequence.

149

SHAPIRO RESIDENCE

WESTPORT, NEW YORK, 1994

Stone Wall

Connections between key points of the greater property shape the lay-out and the form of individual areas.

It is a pleasure to work with artists as clients – be they sculptors, painters or dancers – for they have the capacity to envision spatial relationships and recognize the importance of form, colour and texture in the built environment. The process of design is always an interchange with clients to some degree; with the artistically inclined, this dialogue often acquires a greater depth and is fraught with questions about

all aspects of the process. For this reason, I was delighted to work with the sculptor Joel Shapiro and painter Ellen Phelan on their residence in Upstate New York.

The Shapiro Residence sits atop a low slate bluff overlooking Lake Champlain. The Prairie-Style house – an anomaly in a region where many of the great Adirondack camps of a former era are found along the shore – is set at the

150

RIGHT As one approaches, the house and lake are glimpsed through cedar trunks.

margin of a native white cedar (arbor-vitae) forest, a species typically found banding the shoreline. The house looks east towards the Green Mountains of Vermont, just yards from the waves and a short ferry ride from my office on the other side of the lake. The forty-acre property came with a well-proportioned barn (now a workshop), an aged boathouse (with minimal renovation transformed into a painting studio), a defunct carriage house (currently a storage/service barn) and a tiny ice house. We set about integrating the disparate parts of the property into a unified experience.

The first note of articulated landscape in the approach is a double row of Lombardy poplars that extends the length of the southern boundary, parallel to the road. The poplars, which grow quickly and can reach over ninety feet in height (these already measure fifty feet or so), march side by side for over a thousand feet. They are magnificent. Any severity of form is dispelled by their magical foliage: the leaves are finely crenated and hang from petioles whose engineering causes them to tremble and wave at the slightest breeze (the tree is related to the quaking aspen). Thus, the columnar height of the poplars rustles and dances above the adjacent cornfields. I must note that this species is susceptible to certain diseases and thus tends to weaken and die within several decades. But so do we.

At the end of the poplar *allée*, the entry drive turns ninety degrees due north and follows the margin of the cedar forest. A double row of tea crab follows the drive on its other side, thus bracketing the entrance between low, flowering trees and the taller, evergreen mass. The drive passes between a pair of old stone piers that mark arrival into the domestic precinct; once through, the drive is encompassed by cedars. In the first clearing one comes to is a two-storey barn, now a workshop for study-model fabrication. One side of the barn has been cleared, levelled and surfaced with white crushed stone. This is a sculpture court, with concrete support pads poured in place below the surface. At the north-west corner of the startlingly bright court, we scraped off layers of decomposed

needles to expose a slate outcrop. The purity of the crushed stone sweeps directly up to the lip of the outcrop, heightening the contrast of art (sculpture), artifice (the court within the forest) and (artificially revealed) nature.

From the sculpture court, a fork in the drive continues north to the boathouse and dock. The main branch of the drive veers east and descends over gnarled cedar roots to

151

TOP Master plan, with the poplar *allée* along the southern boundary, studio barn and main house up to the east, and boathouse at the far north.

ABOVE The poplar *allée* is visible through the pergola's vine-covered columns.

152

ABOVE A Joel Shapiro piece, in silhouette against the backdrop of Lake Champlain, stands at one corner of the entry court.

ABOVE RIGHT Visitors drive along the length of the poplar *allée* and then turn at its end to enter the property.

the arrival court. We re-aligned the drive at this point, eradicating a curve in favour of a much stronger configuration: the drive now approaches parallel to, but offset from, the house and porte-cochère. This inaugurates a series of orthogonally related spaces that emanate from the house. The arrival court is a square, sheer plane; it begins at grade, but then is contained by a flush, dry-laid stone wall as the floor of the cedar forest descends to the lake. At its outer eastern edge, the court is a promontory, jutting four feet above existing grade and creating a false horizon line. A sculpture by Joel Shapiro stands in this corner, silhouetted against the waves of Lake Champlain.

At the centre of the court is a thirty-foot-diameter circle of clipped yew with a tiny water jet at its centre. The ingredients of the court are elemental and are used in broad sweeps, creating a space of lucidity beyond its prosaic function. During the design process, we studied the scale of

each integer to derive maximum emotion from minimal form – square, circle, line. The three meet here as individual elements, yet they seem inseparable parts of a whole, particularly when unified by seasonal effects: a golden scattering of cedar needles, the grainy glitter of autumn frost, the drenching of spring rain that coaxes colours out of each material unseen in dry weather.

A walkway of Lake Placid granite leads from the arrival court to the entrance. A wooden pergola extends perpendicularly from the door, linking the interior of the house to the interior of the cedar forest. Just beyond the pergola, a rectangle of crushed stone edged with granite outlines an additional small sculpture court. At its northern end sits a low panel of clipped yew, bisected diagonally by a pathway that leads from the main house to the boathouse. This is a manifestation of the master plan – connections between key points of the greater property shape the lay-out

RIGHT Detail plan of the main house, with entry court at top, arrival pergola to right, garden and *tapis vert* below. Lake Champlain runs along the east face of the building.

BELOW RIGHT The arrival pergola reaches out to connect the house to the surrounding cedar forest.

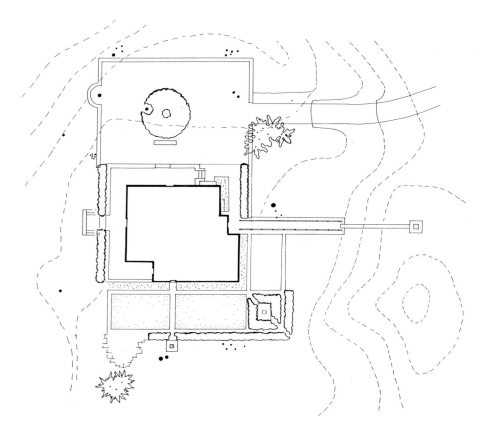

153

and the form of individual areas – and it reinforces the idea of a unified whole brought together by a light touch of order on the land.

A second rectangle parallels the north side of the house; it is a *tapis vert* delineated with granite pavers. At the east end of the clipped grass *tapis*, we found an existing dell of white-blossoming vinca; to integrate it into the design without destroying its essence, we carefully placed granite pieces into the forest ground covers and added ferns and herbs. The didactic simplicity of these spaces is needed to allow the designed landscape abutting the house to communicate directly with the setting. I strove to open the house up to the spirit of the trees and lake – not by imitation or overt framing, but by defining an open stage of sorts that mediates between the two existences. I feel we will have succeeded if the serenity of the cedars pervades.

In addition to crafting spaces around the house and studios, we also worked with the clients on a vegetable/ cutting garden in the field alongside the initial approach, connected to the inner property via pathways. We built a pergola – in essence, a place-maker in the middle of an open field – that established an armature from which to develop harmonically related planting plots. The pergola is eight feet wide and freestanding, with sono-tube concrete columns and a wooden frame. Vines quickly overtook the structure; it now resembles a fragment of Greek history that somehow landed in Upstate New York. The pergola provides a splendid seating area from which to oversee the growing gardens, as well as a place for cocktails at sunset.

LEHR RESIDENCE

MIAMI BEACH, FLORIDA, 1995

The bosque is truly the element that begins an orderly arrangement of the entire back area.

RIGHT The double fronts of palm-tree lines screen the house and frame a parking court.

The detail of renovation and the attentively proportioned spaces of the Lehr Residence belie the fact that its design was relayed almost entirely by telephone and fax, from concept through construction. Initial concept sketches and scribbles on site photographs were sent to illustrate important ideas. In the midst of several conversations, the client responded to design ideas with a quick 'I'll do it!'

More than once, we devised spur-of-the-moment solutions to site conditions. For example, a gentle planted grade change between entry walk and street presented a somewhat ambiguous edge condition, against which the new entry drive's neat sod joints and grid of concrete pavers appeared discordant. We suggested that a concise cut be made parallel to the street to retain the lawn with a single line of

LEFT An early plan of the back garden with, clockwise from the swimming pool at top, house, existing water feature, terrace, palm bosque, waterside pergola.

BELOW Because the steps which negotiate between the three levels are fixed, one is required to move through in a fairly choreographed manner, an exercise which instills a sense of expanding layered space.

155

concrete blocks, painted black. In this way, a refined character began to emerge from existing pieces.

This project represents an excellent and rarely attained working relationship resulting from a kinship of design sensibilities and a sincerely enthusiastic client. I visited the site just once before sending a loose sketch that later provided the underlaying site structure. In that first visit, I noted several extant features that had potential: two royal palms and a gnarled banyan tree at the house entrance; a few more palm trees and groupings of vigorous flowering shrubs at the back of the residence; a rectangular swimming pool wedged between house and waterfront; and, perhaps most crucially, an artist client who shared a zest for life expressed through design.

The *complaisance* of two royal palms at the front façade prompted my strategy for the entry sequence. We strengthened their formal role by adding matching palms at either end of the pair, to form a line across the house front. The line is repeated by a second row of palms parallel to the drive court edge. This second palm screen is backed by a clipped hedge, an element whose role is to ensure privacy, but, more importantly, to create a distinct wall that one passes through, moving from car/parking to inner garden

RIGHT Detail plan of the roof-top 'spa,' with pool, bathtub and sun-deck rooms partitioned by rows of potted trees.

BELOW Royal palms form one wall of the parking court; the drive cuts orthagonally around a grand existing banyan tree.

precinct/house. Together, the palm lines frame the property's brief approach in an ordered, finite volume. An entity is born that did not exist before – the forecourt – and it bestows a spatial elegance that increases the stature of the bungalow on a small lot.

The back of the house faces directly onto Indian Creek, and this back area is primary living space. Early on in the project, we discussed the concern that the central swimming pool and its heavy deck were dividing the area into two unrelated pieces. We strove to work out a diagram of varied but unified interlocking spaces. Here, as in the front of the house, existing palm trees served as the genesis for the area's spatial structure: young royal palms in an eight-foot grid surround and incorporate mature existing trees in a palm bosque. The tightly placed trunks compose a light mass

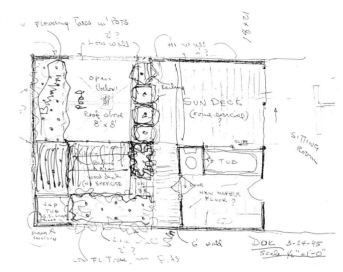

RIGHT Three night-time views of the palm bosque, the pergola and the pool with wall segments.

BELOW Detail plan of the parking court 'room' that illustrates the structural use of palms.

that is dense yet permeable; the living columns filter both movement and view between house and waterfront. The bosque is truly the element that begins an orderly arrangement of the entire back area and establishes the composition in relation to the pool.

We chose to elevate the swimming pool above its conventional azurine character of chlorine and spring boards. The wide wooden decking was ripped up, sliced into narrow strips and laid back down for a finer, lighter effect with a delicate Oriental feeling. The pool is screened on the river side by a free-standing pergola and flanked on another side by eight-foot segments of ten-foot-high, white, textured concrete-block walls. Clothed in bougainvillea, the walls are a lush enclosure mechanism for the swimming area. Wire mesh is strung between the wall segments to provide further armatures for climbing jasmine. These three wall panels shield the neighbours, but let space in and out . . . the boundary line is obscured: you can no longer see it, but it is known and felt.

157

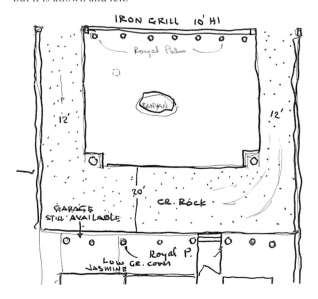

KIMMEL RESIDENCE

SALISBURY, CONNECTICUT, 1996

The challenge was to develop an effective exterior sequence which would respond appropriately to its physical and historical setting.

← NORTH

A

I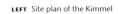

H

B

D

G

C

E

F

J

r

r

K

L

OPPOSITE BELOW Aerial view of the
Kimmel Residence, with main house at
centre; *potager, allée* and tennis-court
pavilion at lower left.

LEFT Site plan of the Kimmel
Residence:

A   GUEST-HOUSE GARDEN
B   ENTRY DRIVE
C   ORCHARD
D   ARRIVAL COURT
E   NORTH TERRACE
F   BEECH-TREE STAIR
G   SOUTH TERRACE
H   *POTAGER*
I   TENNIS COURT
J   BIRCH GLEN
K   SPRULE BOG
L   POND

159

The Kimmel Residence sits atop a low rise above a wetland, on one of the many rolling hills that emanate east from the Taconic Mountain range into the farmlands of western Connecticut and Massachusetts. The fourteen-thousand-square-foot house was designed by a local architect to replace an existing residence, and it now occupies a commanding position within the complex of historic buildings that remains on site. There are remnants of past lives embedded in the landscape, some of which we brought forth and integrated into the site's present order: an old stone foundation complete with broad front steps now serves as an elevated grass pad on which a Flanagan sculpture sits; a well-tended mature orchard is interpreted as a grid of living forms that consummate the northward movement of a new terrace system; a grass tennis court, barely perceptible within a grove of pines, currently hosts successional field growth, but I envision carving out a secret garden there one day.

When I met the clients on site for the first time, I realized that the most important aspect of the project would be to mediate between the residence and the hillside upon which it sat. The challenge was to develop an effective exterior sequence that would allow the house to become part of, and respond appropriately to – as opposed to dominate – its physical and historical setting. At the direction of another landscape architect, the clients had already made initial cuts into the hillside and had constructed several stone walls of significant height and length. Although I might have placed the walls differently, we were able to work them into what we felt to be the best lay-out. What I was not able to accept was the dark wood siding of the house; its colour, texture and proportion not only were inappropriate for the scale of the large building, but the look seemed to violate the regional character and isolate the house from the land. The clients agreed to paint everything white.

LEFT Wisteria vines climb up a pergola (designed by the architect) which extends off the pool room onto the south lawn.

BELOW LEFT At eight feet on centre, the littleleaf lindens echo the pergola columns and create a spatial structure which harmonizes with the house.

RIGHT Water channel above and pond below – human order and nature's carving of the land – share reflections. An edge of the beech-tree stair is seen at left; the Taconic mountain range is visible in the distance.

BELOW RIGHT A Naumann sculpture sited on a grass pad beside the pond is seen here in silhouette alongside young willows.

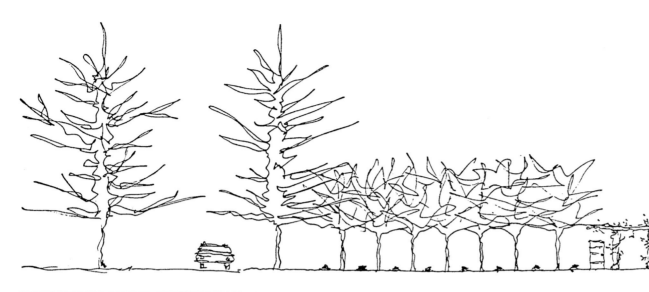

LEFT An early version of the entry scheme called for a ginkgo-lined drive to meet a tea-crab bosque, interspersed with tiny water jets, at the arrival court.

BELOW LEFT Twin eighteen-inch-calliper copper beeches provide instant drama.

BOTTOM LEFT A vine gallery outlines the tennis court.

162

Our second move was to construct a series of retained terraces to flank the length of the house's west (down-slope) side. These terraces, just inches below the first-floor elevation, begin to balance the voluminous scale of the house perched against the hillside. The terraces form a plinth that is absolutely crucial to the design; without them, the building would not have a proper relationship with the land. The north terrace stretches more than eighty feet out from the library and bar on the north end of the first floor. Here, the retaining-wall system slowly rises above grade as it moves down the hillside. At its height, the poured concrete is nine feet high; we planted Boston ivy along its base, which now covers the wall with lush greenery in summer and brilliant scarlet tracery in fall.

The north terrace is a smooth grass plane that doubles as a croquet court. A wide pergola (with sono-tube poured-concrete columns and a wooden frame) at the back of the terrace provides a seating area for viewing sunsets and games. The pergola also conceals HVAC units. Twin four-squares of honey-locusts bracket doors into the house as well as frame the view out. The north terrace is edged in an eighteen-inch-wide, three-inch-deep water channel that runs flush with the lawn. Sheathed in copper with a black slate bottom, the channel creates a crisp line that accents the raised terrace's orthogonal lay-out as an extension of the house. Water spills out of the channels into narrow side troughs and is recycled. The channels also feed a shared pool at one corner of the terrace. The pool's wind-sensitive fountain erupts in a roiling mass of water, which is spectacular when lit at night. During the day, the bands of water at the terrace edge reflect

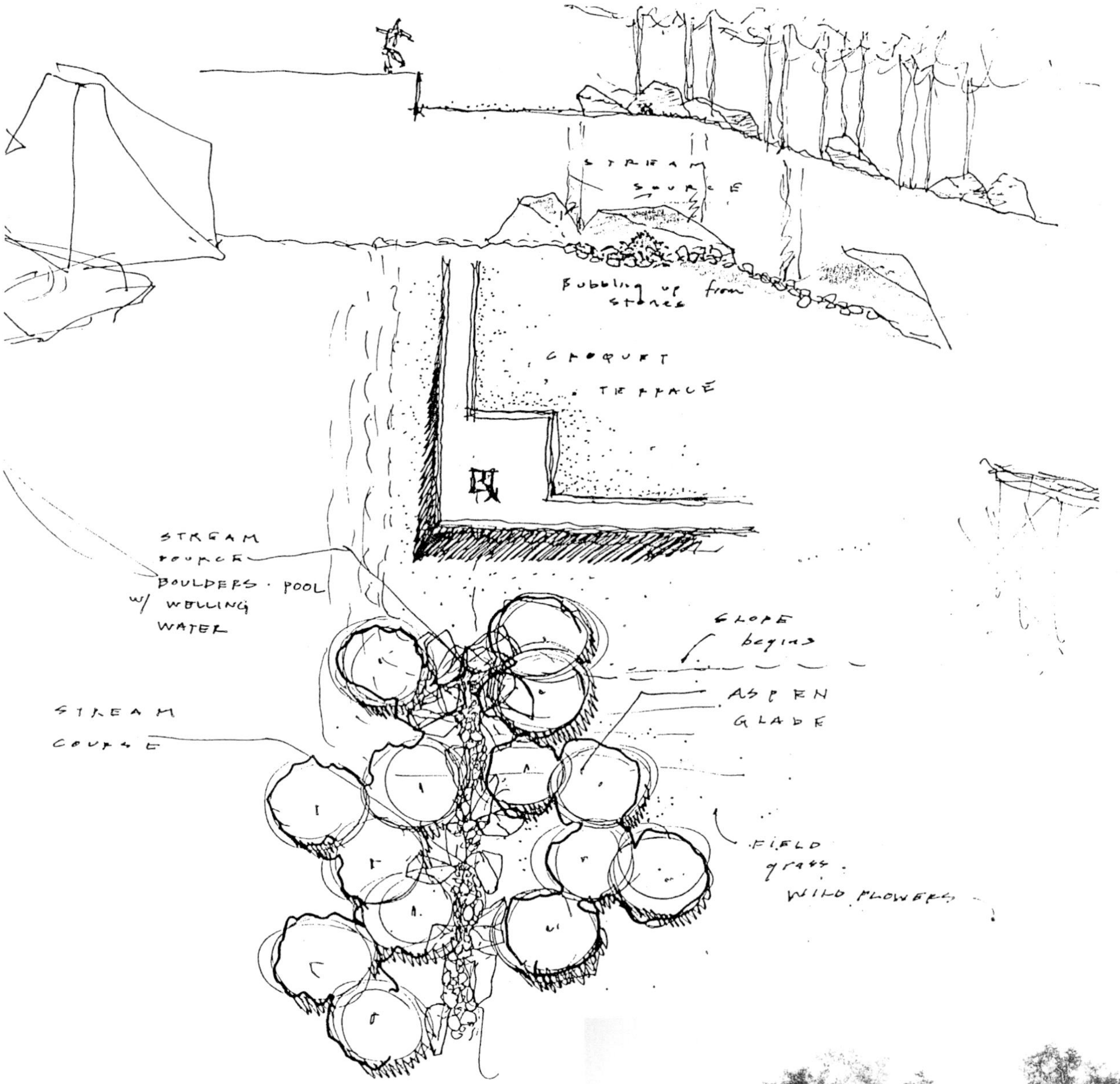

The sketch includes the following handwritten labels:

STREAM
SOURCE

Bubbling up from
stones

CROQUET
TERRACE

STREAM
SOURCE
BOULDERS · POOL
w/ WELLING
WATER

STREAM
COURSE

SLOPE
begins

ASPEN
GLADE

FIELD
grass ·
WILD FLOWERS

LEFT Section and detail sketch plan of the birch glade. A series of drops and pools brings a small stream to a spruce bog at the pond's northern end.

BELOW The water channel leads the eye from the north terrace towards the entry drive.

163

sunlight and cloud movement, tree canopies and the distant mountains.

On the south end of the house, just off the indoor swimming pool, another grass terrace extends out from the foundation. A raised sculpture pad, thick with vinca, sits at one corner, echoing the fountain on the north end. Yet here, it was necessary to release the continuous retaining-wall system from its strict angularity. In the office, we spent days sketching sinuous s-curves that would allow the built-up tension to flow out, but that would remain fully integral to the site diagram. A ring of larches occupies the lee of the

curve on the terrace; below, where the second curve opens out into the sloping field, there is a ring of Kousa dogwoods with winterberry below. Six trellis columns, custom-built out of reinforcing bar, support hydrangea vines and provide a green curtain along the terrace's east side (which abuts service parking).

Between the north and south terraces, the system narrows and closely follows the protrusions and recesses of the west façade. At the living-room, immense glass double doors slide open towards the Taconics. To frame this event, we planted matching copper beeches, eighteen-inch diameter at installation, in massive drums that are a protrusion of the retaining wall system. The rotundity of the drums relieves the linear edge for a moment; between them a set of granite steps fans out to connect house and hill. The beeches and other

trees on this side of the house play a dual role: they regulate the spatial flow of the landscape and protect from exposure to sun and wind.

In front of the conservatory, we designed a small seating/sculpture area beneath a quartet of clipped horse chestnut trees. The original horse chestnuts failed and were replaced with four littleleaf lindens, trees of similar formality. At this point, the terrace system, now topped with an eighteen-inch-high seat wall of carnelian granite, is as much an outdoor corridor as it is a series of interconnected rooms.

After resolving the primary issue of creating a base for the house, a tennis court, a three-hole golf-course and additional sculpture locations were created around the estate. The tennis court is surrounded by a delicate double wall of steel mesh, which we planted with ivy; eventually, it should

OPPOSITE Painted ribs and panes of antique glass articulate the ceiling of the tennis-court pavilion.

BELOW Two giant ginkgoes, set in vinca, occupy the centre of the arrival court and punctuate the horizontality of the oil-and-stone surface.

164

grow into a green gallery. A copper-roofed courtside pavilion
with granite steps provides a comfortable viewing platform.
In this area, as in that directly surrounding the main house,
we paid close attention to the grading. The shape of the
land has everything to do with successful integration of
disparate elements. In addition, a tiny shed serves as a garden
pavilion. It now sits on axis at the head of bi-level vegetable
and cutting beds. A Sergeants cherry tree is set at each corner
of the garden.

The arrival court was designed to accommodate traffic,
but also to be used as a comfortably scaled courtyard when no
guests were present and the owners would be passing through
as well as looking out onto this area. I envisioned the court as
a plane of crushed stone; it is gently graded to carry drainage
into catch basins. Along one side, a clipped hornbeam hedge
fronts a stone retaining wall above which steps lead to an
upper lawn and the guest house. The main entrance to the
house is called out with a porte-cochère, which is designed to
be a clean-lined, simple addition to the façade. Black steel
columns rise out of the carnelian granite flooring of double
parking bays. Overhead, pyramidal glass skylights pop up
above the flat roof. At the centre of the arrival court, we
planted twin ginkgoes in circular beds of vinca. A bosque of
tea crab-apple trees, with vinca and cotoneaster below, forms
a block around which one swings to approach the entrance.

The entry sequence is always a vital introduction to a
site's overall structure. In this project, the entry drive is lined
with an *allée* of quick-growing red maples, a species often
found marking the rural roadways of New England. As the
house is set into the hillside to some degree, it is not fully
visible from the entry gate. We selected materials and a
language for the gate, the drive surface and the plantings
(American holly, dogwood, birch and pine) that would meet
the town road in an appropriate way and thus mediate
between the boldness of the house and the historic context.
Given the juxtapositions of new and old on this site, our
design employed structural elements of the classic with
spatial dimensions of the modern to bring forth fluid order
blending the vernacular and the exotic.

KIMMEL RESIDENCE

RIGHT Studies for the north terrace pool and fountain.

BELOW View towards the library wing of the house over the water channel and through the pergola at the north terrace.

FAR RIGHT The water edge runs flush with the lawn. The grade drops sharply on the outside to a lower turf platform upon which sits the terrace plinth.

KUSKO RESIDENCE
WILLIAMSTOWN, MASSACHUSETTS, 1996

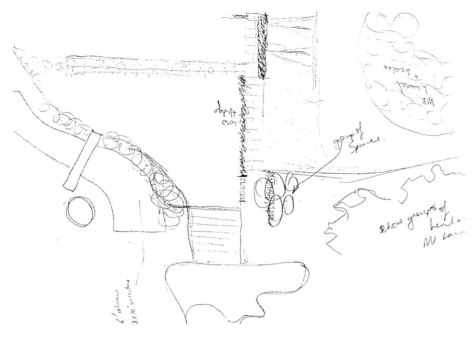

At issue was how to integrate the property's impression of wilderness with the house's tastefully appointed civility.

The Berkshire mountain range hugs the border of western Massachusetts. Its low peaks are a continuation of the Appalachian mountain chain that ripples the length of America's Eastern Seaboard, from Georgia all the way to Maine, at which point its granite outcrops subside into the flat farm lands of the St Lawrence River valley in Quebec.

168

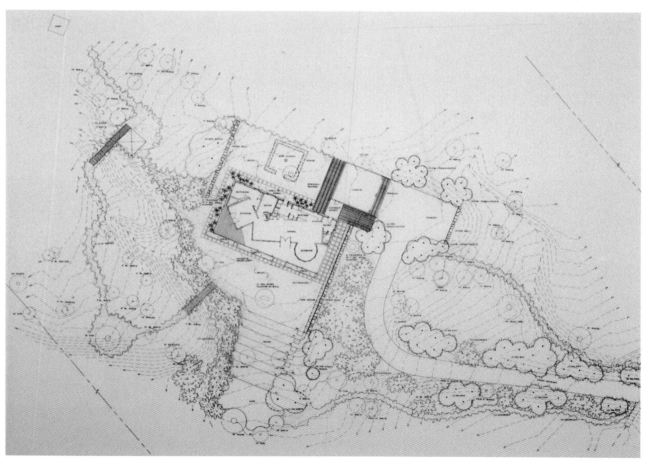

RIGHT Site plan of the Kusko Residence with house at centre, grass steps and pool below, entry drive to right.

The Berkshires are a gentle link in the Appalachian catenation and host diverse cultural and recreational activities. Tucked within these forested hillsides, the Kusko Residence is situated as a private sanctum from which to enjoy the lively regional offerings.

In 1994, the owners invited me to visit their mountainside house, recently completed by architects Burr McCallum. The building is a unique aggregation of readily visible geometries: the dining-room, living-room and master bedroom are individual glass-faced blocks that protrude

ABOVE The site is carved out of a densely forested mountainside.

BELOW LEFT North–south section of the site, with house above and forest pool below.

ABOVE A sketch of the woodland pool from atop the grass steps.

RIGHT My vision is of a pocket of cold, clear water held momentarily against the mountainside; it then drops away so cleanly that no edge is visible – one sees just a rhythm of trunks and a brief, glimmering surface.

170

from a solid bar housing the kitchen, bath and library. At issue was how best to assuage the site's post-construction condition and, more importantly, how to integrate the property's impression of wilderness with the house's tastefully appointed civility. I saw an opportunity to mould the sylvan site, to eke out the bones of an order that would unify the built and the unbuilt. As at Currier Farm, in this project I strove to reveal the human touch so lightly but truly that the boundary between nature's shape and our work would be understood as the result of equal participation on both sides.

The planting palette comes from the surrounding upland ecosystem – a typical mix of evergreens, birch, elm, poplar, beech, maple, shadbush, ferns and hardy ground covers. Under the guidance of project manager Peter Meyer, we planted tightly spaced hemlocks along both sides of the entrance to create a dense green tunnel. The tunnel encompasses the first third of the driveway's length; it then stops abruptly, and visitors emerge, aware for the first time of the expansive surrounding forest. Acres of ground debris and weak understorey trees were cleared to emphasize the majesty and spatial volume of the forest. A variety of ferns (hay-scented, Christmas, cinnamon, ostrich and interrupted) carpet the ground. A low area adjacent to the drive is planted with moisture-loving flowering shrubs, such as Viburnum *alnifolium* and Azalea *viscosum*, as well as clumps of larch. The general effect of the entry sequence is one of breaking through an intense forest edge, diving off the highway into a different environment of soaring trunks, leaf-filtered light and secret mountain brooks.

The small parking court is elevated just enough above the surrounding forest that there is a sense of prospect as one exits the car, steps out into the cool air and peers into the multitude of trunks and gullied, leaf-strewn slopes. An overhead steel-mesh trellis connects the garage with the house; beneath it, a walk of pressed-concrete squares set in local crushed stone leads to the entrance. Eventually, wisteria vines should spread over the thin steel supports of the trellis to create a leafy vestibule.

One of the first gestures of the site diagram was a stone retaining wall that leads from the entry walk out onto the front lawn. The wall establishes a level platform on the slope, and against it rests the filled earth around the house. It is a bold, singular move that serves as a primary unifying element for the design. The wall's line is parallel with, and extends the orientation of, the house and detached garage outwards into the forest. This wall is the signal element that initiates arrival into the heart of the site. Its top runs flush with the front lawn; its height grows from eighteen to thirty-six inches as the grade drops along its base. The wall is backed on the upper level by a line of clipped yew that forms a strong edge to the open lawn. We hesitated to use yew here

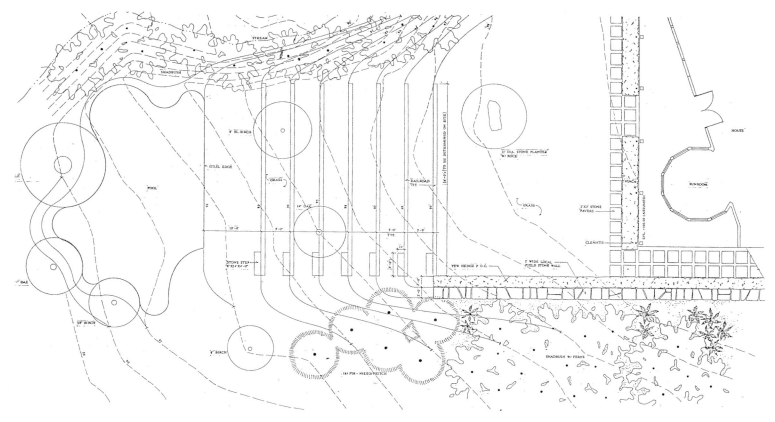

BELOW As one approaches, the orientation of the house is successively reiterated by vinca bed, walk, yew line, wall and shad grove.

173

OPPOSITE ABOVE Just after installation, the yew had not yet spread to form a solid evergreen bar.

OPPOSITE BELOW Partial plan of front lawn, glass steps and forest pool.

as it is highly susceptible to deer; however, to our delight we discovered that, when controlled by protective (almost invisible) netting draped over the plants, the deer's chewing actually keeps the yew clipped to a perfectly sheer top. A grove of multi-stem shad is planted along the base of the wall to bring depth to the diagram and screen views between the entry drive and the main lawn. Shadbushes are native understorey trees; they grow along forest margins, and their tiny white blossoms are one of the first to appear each spring.

Off the south side of the front lawn, perpendicular to the long stone wall and directly in line with the house's southern orientation, we constructed a series of broad grass/moss steps edged with railroad sleepers. The terraced steps descend eight feet from the lawn to a serene mountain pool. At the foot of the steps, the pool cuts a straight line parallel to the face of the house whose reflection glimmers from above in the dark water. As it moves away from the grassy steps, the pool edge of semi-submerged, mossy cleft stones undulates in and out of existing trees. The pool is fed by a nearby artesian well, siphoning off a miniscule percentage of the mountain's hydrologic energy. In the summer, the pool offers a bracing quick dip; in the fall, it catches bright red, yellow and orange

ABOVE Like snow in the winter, leaf drop in the fall covers surfaces indiscriminantly and unifies everything visually.

OPPOSITE Railroad sleepers retain the grass tiers which descend from house to pool; a narrow set of pre-cast steps marks the northern edge and separates the open slot from a thick spruce stand.

foliage; in the winter, its still surface ices over with a translucence that magnifies the decomposing leaves below. The water appears to hover at the edge of the slope, captured for a moment before answering the call of gravity.

Just west of the pool, seasonal mountain brooks continue to rush past. From the lawn above, a wooden bridge crosses over to a promontory covered with beech, birch, hemlock, ferns and partridgeberry. Once across the bridge, wanderers are pressed immediately into the mountainside, removed from the house and surrounded by water channels and the smell of moist humus.

On the north side of the house, a clipped rectangle of grass is separated from the forest by a stone retaining wall and an arbor-vitae hedge. A twenty-four-inch-wide canal, currently under design development, is planned to parallel the arbor vitae and edge the *tapis vert*. A five-foot-wide opening in the hedge line will reveal a glimpse of Diana or another figure, set back in the forest within a hemlock exedra. This nymph of the forest and moon, partially primitive yet certainly a product of human culture, is an apt symbol for the entire project. It is a mountainside site of untamed spirit from which civilized terrain is carved, a landscape established not as a blemish or intrusion, but as an extraction of nature's cycles and forces, which shape and colour the land continually.

OUT ON A LIMB:
THE PROCESS OF DISCOVERY

The best part of design is that there are no rules. One can do something different each time, start fresh (but with added depth of experience) on each problem, see the site with open, clear eyes that allow the highest solution to come forward. Design is truly a process of discovery. It is an exciting dialogue that draws upon all of one's knowledge, intuitions, values and inspirations. To be good, the designer has to trust his or her instinct and go out on a limb to propose the best scheme, even though nothing like it has been done before.

As the turn of the millennium draws near, there are several projects in my studio that suggest a fullness and complexity of weaving and layering that goes beyond earlier work. The MID-Kyoto garden plaza is a study of this intensification of ordering systems. Other projects, such as the Columbus Circle proposal and the Agnes R. Katz Plaza, go the other way, presenting a geometric simplicity that is refreshing in plan. There are other works that are idiosyncratic compositions built around site-specific features, as at the du Pont Residence and the PO+LE House. At the Milwaukee Art Museum, we are reaching for a reduction of elements, tensile relationships and materials to achieve the purest connection to the breath-taking museum addition.

A connection so pure, perhaps, that it is only suggested. What exists and what one experiences comprise a parallel movement; there is no literal contact – the addition and the garden are divided by a road. So, the powerful link between the two designs is implied, and, as such, it is stronger than what is known and present because it revels in potential, free from boundaries, definitely spiritual in nature. In these projects and in those to come, I am seeking the nature of unified spirit; the tools remain order and scale, form and balance, unity and dynamic rhythm. This goal, I believe, is a compelling reason to reach out to that which is as yet unexplored, both in life and in design (because, after all, they are the same) – it means going out on a limb, and that is the best place to be.

OPPOSITE Early study for Columbus Circle

PRIVATE RESIDENCE

NEW YORK, 1997

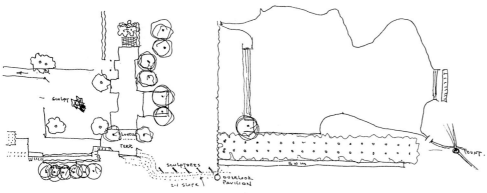

The drive suddenly emerges into a cathedral-like space: a crowd of soaring spruce trunks, slicing and dancing in the air.

I first saw this three-hundred-plus-acre site from the precarious passenger seat of a bouncing golf-cart. The mode of transport was appropriate, as the grounds of the estate had been moulded into an eighteen-hole golf-course sixty years earlier by Lowell Thomas, the popular radio personality. By the time the current owners purchased the property, it had sat vacant for thirteen years. Most of its features were overgrown,

deteriorated, transmogrified into half-tamed, half-wild vestiges of a past way of life. Traces of the golf greens were perceptible only when pointed out, their pate of bent grass long ago consumed by coarse lawn and field species. The true legacy of the old golf-course was a series of astounding turf boulevards, lined by hundred-foot-tall Norway spruce trees. Planted in the 1920s, the towering stands of spruce now

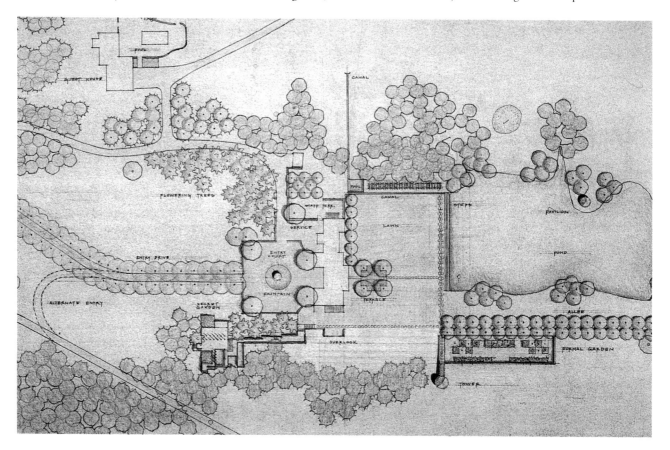

RIGHT Site plan with main house at centre, arrival court/entry drive to left (with secret garden below), south lawn terrace, pond and ginkgo *allée* to right.

RIGHT Site plan with guest house at centre, guest barn and service barn to upper left, swimming pool and arrival court to right.

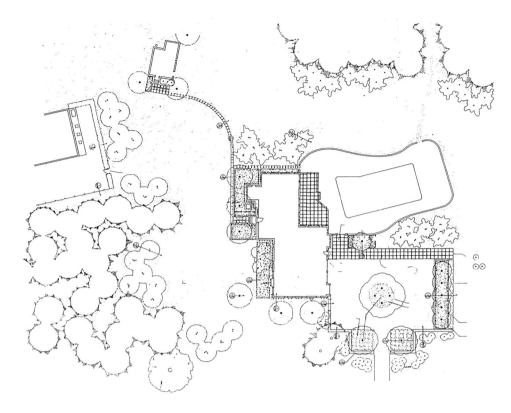

RIGHT Site plan with guest house at centre, guest barn and service barn to upper left, swimming pool and arrival court to right.

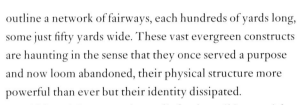

outline a network of fairways, each hundreds of yards long, some just fifty yards wide. These vast evergreen constructs are haunting in the sense that they once served a purpose and now loom abandoned, their physical structure more powerful than ever but their identity dissipated.

Although I cannot take credit for the striking spatial effect of the spruce stands, there was no question that they would be not only a reference point, but a fundamental generative factor in the design process. Our client, eager to bring order and care back to the grounds, limbed up hundreds of the spruces with dramatic results. The property is entered via the original entry drive, which we renovated with an oil-and-stone surface. Although gouged and scarred from decades of neglect, the old drive had a stable base of unusually large cobbles that we were able to use and update with the latest in lighting and security technology. At first, it seems as if one has stumbled onto a narrow country track within a forest of birch and beech. Then, the drive suddenly emerges into a cathedral-like space: a crowd of soaring spruce trunks, slicing

179

and dancing in the air, a place that reverberates with the silent presence of immensity. We have planted thousands of hay-scented, cinnamon, Christmas and other ferns to carpet the forest floor and provide a continuous, unified surface out of which the trunks rise.

The entry road then climbs up a steep hill, at the top of which rests the house. As one negotiates a tight hairpin turn around a lily pond, the severity of the hillside is noticeable. Passage over this terrain serves as a reminder that the Appalachian Trail and the mountainous ridges that it traces are nearby. Yet the site is equally representative of the Hudson River Valley above which it hovers, whose rich soils

BELOW There is a thirty-six-inch window between the top of the holly hedge and the branching height of the littleleaf lindens so that one can look south out of the arrival court.

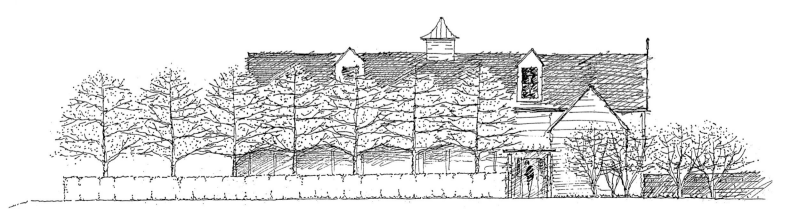

ABOVE An initial study of thresholds, screens and planting at the guest-house entrance.

RIGHT Aerial view of model from the north, with main house and pond visible at top.

and busy wildlife corridor it shares. Due to its exposed terrain and active, temperate climate, the site is prone to intense hydrological occurrences. One of our primary concerns in revamping existing structures – the entry drive, weakened stone walls, eroding shorelines along the pond – was a well-researched storm-water management programme.

Although currently on hold, the essential ingredients of the main-house master plan included the arrival sequence (the creation of an ordered spatial context) and the harmonic integration of the house (its mass, proportions and orientation) into the landscape. On the south side of the house, an existing pond became the zone of transition between ordered space and the outer grounds. We proposed to cut the shoreline closest to the house into a crisp line, its link to the domestic realm manifest as three broad grass steps, edged in stone, which descend from the lawn to the water. The architectonic shoreline continues along the pond's west edge for seventy-five feet, then relaxes into a lentic rhythm of bulges and reed-filled recesses. A two-hundred-foot-long ginkgo *allée* parallels the west shore; on axis with the library portico, it is a datum for the entire composition.

Our design for the nearby guest house has been nstalled under the direction of project manager Peter Meyer. As at the main house, our intent here was to create an elegant entry sequence, then create appropriate living spaces that would mediate between the building and the greater landscape context. The entrance passes between two stately London plane trees set in panels of clipped yew, then opens into a eighty-by-eighty-foot court of crushed stone.

Four more plane trees, with their mottled bark and full crowns, anchor a circle of ground cover at the court's centre. A line of five littleleaf lindens, set ten feet on centre, define the south side of the court. A dry-laid stone wall retains the north and west sides and holds the two sentry plane trees in individual alcoves. The wall becomes a tight hedge of

evergreen American holly as it returns south. To frame a view out towards the main house and pond, the holly is clipped to four feet high, while the lindens above are limbed up to a seven-foot branching height. A hundred-foot steel pergola lines the court's east edge. This airy walkway/vine armature plays the role of a Japanese screen – it exists not to prevent views or block passage but to entice with hints of things beyond.

Groupings of Kousa dogwood and Japanese lilac provide colour and subtle structure around the swimming pool. In contrast with the crisp geometries of the entry area, the north side of the guest house is loosely structured and without overt programme. A line of four honey-locusts set ten feet off the façade balances the house and translates its mass to the exterior. A grove of multi-stemmed white birches, rising directly out of grass, flows through the unclaimed area between the adjacent forest margin and

the house. The birches are a species capable of fulfilling dual ornamental and natural roles, depending on how they are situated. We used them here in both – this is the forest reaching inwards and the cultured environment spreading outwards.

In 1998, my office began to work on this client's townhouse in New York City. On the ground floor, in a thirty-by-twenty-foot court connected to the main living-room via a wall of French doors, we are planting two littleleaf lindens balanced at twelve feet apart. The trees' placement is tricky, as it must be attuned to a large piece of sculpture in the court's centre. We have consulted with the architect, Office of Peter Rose, on a water wall that is the outer boundary of the court. On an upper level, a second (tiny) roof garden contains a single flowering tree and tapestry of vines.

ABOVE Model view over main house to pond and ginkgo *allée.*

BELOW View north to the guest house; new plantings are used not only to order the landscape but to link it spatially with the existing mature spruce stands (on right).

181

MID–KYOTO

KYOTO, JAPAN, 1998

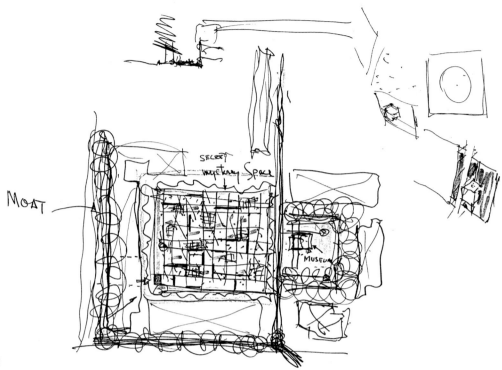

The materials of nature are intensely compacted and formed by human order, while the necessities of urban life are dissipated by organic filters.

Under the direction of Mr Tsuneo Sekine, the Matsushita Investment and Development Company invited four architects each to design one element of a multi-use commercial development in the heart of Kyoto. An eight-acre parcel wedged between the new bullet-train station and National Route #1, the site is on the southern edge of the city's centre and historic garden district. Henry Cobb (Pei, Cobb, Freed), Mario Bellini (Mario

RIGHT Plan view of an early site model, with proposed building sectors for the collaborating architects: Cobb at bottom, Bellini at left, Nikken Sekkei at left and top, KPF to right.

LEFT Detail shot of the model illustrating the ordered ground plane with layer of loose canopy above.

BELOW The site section shows the continual grid of plum trees, which establishes a strong spatial order that pulls the buildings together.

183

Bellini Associates), Gene Kohn (Kohn Pederson Fox) and Nikken Sekkei of Japan contributed office space, a visitors' centre/hotel complex, a conference centre and additional retail/office space, respectively. Harry Cobb devised an initial master plan and then invited me to bring that framework to life as a master landscape plan that would give the entire project a distinctive identity. MID asked me to propose a site plan that would knit all the buildings into a singular, comprehensible development and embrace 'variety within variety'. 'The element of landscape,' Mr Sekine stated,

should respond to the truth that 'the collective of the individuals is not the whole, the division of the whole is the individuals. The whole is something special.'

It is said that the Japanese tea ceremony is distinguished from other art forms in that it takes a simple, everyday activity and elevates that act to the level of an art that embodies the beauty of form. Our master-plan proposal reinterprets those and other harmonic relationships, rhythms, spatial proportions, symbolic associations and materials of Kyoto's traditions at a huge, contemporary scale. As stated in

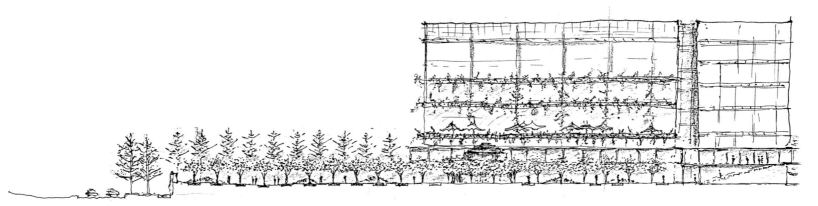

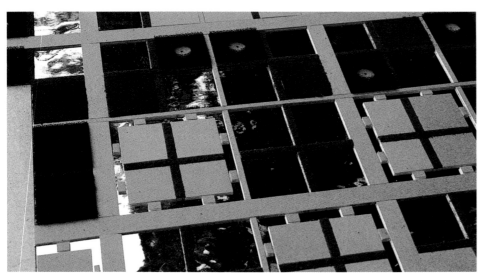

TOP Perspective view from within the garden.

ABOVE Detail shot of the model showing the modular interplay of water and solid.

OPPOSITE Schematic site plan indicates the canopy checkerboard. National Route #1 borders the site to the left; the train station is at top (not seen).

recreational use as an urban amenity and, finally, its cultural contribution as a cherished component of Japanese gardens. At MID-Kyoto, water permeates all. The substance of water is malleable, and as such we employ each expression as a programmatic device: quiet pools for rest and contemplation; gushing fountains at gathering and café areas; long water walls to abate traffic noise; tiny misting heads throughout the plant beds to cool the air. We want activated water, not static building façades (which surround and tower up to 150 feet over the garden) to be the defining image of the development.

The primary layer of the site structure is human order, inscribed as a grid of walkways and moss lines across the plaza. This organizational system covers the majority of the site (all of which is over parking structure) and sections it into alternating panels of grass, ground cover, paving and water. The second layer is spatial volume, an ordered flow created by quartets of flowering trees set in a checkerboard pattern over the walkway grid. The scheme of green structure is envisioned to continue outwards, to act as a catalyst to forge links with a tree network throughout the southern zone of Kyoto. The third layer of the site structure is loose spirit, the mark of freedom and energy and mystery of the unknown. This is found in curving, linear mounds of moss and sheared azalea that move in a serpentine continuum across the grid, pulling the eye and the curious mind through the regularized framework of tree trunks. Up to eight feet high, the mounds crash through the site order to find a sinuous, organic balance of their own.

A grand staircase and festival plaza on the site's north side act as an infrastructural/circulation core, but also as an observation deck of sorts that encourages the spectacle atmosphere of the public place. The surrounding office and hotel walls are in a way vertical extensions of the plaza. Their windows and balconies allow visual interaction with events on the ground plane, as well as views out to the neighbouring landmarks, and thus provide information and institute a perceived knowledge of place beyond what is known below. The idea of multi-level activity is carried throughout the site: on the eastern parcel, an elevated water garden provides gathering space that integrates access to parking below.

The best works of design are born from clarity of structure and brought to life with nuance of detail. At MID-Kyoto, nuance springs from the interplay of textures and

the initial project documents, the master plan was intended to grant 'primacy to figural space over figural volume'; in other words, the buildings would frame a central, public garden plaza to 'celebrate the landscaped space rather than the buildings as objects'. I was honoured indeed to be presented with such a challenge. I felt that this was a project of significance far greater than the typical urban development. This would truly be something new, a landscape and a garden model for the twenty-first century – a rich weaving of park, plaza, nature and building that would emerge as a form of ordered space and articulated energy.

Water is an essential element in Kyoto, for its historic associations of transport and commerce, its ecological ramifications of sustenance and cycles of nature, its movement amongst the various materials across the spectrum of the seasons. In the late spring, the trees' white blossoms will be caught in the still pools that surround the conference centre. The sun's daily journey will be reflected in the waterworks and in tree shadows cast over the gridded walks. The grinding crunch of crushed stone or the silent springiness of grass will accompany one's journey across the plaza. Visitors will experience the presence of nature within the burgeoning city: here, the materials of nature – water, trees, stone – are intensely compacted and formed by human order, while the necessities of urban life – looming buildings, traffic, parking, noise – are dissipated by the organic filters of waterfalls, foliage and laughter. As such, distinction between the two will blur; the duality of Nature and City will merge into one enlightened space. The division between indoor and outdoor will be faint and cloaked in intermediate devices of café pavilions, groves, pergolas. The garden will be invigorated with twenty-first-century energies and technology, yet remain attuned to the profound history of Kyoto.

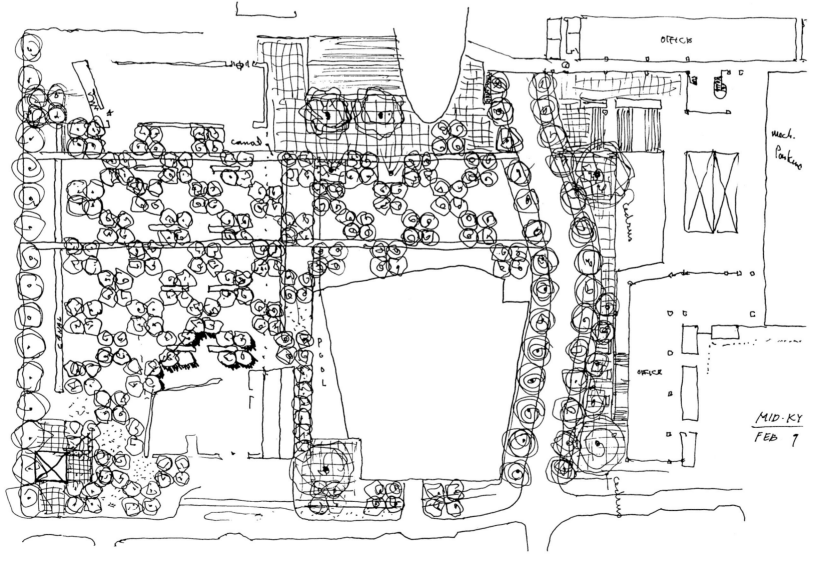

COLUMBUS CIRCLE
NEW YORK, NEW YORK, 1998

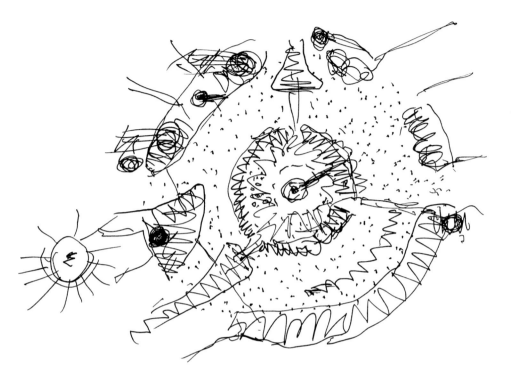

The successful proposal would enact a fundamental change – from seedy traffic island to a realm of vitality and urban integrity.

Early in 1998, we were invited, along with five other teams (Kennedy & Violich Architecture, Machado and Silvetti Associates/The Olin Partnership, Michael Sorkin Studio, Rafael Viñoly Architects and Weiss/Manfredi Architects) to present 'inspired but practical' plans to be used as the basis for a long-overdue renovation – or reinvention – of New York City's Columbus Circle. Conceived of and sponsored by the Municipal Arts Society, the competition was grounded in a

RIGHT Plan view of schematic model. The Christopher Columbus statue stands at the centre.

LEFT Plan view with tree canopies and fountain ring at centre. The entrance to Central Park is at the upper right; Broadway comes in at the upper left.

BELOW A sectional study of street architecture: clipped tree forms.

187

wish to realize the site's latent potential: to move beyond its current incarnation as a complex traffic round-about that repels pedestrians towards a more-than-cosmetic transformation into a grand civic plaza on the order of Place de la Concorde in Paris and Trafalagar Square in London. The jury asked participants to incorporate a philosophical future vision of the site with a thoughtful examination of a myriad of use issues. The successful proposal would enact a fundamental change in public perception of the place – from seedy traffic island to a realm of vitality and urban integrity.

The Circle itself is over four hundred feet in diameter, with a 180-foot-diameter island at the centre. A narrow, ascending statue of Christopher Columbus rises from the centre, its symbolism lost in the chaotic activity around it. The fixed elements of the design (to which all teams were instructed to adhere) include the road alignments, the circumferential property line, three subway entrances and a limited depth of ground resulting from shallow utilities and subway tunnels. The site's location is paramount as it occupies the crossroads between downtown and the Upper

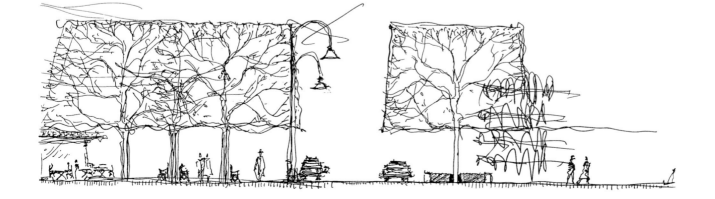

ABOVE A schematic cross-section through the Circle, looking north.

BELOW Detail plan of a typical sector of the central island, showing tree placement, café tables, kiosks and perimeter bubble canal.

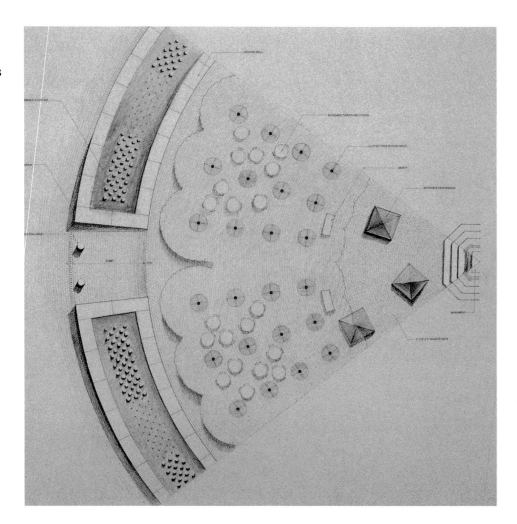

West Side; it also can be seen as a threshold into the performing arts district, with Lincoln Center to the north and Broadway to the south. Central Park spills out from the Circle's north-east quadrant, offering a proximity to parkland unusual within New York City. The huge buildings that surround the Circle present a cacophony of clashing architectural styles – unlike famed plazas elsewhere, there is little or no continuity in the site's perimeter.

In my mind, the missing ingredient of Columbus Circle was one on which almost all works of design depend, an aspect so fundamental that its effect is intrinsically sensed rather than overtly tangible: unity. Instead of intensifying the existing chaotic built environment with more 'jazz', we wanted to bring out what was already there – the traditional form of the civic circle and an enviable location – then inject the new textures, colours and life that would truly make the urban space come alive. Our strategy was to bring forth a sense of cohesiveness via a loose but palpable order, and our tool was living architecture – the material of the Park (trees), the language of the City (architectural form). In a functional and aesthetically lucid manner, this solution was clearly the most 'apt' (the guiding principle of Frederick Law Olmsted, architect of Central Park).

Our scheme relies upon a singular structural device to dramatize the Circle: a triple row of clipped littleleaf lindens, which emanate concentrically from the centre out into the city in a refreshing and enduring application of spatial infrastructure. The trees are set fifteen feet on centre and

RIGHT Perspective view of the fountain
arc in front of the Coliseum.

OPPOSITE BELOW View through tree
rings from the pavement.

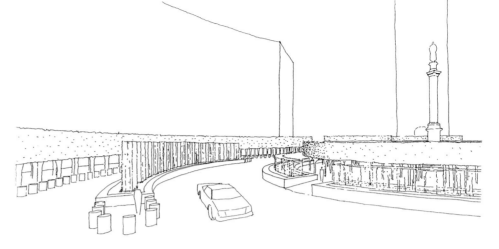

are precisely trimmed for architectural clarity; branching
begins at eight to ten feet, so that sight-lines and passage
are unhindered. The structure is formal but open-ended; it
establishes Columbus Circle as a specific place, yet implies
ongoing expansion in both place and time.

The central island is rimmed with a ten-foot-wide water
canal out of which spring thousands of bubblers that can
be programmed into fountains and water curtains of various
heights and shapes. The inner circle is repeated with
additional rings of trees that circumscribe the site and
define the sidewalk. In front of the soon-to-be-renovated
Coliseum (a venue for large events and expositions), an arc
of water columns calls out the entrance and drop-off area.
We encourage cafés and outdoor markets to fill the wide
sidewalks and the central island, for year-round activity
is essential to urban vigour. At night, the rings of trees and
the fountains will be illuminated to create a festive meeting
place and usher theater-goers into the district.

It is critical to establish a continuous surface across the
entire site, as this will create a comprehensive base for unified
space. We proposed a stone carpet of 2½-by-2½-inch basalt
cobbles, set in asphalt where necessary. This small but
constant module will provide a distinct texture and planar
rhythm, with variations in colour or elevation to distinguish
crosswalks. I feel strongly that there should be no curb
announcing separation – instead, bollards will keep
pedestrians and vehicles apart, yet not interrupt the
flow of the ground plane.

As designed, Columbus Circle will grow from the
core outwards and from the ground upwards as a living
embodiment of dignified structural order, from which civic
identity emerges. The Circle holds resonant history and

plentiful urban potential, here redefined as one harmonious
entity that communicates directly and equally with
pedestrians and cars; natives and visitors; daytime use and
night life; functional necessity and poetic visions; complexity
of use and simplicity of form. The Circle must have a charged
atmosphere of activity in which the conflicting energies of
individual monuments and buildings are subsumed by the
greater living whole.

ABOVE View towards the central
island from the pavement.

189

PRIVATE RESIDENCE
NEW YORK, NEW YORK, 1998

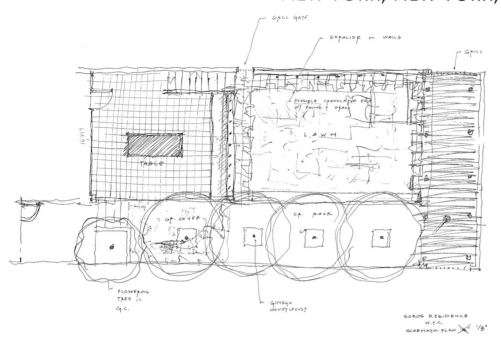

SOROS RESIDENCE
N.Y.C.
SCHEMATIC PLAN

With a site of this size, the only true response is to make one move, and everything else plays off that.

Although not all of the proposed aspects have been realized, this attention to intermediate spaces should result in a more fully integrated overall experience of the living quarters.

The garden is a rectangle of less than fifteen hundred square feet; its north–south dimension is just shy of sixty feet, and from east to west it is just over twenty-five feet. A two-sided fence encloses the east and west property line (the two sides allow for variation in material between the client's side and the neighbour's), while the north boundary, which needs to be visually strong as it faces the house and anchors the garden, is a sturdy brick wall. From the living area on the brownstone's ground floor, doors open into an exterior vestibule of sorts, which is eighteen inches above the garden elevation. A custom-designed stone bench and a raised plant

Tucked behind a handsome brownstone on a quiet side street in lower Manhattan, this private garden is so small that we approached the design almost as if we were creating a room inside the house. Our involvement in the project began in the midst of the design-development phase of interior renovation. As details were not yet fully resolved, we were able to collaborate with the architect and owner on several transitional areas between indoor and outdoor space.

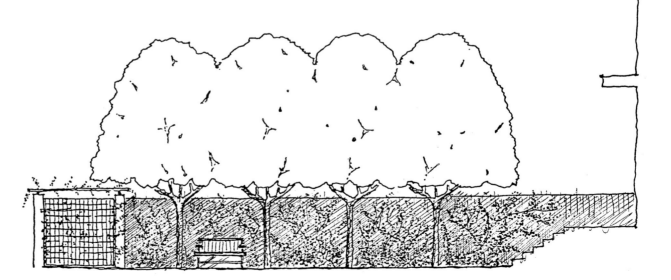

RIGHT East elevation of garden, with pergola on left, house on right, clipped lindens between.

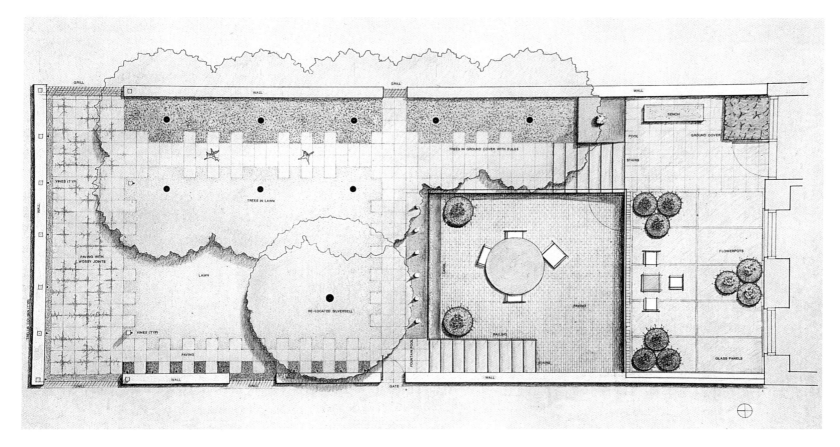

bed occupy the area. The flooring at the door is paved with twelve-by-twelve-inch cut stone that becomes a unifying element as it extends throughout the site. The remaining two-thirds of the floorspace at this upper level is covered with reinforced glass panels that allow light into the kitchen area below.

The garden level is a simple lawn panel framed by stone walks that parallel the perimeter walls. With a site of this size, the only true response is to make one move, and everything else plays off that. One cannot afford to decorate with lots of flowers or forms or variety of plants or paving. The shape of the space was perfect for a pergola at the far end, to draw people away from the house to a shaded spot. We were sure from the beginning that the centre should be plain, pure, clipped grass – like a table wine in some village in Italy, the simplest things would be best.

We explored several schemes for tree placement within the garden. At first, I thought that a double row of littleleaf lindens, on line with the upper entry, worked best. In the final version, just three flowering dogwoods are shown along the east wall. Beneath the trees, a lush bed of vinca with seasonal bulbs springs up as a darker, higher, more textured surface that complements the central lawn panel. As the walk has a crenellated edge, both the ground cover and the grass merge in and out of the paving for a loose but ordered effect.

An espalied firethorn is planned for the west wall, directly across from the flowering trees. From here, one can descend a set of steps into a sunken dining area, which is an extension of the kitchen/dining area on the brownstone's lower floor. The garden level and this sunken area are connected by water – an active element that relieves the potentially static structure of the place. A shallow pool on the south end of the garden is engineered to spill over and trickle down a moss-covered stone wall. The water is collected in a narrow trough and recirculated. To get access to this part of the project, a mature silverbell tree was removed from the garden level by crane.

I enjoy this scale of project as it allows one to focus intently and work almost everything out to the last detail.

ABOVE Site plan, with lawn panel at left centre and sunken terrace at right centre, separated by linear pool and water wall.

MILLENNIUM TOWER
MIAMI, FLORIDA, 1998

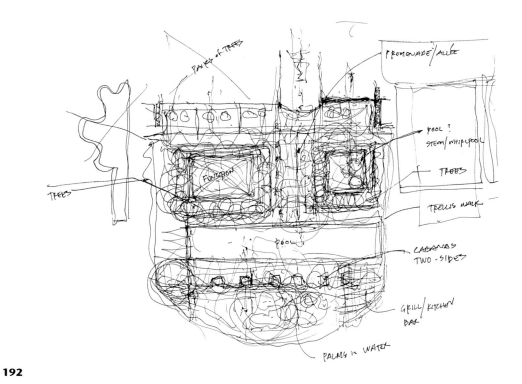

The soaring hall of palm trunks forms a dynamic curtain which becomes a backdrop for the rest of the garden.

The Millennium Tower is a mixed-use development in the heart of Miami. Designed by architect Gary Edward Handel and Associates, the tower has retail and parking on the ground floors and a combination of residential units and hotel on the upper levels. We designed a one-acre roof-top garden that opens off the hotel's seventh-floor restaurant and banquet rooms. The garden is also accessed directly from the hotel's eighth-floor lobby via interior stairs. Although the site is over a parking structure, it is engineered such that we had no limitation on plant depth or weight. In fact, the garden includes over seventy palm trees, a café, an eight-thousand-square-foot swimming pool and an equally expansive aquatic palm court.

The perimeter of the roof deck is ringed by a broad strolling promenade. The circuit, which will also serve as a jogging track, is shaded by an overhead trellis system that doubles as an armature for flowering vines. The trellis widens along the garden's west side, at the entry point from the hotel, but otherwise provides a consistent depth of frame around the space that disguises the deck's precarious edge above busy Brickell Avenue.

The garden is organized into interconnected, well-defined spatial volumes by blocks and lines of trees. These

RIGHT An early site plan with hotel at top, palm water-bosque at bottom.

volumes serve as rooms that address specific programmes: the south-west corner is open terrace that provides a gathering and entertainment area as an extension of the adjacent banquet room; the north-west corner is a children's pool; the central volume is an open gallery that contains the swimming pool overlooked by a small café and open-air dining area; the eastern third of the site is a towering bosque of royal palms, rising fifty feet out of a plane of water.

Although set on the outer side of the roof-top, the water bosque is in a way the centre of the garden. The surface pool is shallow and dotted by low fountains that bubble up

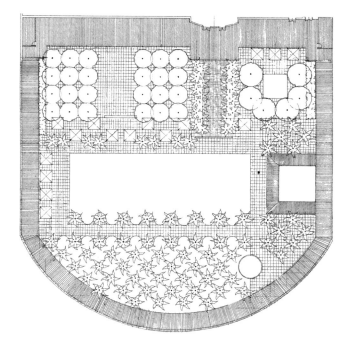

RIGHT Site section/elevation which illustrates the intimate spatial effect of low flowering trees versus the airy ceiling of palms.

BELOW RIGHT Perspective sketch looking from the hotel banquet room out to the roof-top garden.

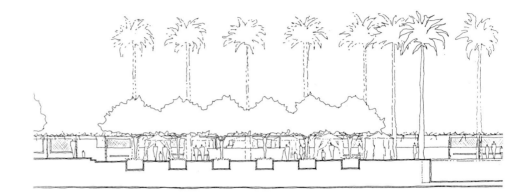

between trunks. The trees are planted in eight-to-ten-foot-diameter concrete drums that extend well below the pool's bottom, to provide a generous planting condition in which the palms can develop adequate root systems. The soaring hall of trunks, set in a grid at fifteen feet on centre, forms a dynamic curtain that becomes a backdrop for the rest of the garden.

The impressive height of the unfettered palm trunks is contrasted by the lower, fuller, more textured flowering trees that we use in blocks to define spaces in the east half of the garden. Our initial plant selection for the flowering trees includes Hong Kong magnolia with hedges of podocarpus and fragrant star jasmine. Ground covers and flowering vines such as English ivy, rosemary, creeping fig, bougainvillea and glory bower will adorn the many cabanas placed around the roof-top and will alternate with paving to define the ground plane. Vines will also drip over the edge of the decking and spill down over the parking structure beneath.

193

RIGHT From within the water-bosque, the palms create a cathedral effect. All drawings by T. Lee.

MILWAUKEE ART MUSEUM EXPANSION
MILWAUKEE, WISCONSIN, 1998

The water curtain and ribs of hedge move in a harmonic contrapuntal gesture in relation to Calatrava's magnificent addition.

On the shore of Lake Michigan, the new addition to the Milwaukee Art Museum, designed by architect Santiago Calatrava, is a splendour of engineered grace and material simplicity. It presents a rare opportunity to shape the surrounding landscape and shoreline into a work of equal resonance. True integration of building and land will realize a spatial order that can synchronize the cultural qualities of the city with the beauty of the lake.

Our design for an arrival-plaza garden is inspired by the articulated purity of Calatrava's work (which itself responds to the original War Memorial of Eero Saarinen and the subsequent David Kahler museum addition). The garden site is a rectangle, six hundred feet long and a hundred feet wide, that parallels the most recent expansion and lies between the museum and the city grid. A series of four-foot-tall evergreen hedge lines sections the garden into five lawns, with a paved plaza at each end. Monumental fountains anchor the centre of each plaza; these two end-pieces are connected by a narrow (three-foot-wide) water channel that bisects the entire length of the garden. Water jets within the channel are programmed to create a solid water curtain that can dance up at various levels or be illuminated to create a shimmering band at the museum's most public face.

The plane of each lawn parcel breaks diagonally across its width, with the inner half descending at a five-per-cent slope towards the spine of the canal. This manipulation of grade reveals low retaining walls that parallel the base of the hedge lines, on top of which walkways cross the garden and intersect the museum's broad entry plinth. The walks meet the new building perpendicularly and can be seen as a

194

RIGHT Aerial view of an initial study model, with museum on left and serial hedge segments at centre.

RIGHT A view towards the museum addition from the entry garden.

BELOW RIGHT The garden's hedge segments stitch together the city grid and the shoreline of Lake Michigan.

BOTTOM RIGHT An early site plan shows the rhythmic triangulation of the ground plane.

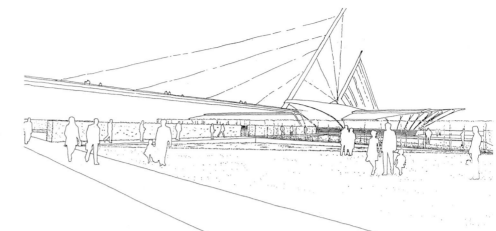

continuation of the city grid, reaching through the site to the lake. The outer, level lawns – at street grade – are a very fine-textured grass; the inner, inclined lawn planes are a rougher grass species; the contrast sets up a subtle diagonal rhythm.

Together, the water curtain and ribs of hedge move in a harmonic contrapuntal gesture in relation to Calatrava's magnificent addition. The scheme's open nature invites visitors to enjoy the energy of a unified spatial experience. Plant and paving palettes are quite minimal: there are no trees, no flower-beds or other ingredients to relieve the elementality of the composition, particularly in plan view. Yet once defined with unambiguous structure, the spatial energy will be built up and released. Minute variations of material, grade and light will become audible, much like the subtleties of poetry that can only be heard when one concentrates fully on the spare arrangement of words, or the importance of hue variation in a painting, which becomes apparent only when the piece is hung in a gallery space of the highest order.

On its east side, the museum faces Lake Michigan. We are currently consulting on the design of a new sea-wall and pedestrian/bike path along the shore. The plan calls for a broad, paved corridor to link a series of sculpture lawns and terraces, continue on to picnic gardens and eventually connect with a greater lake-side path system. Outlaying areas around the museum will be defined by *allées*, groves and large tracts of a rugged, loose shrub such as Rosa *rugosa*.

195

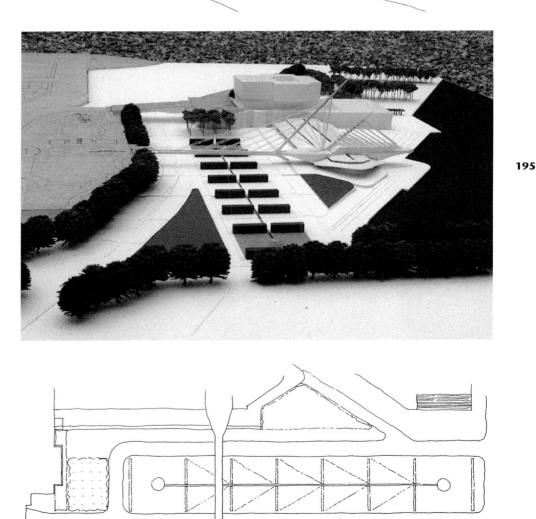

THE AGNES R. KATZ PLAZA

PITTSBURGH, PENNSYLVANIA, 1998

Our intent was to create a plaza of the utmost simplicity, a space which is a pleasing interlude from the city street.

The city of Pittsburgh has a marvelous commitment to the promotion of culture within the civic realm. As part of the gradual renovation and development of a cultural district within the heart of downtown – a laudatory synthesis of urban design and the arts – I was invited by Carol Brown, president of the Cultural Trust, to participate in the design of a small plaza at the corner of Penn Avenue and Seventh Street. Conceived as open space for the new, nearby Theatre Square Project (by architect Michael Graves), the plaza was to be formulated to accommodate a large Louise Bourgeois sculpture as well as a number of her 'eye' benches. At under fifteen thousand square feet, the scheme would have to be rich in effect but reduced to the simplest forms and relationships.

Early on in the project, we all met at Bourgeois' studio to view her maquettes. The piece destined to be the plaza's centrepiece was a connected pair of ascending, narrowly terraced cones that reach a height of twenty-five feet above a thirty-five-by-fifteen-foot base. As Louise explained that water would emit from both peaks and trickle down the pitched, grooved sides, it became clear that the statue should be set in a pool. In initial schematic studies, we played with placing the piece at the rear of the site (to take advantage of the strong background effect of the abutting high-rise's solid walls), but then agreed that it would work best at the plaza's centre, a location that would allow free circulation from any point of access.

To passers-by, the Bourgeois piece appears to rise out of a four-inch-deep basin of water (like an iceberg), which itself occupies most of a central sunken terrace. The pool's edge is fractured into an irregular but balanced border. We purposefully kept the pool's dimensions limited so that visitors could approach and interact with the artwork. The terrace is paved in two-by-two-inch granite sets and is depressed just eighteen inches below plaza grade. From the upper level, paving and the sense of spatial volume flow uninterrupted towards the sidewalk and street with the sculpture as the dominant element. Our intent was to create a plaza of the utmost simplicity, a space that is a pleasing interlude from the city street yet is an integral part of the urban circulation pattern.

Three sides of the plaza are marked by concise lines of littleleaf linden trees, to form a U-shaped volume that opens onto Penn Avenue. The lindens are clipped for formal,

architectural clarity and branch well above passage and sight lines. In a way, the trees are an extension and indentation of the arcade that extends towards the plaza from the theatre further up the block. They frame the Bourgeois sculpture and encapsulate the sense of specific space at the corner of two busy streets. Yet the high branching and regularity of trunk placement act to receive passers-by and encourage unrestricted circulation.

Night lighting, Louise Bourgeois' crafted benches and commemorative plaques each contribute to the detailed experience of the plaza. Ivy will be planted against the Century Building at the back of the plaza; once established, it will reinforce the linden's verdant backdrop effect.

ABOVE The clipped lindens build spatial volume which receives the Bourgeois piece.

RIGHT A sketch plan of the plaza with Bourgeois piece at centre; Seventh Street runs along the bottom, with Penn Street along the left side. Graves's related theatre project is at upper left (not seen).

OPPOSITE In one of the earliest schemes, the floor plane slipped and shifted as it moved inwards towards the sculpture from the street.

197

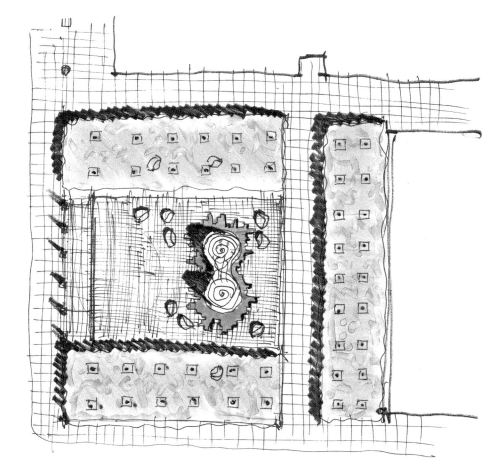

PO+LE HOUSE

ASPEN, COLORADO 1998

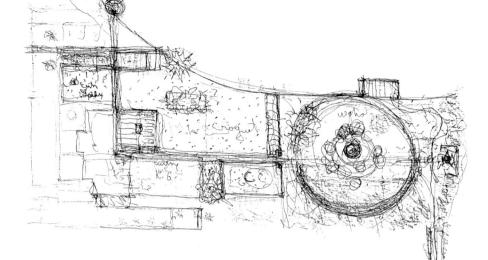

At its simplest, the scheme is a co-dependency of two paradigms: forest and garden.

In the heart of Aspen's historic residential district, the PO+LE House site perches on a bluff of glacial deposit overlooking Hallam Lake and the Aspen Center for Environmental Studies. At under two acres, the property's size dictates an intimacy between interior and exterior spaces that is heightened in juxtaposition to the enormous

view of gravelly mountainsides that looms across from the site's open north face. The house was one of the first in Aspen, originally built in the 1800s and added onto over successive generations. A mélange of architectural styles from Victorian to bungalow, the main house and its outbuildings were purchased by a family instrumental in the development of the ski industry in Aspen. I acted as a consultant in the resort's early planning stages and in the process became warm friends with the owners, who eventually sold the house to our current client.

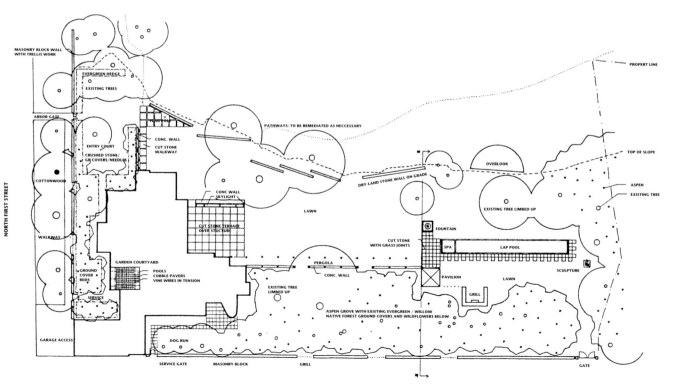

RIGHT Site plan with terrace and open lawn at centre, pool/pavilion complex to right, and entry garden at upper left.

Architect Michael Ernemann's renovation plans were near completion when we signed on. Our goal was to discover a scheme for the site that served the current owner's needs while respecting the delicate environmental concerns and weaving in an interpretation of the property's historic role within the tightly knit Aspen community.

The site is surrounded by and infilled with stands of spruce mixed with occasional groups of quaking aspen, bristlecone and lodgepole pine. The spruce stands form an evergreen envelope that shrouds the site on all but its northern exposure, leaving a central open 'room' on the east side of the house. In the past, this inner sanctum had been lawn with a series of perennial beds; our scheme called for a clarification of the green structure and an amplification of the site's inherent tension between wild and cultivated. At its simplest, the scheme is a co-dependency of two paradigms: forest and garden. The two types are not blended; they are lucidly independent yet intrinsically involved with each other. As the property is nested within the immensity of the Rockies, so the scale of the garden is understood within the realm of the forest.

The entry sequence draws pedestrians from the street inwards, the first portal being two pines between which the walkway dives. The walk passes beneath an arbour gate of black steel and flowering vines designed as part of a reconstruction of the existing property-line wall. Breaks in the wall (obsolete entrances) that had to be maintained in adherence with strict local codes became sections of six-foot-high steel grill that punctuate the length of its white concrete face. The rhythm of alternating solid and open grill continues around all but the northern edge of the site, leaving that exposure open to the vast view. Aspens will be planted to create a filigree of foliage across the house's street façade, also to cast light and shadow onto a tiny entry court of crushed stone, needles and ground covers below.

The reconfiguration of the house's interior is founded upon the intersection of two perpendicular concrete walls at

the heart of the structure: it is both a datum (the primary circulation corridor off which interior volumes open) and a cross axis that extends into the site. This axial armature continues into landscape structure as a hundred-foot-long pergola that connects the garden to the house. The pergola plays a crucial role in clarifying the relationship of the various site elements; without it, the site would consist of disparate zones. We want to illuminate the inevitability of movement from interior to exterior. With two-by-two-inch steel tubing, wire cables and narrow-gauge grillwork, the pergola is a diaphanous structure like those used throughout history to provide subtle spatial definition, to formulate acts of passage and connection. It will blend with tree branchings behind it in the winter months and be covered with vines in the summer. One can think of the pergola as the transformation of foliage and trunks into the ordered space of the open lawn.

The pergola leads to a ten-by-ten-foot pavilion, fire pit/grill and sculptural fountain (the water feature is centred on the living-room terrace). A central grass panel moves out from the pavilion, held on its north side by a lap pool – a sliver of shimmering cool liquid in the forest – and on its left side by the forest edge. Ground covers, ferns and spring bulbs fill the ground beneath airy aspens and mark the boundary between cultivation and untended ground.

A forty-foot flag pole rises up from the far eastern edge of lawn, pinning down the point at which the axis of the house's circulation corridor intersects the axis of an historic route that used to lead to the lake from downtown Aspen. On the site's north face, we replaced an existing overlook with teak decking of narrow strips steamed and bent to fit a fifteen-foot radius. A series of eighteen-inch-high dry-stone walls is set at intervals along the top of the north slope for minimal spatial definition of the edge as well as to provide seating.

199

ABOVE Preliminary thoughts on the fountain sculpture.

BELOW An early site elevation looking south.

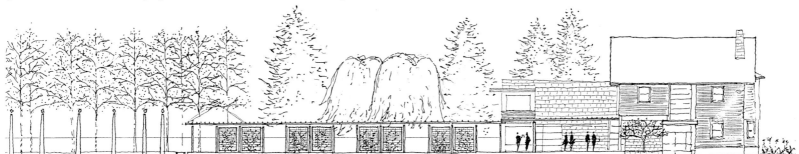

DU PONT RESIDENCE

WILMINGTON, DELAWARE, 1992–98

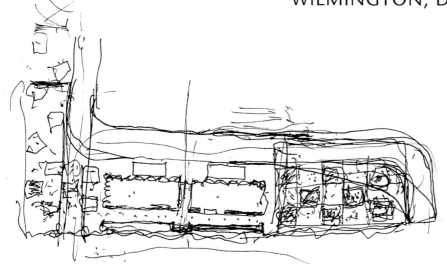

Much of our early master-plan work looked to existing landscape features for suggestions about lay-out and spatial arrangements.

Our initial master plan for this estate included a series of themed gardens linked by a network of paths and well-proportioned intermediate spaces: a master-suite terrace and arrival court directly adjacent to the house, a children's garden, an 'adventure playground' and theatre for children, a maze with a 'Rapunzel' tower, a *potager*, a hillside garden, a bog garden, orchards and a tea-house tucked into the outlaying grounds. It was decided that rather than construct everything at once, the development would take place over a decade. This year, we have seen the *potager* and the entry drive/arrival court implemented. The owners anticipate that once the master plan is fully realized, there will be frequent visitors touring the estate.

The existing condition of the site was quite beautiful, although frank in its unmet potential. The native forest tracts were outstanding – in particular, the stands of mature tulip-poplar and beech provided an inspiring organic spatial construct off which to build. In part to connect the new element to the site's intrinsic composition, we selected tulip-poplars to line the new entry drive. Set fourteen feet on centre in double rows along both sides of the roadbed, the poplars are a species that will grow quickly to a massive size and thus create a grand entry corridor.

Much of our early master-plan work looked to existing landscape features for suggestions about lay-out and spatial arrangements. The forest species mentioned above is one

RIGHT An early detail section cut through the *potager* slope, with outline hedges in the distance.

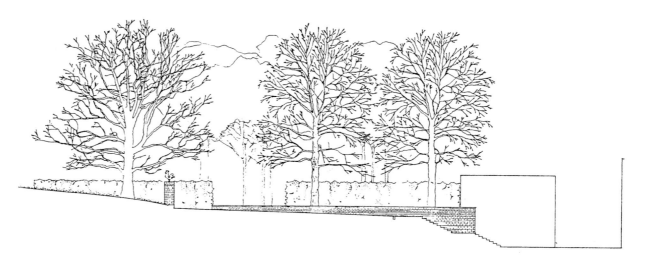

ABOVE The original master plan, with house at centre, *potager* at far left. Pathways cut through forest and field connect various features of this decentralized plan.

example of this approach: we proposed to create an open seating area at the base of the most outstanding specimens, with *allées* connecting one majestic old tree to another across the woods. Another example is the incorporation of the old stone walls, which for years had divided the property into oddly shaped parcels and paddocks. Several of the new pathways follow existing walls, and at one point where two low walls intersected, we drew a hypotenuse to complete a triangular shape that became the outline for the maze. The master plan also integrated and reinterpreted built aspects of the original estate, such as an upper-level pool and various outbuildings.

The *potager* was conceived as a walled garden, set on the edge of a gentle, architecturally cut slope. At two hundred by sixty feet, the available planting area for vegetables, annuals and perennials is extensive, yet the *potager* is as much a place to wander amongst beds, to sit and consider the surrounding landscape, as it is an intensive work space (a similar circumstance to Thomas Jefferson's hillside plots at his homestead, Monticello, in Virginia). A wall of holly hedge

skirts the garden; it is perforated at regular intervals with a delicate steel grill to let sight-lines in and out. A central canal, just twelve inches wide, bisects the *potager* and is anchored at each end by a twelve-foot square pool. The canal is both a compositional and a functional feature – it is a handy place to rinse herbs and freshly harvested vegetables. The pools, in contrast, relate less to the garden's productive endeavours and more to its capacity to offer relaxation, a place for conversation and respite from the sun. An overhead steel trellis shades the pool areas; beneath them are benches and tool-storage space that again serve both gardener and observer. A linear section of the trellis extends the length of the canal, paralleling its alignment eight feet above grade.

VITA

DAN KILEY was born in Boston, Massachusetts in 1912. His mother, Louise Baxter, cared for the family and house; his father was a construction manager by trade and a boxer by calling. Kiley's childhood was spent in the Roxbury section of Boston, where he attended Jamaica Plain High School and often walked home through the Arnold Arboretum. Many of Kiley's summers were spent at his grandmother's upland-pasture farm in New Hampshire. In his late teens, Kiley caddied at the Charles River Country Club and hoped to open his own landscape design practice. At the age of eighteen, in the midst of the Great Depression, Kiley wrote letters to a number of Boston-area landscape architecture and planning firms to seek an apprenticeship. All wrote back, but only one offered a position: Warren H. Manning, the pre-eminent co-founder of the American Society of Landscape Architects and past associate of Frederick Law Olmsted, Sr.

Kiley apprenticed for Manning without pay for several years and was then promoted to associate and given a pay-cheque. Past employees of the firm with whose work Kiley became familiar included Fletcher Steele and Arthur Sylvester. After six years at Manning's Brattle Street offices in Cambridge and in the field, Kiley was accepted as a special student to the Harvard Graduate School of Design's Landscape Architecture programme. Kiley was twenty-four when he matriculated in 1936; he was full of energy and possessed extensive plants and construction experience in place of a college degree. He continued to work up to thirty hours a week at Manning's studio while enrolled in school. At Harvard Kiley consorted with classmates Garret Eckbo and James Rose in the quest for modern expression in the practice of landscape design. While their efforts in that direction were not supported within the Landscape or Architecture departments of Harvard at the time, the tide of modernism was rising. Once out of school, the three launched themselves onto the crest of the wave.

In 1938, Kiley left Harvard without a degree, partially due to disillusionment with the curriculum and pedantic style. Soon afterwards, he headed north to New Hampshire, where he was employed by the National Parks Service for several months. He subsequently prepared the first master plan for the City of Concord for the Concord Planning Commission . In spring 1939 via a connection to the New Hampshire senator's son, Kiley took a job in Washington, D.C., as Assistant Landscape Architect at the Procurement Division, Public Buildngs Branch at the Treasury Department. By the summer, he had transferred to the position of Associate Town Planner at the United States Housing Authority under Elbert Peets, working on low-income housing estates. Although discouraged by the unwillingness of his superiors to incorporate new ideas, Kiley was thrilled to be in a place of social and professional opportunity.

In those pre-war years in the capital, Kiley befriended colleagues and was introduced to eminent figures in the design field. In later decades, those early contacts evolved into a network of figures crucial to the success of Kiley's career. Fertilized by the intellectual curiosity and budding internationalism of the modern era, in the construction boom after World War II the acquaintances Kiley had made in Washington (and to some degree at Harvard) became professionally productive relationships with star architects and a self-perpetuating list of prominent clients.

In 1939 and 1940, Kiley co-researched a manifesto with Eckbo and Rose which was published in the *Architectural Record*. The piece, 'Landscape Design', was presented in three parts over a nine-month period. This publication, in addition to a number of contempory books and articles by various authors, including Lewis Mumford, Fletcher Steele, Christopher Tunnard, Margaret Goldsmith, Rose and Eckbo, were instrumental in the dissemination of the notion of modern and modernized landscape architecture.

In 1941, Kiley took up residence at Charles and Nina Collier's estate in Virginia, where he explored design expression in situ. The Collier job was Kiley's first major project, and with it he opened the Office of Dan Kiley in Washington, D.C., and Franconia, New Hampshire. A year later, Kiley married Anne Lothrop Sturges. In fall 1942, while on their honeymoon in the Grand Tetons of Wyoming, Kiley received word that Louis Kahn wanted him to join the design team for Willow Run Housing Project. Although this change of plan cut the honeymoon short, it also prevented Kiley from reaching his intended destination: joining the ill-fated 10th Mountain Division training camp in Colorado.

After collaborating for several years with Kahn, Kiley joined the armed forces and was sent to Texas as a member of the United States Corps of Engineers. He then returned to Washington to the Fort Belvoir training centre. At Eero Saarinen's behest, Kiley took on the assignment of Director of Design for the Presentations Branch of the Office of Strategic Services (OSS) in 1944, and in 1945 was sent to Nuremberg, Germany to design and rehabilitate the Palace of Justice into a courtroom and offices for the post-war international tribunal.

On his return from Europe, Kiley reopened his office in New Hampshire and became a registered architect (with Eero Saarinen and Louis Kahn as references). Some of his early work – primarily houses, as landscape work was scarce – was published in *Architectural Record* and *Interiors*. In 1951, the Kiley family transplanted to the Green Mountains of Vermont, where Kiley opened an office near their sprawling house on Lake Champlain. For the next four decades, the practice grew, expanding up to thirty-five employees (including landscape architects, architects and engineers) at its largest. In that time, the firm was known as Dan Kiley and Partners (1951–74); it then moved ten miles east and became Kiley/Tyndall/Walker (1974–79), then Dan Kiley/Peter Ker Walker (1979–85). Since the mid-1980s, Kiley has practised alone with associates.

Kiley has been honoured with more than sixty state, national and international awards, and has participated in numerous juries, lectures and advisory councils. A selection of these are listed here. In addition, his work has been shown at the Museum of Modern Art in New York, The Library of Congress in Washington, D.C., the Architectural Association in London, Harvard University in Massachusetts, the Urban Center and the American Academy of Arts and Letters in New York, and has been presented as a travelling exhibition.

AWARDS

1944	U.S. Air Force Special Commendation: Transport Command, Washington (DC), International Airport
1945	Legion of Merit, U.S. Army: Nuremberg Courtrooms, Nuremberg, Germany
1947	First Prize, Jefferson Memorial Competition (architect: Saarinen), St Louis (MO)
1949	Chicago Tribune Honourable Mention: 'Better Homes for Living', Chicago (IL)
1957	House and Home Award: Residential Design
1959	Progressive Architecture Design Award: Filtration Plant, Chicago (IL)
	First Honour Award: Concordia Senior College, AIA/Fort Wayne (IN)
1962	Award of Merit: Residential Design, ASLA/Columbus (IN)
1963	First Honour Award: SW Redevelopment Capitol Park, FHA/Washington (DC)
	First Honour Award: Stiles and Morse Colleges, Yale University, AIA/New Haven (CT)
1964	Award: Concordia Senior College, AAN/Fort Wayne (IN)
1966	Gold Medal Award: Independence Mall – Third Block, AIA/Philadelphia (PA)
	Award for Kenwood-Hyde Park Housing, AIA/Chicago (IL)
1967	Bard Award: North Court of Lincoln Center, New York (NY)
1969	Award: Oakland Museum, AAN/Oakland (CA)
	Award: Ford Foundation Atrium, AAN/New York (NY)
	Governor's Award: Oakland Museum, Oakland (CA)
1970	Landscape Architecture Award of Merit: Oakland Musuem, Oakland (CA)
1971	Allied Professions Medal, AIA Washington (DC)
1972	Collaborative Achievement in Architecture Award: RIT AIA/Rochester (NY)
1973	Honour Award: Miami River Corridor Study, AIA/Dayton (OH)
	Architectural Record Award: Squibb Headquarters, Lawrenceville (NJ)
1975	American Academy in Rome, Landscape Architect in Residence, Rome, Italy
1978	Award for Design Excellence: Indiana Bell Building, Columbus (IN)
1983	Citation for Outstanding Contribution to Landscape Architecture, American Horticulture Society
1985	Daniel Kiley Lectureship established, Harvard University
1987	Merit Award: Fountain Place, ASLA/Dallas (TX)
1988	Distinguished Designer Fellowship, NEA/Washington (DC)
	Thomas Jefferson Medal in Architecture, University of Virginia
1990	Dallas Urban Design Award, Dallas (TX)
	Academician: National Academy of Design, New York
	The Year of the Landscape: A Celebration to Honour Dan Kiley, American Academy in Rome
	National Landscape Award: Ford Foundation Building, Washington (DC)
1991	ASLA Merit Award: Henry Moore Sculpture Garden, Kansas City (KS)
	Governor's Award for Excellence in the Arts, Vermont
1991	Chicago Architecture Award, AIA/Chicago
1992	Outstanding Lifetime Achievement Award, Harvard University
1993	Honorary Degree: Green Mountain College, Vermont
1995	Arnold W. Brunner Prize in Architecture, AAAL/New York (NY)
	25-Year Award: Ford Foundation Building, AIA/New York (NY)
1997	Tribute to Dan Kiley/Flag flown over the U.S. Capitol, Washington (DC)
	Daniel Kiley Exhibitions Fund established, Harvard University
	National Medal of Honour in the Arts, NEA/Washington (DC)

COMPLETE WORKS AND PROJECTS

KEY

A	Architecture	**MP**	Master Plan
C	City Planning	**N**	Consulting
CM	Campus Master Plan	**P**	Panel
CO	Competition	**PR**	Prospective
H	Honorarium	**RP**	Resort Planning
HP	Historic Preservation	**S**	Site Planning
L	Landscape	**UD**	Urban Development

1931
Frederic Stewart, West Roxbury (MA), **L**

1935
Mrs George E. Kunhardt, North Andover (MA), **L**

1936
Mr Felix Knauth, Sandwich (MA), **L**

1937
Mr Herbert Swett – Summer Theatre, Skowhegan (ME), **L, S**

1938
Bear Brook Park – State Rec. Area, Allentown (NH), **MP**
Concord City Planning Board, Concord (NH), **C**

1939
Public Buildings Admin., Washington (DC), **L**
U.S. Housing Authority, Washington (DC), **L, S**

1940
Charles Collier, Falls Church (VA), **L**
A.A.S. Davy, Middleburg (VA), **L**
Mrs W. S. Donovan, Berryville (VA), **L**
John Collier, Falls Church (VA), **L**
Kenneth Kassler, Princeton (NJ), **L**

1941
Elizabeth K. Bauer, Princeton (NJ), **L**, *Mock*
Ralph Hetzel, Falls Church (VA), **L**, *Howe*
America House [store], Washington (DC), **L**
Mordecai Ezekial, Washington (DC), **L**
Edward Hollander, Washington (DC), **L**, *Berla*
Clark Foreman, Washington (DC), **L**, *Kastner*
Clark Foreman, Washington (DC), **L**, *Wagner*
Harvey Bush, Alexandria (VA), **L**
Lyle S. Garlock, Alexandria (VA), **L**
Mrs Herbert S. Moyer, Washington (DC), **L**
Dorchester House Apartments, Washington (DC), **L**
Mrs Burton Oppenheim Garden, Washington (DC), **L**
Frederick Gutheim, Mt

COLLIER RESIDENCE FALLS CHURCH, VIRGINIA, 1940 **L**

My first major clients, the Colliers, were wonderfully open to new ideas of the modern landscape. I lived with them for the project's duration, from on-site design through on-the-spot grading from atop a bulldozer. The plan is a collection of elements, spontaneous rather than ordered: interior living space is extended outwards in several terraces; an arc of weeping cherries borders the sloped lawn; a saw-toothed entry hedge echoes French architects such as Legrain.

FOREMAN RESIDENCE WASHINGTON, D.C., 1941 **L**

Reflective of the times, this residential design focuses on the delineation of programmed outdoor rooms. Laundry, vegetable garden, cutting garden, play yard, badminton court and dining terrace are arrayed around the house, each valuing direct access to the indoors over self-contained volu-metric expression. An orchard encloses the west side.

NUREMBERG COURT ROOM NUREMBERG, GERMANY, 1945 **A**

As Chief of Design of the Presentations Branch of the OSS, I was sent to Germany to reconstruct the Palace of Justice into a highly efficient complex with the capacity for six hundred personnel plus a court room for the international tribunal with its throng of journalists and high-tech communications systems. We re-opened brick and plywood factories, we scoured the country for glass and plumbing, we brought theatre seats from nearby towns and purchased a rug on the black market. On average, the renovation entailed 875 workers daily.

Ephraim (MD), **L**, *Berla*
Julian Berla, Washington (DC), **L**, *Berla*
Edmund Bacon, Phoenixville (PA), **L**, *Bacon*
Mrs Kingsley Hubby, Princeton (NJ), **L**
Walker Bleakney, Princeton (NJ), **L**, *Kassler*
Stanley Surrey, McLean (VA), **L**, *Berla*
Princeton Community Gardens, Princeton (NJ), **L**
Frederick Beckman, Princeton (NJ), **L**, *Kassler*
Pennypack Woods Housing Project, Philadelphia (PA), **L**, *Howe, Kahn*
Cabin John Housing Project, Cabin John (MD), **L**, *Berla*
Cameron Valley Housing Project, Cameron Valley (VA), **L**, *Kastner*
Coatesville Foundry Housing Project, Coatesville (PA), **L**, *Stonorov, Kahn*
Coatesville Lincoln Homes Project, Coatesville (PA), **L**, *Stonorov, Kahn*
Middletown Community Building, Middletown (PA), **L**, *Kahn*

1942
Willow Run Housing Project Townsite, Detroit (MI), **L**, *Stonorov, Kahn*
Lily Pond Housing Project, Washington (DC), **L**, *Howe, Kahn*
Edward Hollander (Blackout Room), Washington (DC), **A**

1943
Ft Belvoir Demonstration Area (VA), **A**
Ft Belvoir Administration Building (VA), **A**

1944
Air Transport Command Int'l Airport, Washington (DC), **L**, *Goodman*
Quito, Ecuador, Competition, **S**, *Saarinen*

1945
Nuremberg Court Room, Nuremberg, Germany, **A**

ATHERTON HOUSE ARLINGTON, VERMONT, 1946 **A**

This was one of the first projects I did after the war, and it really was the first house I designed. The client was a distinguished painter; we had a good time discussing the possibilities of the interior materials, light and space. He was a friend before the war, and I did a portion of the drawings for the house while in Nuremberg. I also did some work on another, old house of his, a little one called Red House.

HAMILTON RESIDENCE COLUMBUS, INDIANA **L**

Situated in the same town as the Miller House, and completed just a few years after it, this project is in many ways a continuation of our exploration of geometrically related spatial volumes. Major elements include a gridded bosque of littleleaf lindens set in squares of geranium on a crushed stone plane; a raised water channel with jets; and a honeylocust *allée* which defines the pool and garden lawn.

JEFFERSON NATIONAL EXPANSION MEMORIAL **L, S**
ST LOUIS, MISSOURI, 1947

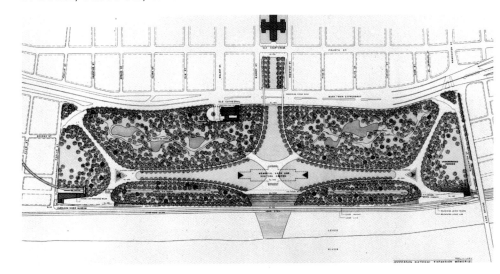

This was the biggest, brightest competition after World War II; it was a stage for the broadening scope of modernism in the U.S. Eero Saarinen's team won (myself, Lily Saarinen, Jay Barr, Sandro Girard) with a catenary arch rising out of the eighty-acre park; I set undulating lines of tulip-poplars (changed to lindens by the Forest Service) along the walks to open up to the archway.

205

MACOMBER HOUSE NEWBURYPORT, MASSACHUSETTS, 1948 **A**

The existing house was an imposing early Colonial structure built in the 1700s. Out in back there was a big Federal-period barn which I remodelled into living quarters. The client picked up an entire boat load of Parana pine, which I used as panelling.

FINE RESIDENCE STAMFORD, CONNECTICUT, 1950 **L**

Earth was moved and shaped in a sculptural mode; we played with the contours and wall segments to create separate but linked outdoor areas. Hedge lines of barberry, mugo pine and cotoneaster further compartmentalize the gardens, while amorphic beds of ferns, vinca and other ground covers emanate from the angular elements in billows of colour and texture. Tree rings surround planted nooks, boardwalk, lawn and pavilion at a pond near the site entrance.

ALCAN CITY PLAN KITIMAT, BRITISH COLUMBIA, 1951 **C**

The mayor of Calgary asked: 'What do you think of our fair city?' I answered, 'It's fine, but don't you know it's in the wrong place?' The city was in a katabatic zone; I recommended that they move it up the mountainside a few hundred feet. At the time, I was participating in planning a new city for fifty thousand for the Aluminum Co. of Canada. The work, in collaboration with Mayer & Whittlesey and Clarence Stein, included analyses of climate, topography, wild life, transportation and industry.

BAKER RESIDENCE GREENWICH, CONNECTICUT, 1951 **L**

In 1951, *Architectural Forum* presented this house by architect Minoru Yamasaki as an example of steel-structured Japanese modularity, irregular form and indoor/outdoor transparency. My plan extends these concepts, yet adds a touch of order to articulate the space outside just enough to allow it to flow in harmony with the house. Evergreen and flowering hedges and screen/grills encompass distinct areas and filter views. The BBQ pavilion has an oak section/ground-cover mosaic.

HOLLIN HILLS ALEXANDRIA, VIRGINIA, 1953 **S,L**

Architect Charles Goodwin designed several prototypes for this post-World War II housing project. We met with each owner and, based on their stated programme, house type and individual site characteristics, produced schematic designs at a rate of one per day – a system which may have helped to codify my design language. Originally conceived as a unified community within a continuous, wooded landscape by Barney Voight, each site was part of a greater whole.

OSBORN RESIDENCE SALISBURY, CONNECTICUT, 1954 **L**

The house by Ed Barnes is a modern structure, flat-roofed with extensive glass walls. A sunken court and an *allée* of elms lead to a small entry courtyard set within hedge and carport. The entry walk passes through a rectangular bosque of clipped maples, then between two fountains which flank the front door. Other elements include a patterned herb garden (designed by Elodie Osborn), a play maze and a pond that extends off the house.

SALTONSTALL RESIDENCE STRATFORD, NEW HAMPSHIRE, 1954   **L**

Short lines of trees (apple, pear, ginkgo and elm) are staccato gestures which break the site into an interplay of activated spaces. The detail of the ground plane provides seasonal interest, with groupings of mountain laurel, viburnum and azalea in beds of ferns. Existing lilac hedges were incorporated into the site structure.

STOKES RESIDENCE HINGHAM, MASSACHUSETTS, 1954   **L**

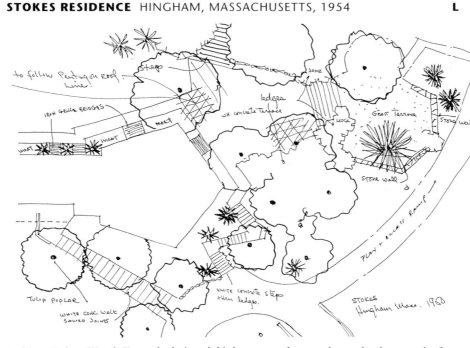

Architect Robert Woods Kennedy designed this house on a five-acre lot on the shore south of Boston. An eight-foot-high wood-slat fence smothered with climbing roses greets visitors. A line of flowering crab leads towards the house, and another up into the site. The pentagonal roof-line originates the shape and dimensions of several terraces lodged into the ledge outcrop adjacent to the house. Stairs climb from the ledge to higher picnic lawns and garden.

BRIDGEMAN HOUSE STOWE, VERMONT, 1957   **A**

207

Richard Thurber, Charlotte (VT), **S**
Chicago Filtration Plant, Chicago (IL), **L**
Bridgeman, Stowe (VT), **A**
O'Hare Field, Chicago (IL), **L**
Richard Davis, Wayzata (MN), **L**, *P. Johnson*
Tanglewood, Lenox (MA), **L**, *Saarinen*
Seymour Krieger, Bethesda (MD), **L**, *Breuer*
National Academy of Science, Washington (DC), **L**
Kenneth Dayton, Minneapolis (MN), **L**, *Giurgola*
Douglas Dayton, Minneapolis (MN), **L**, *Bliss*
Bell Laboratories, Holmdel (NJ), **L**, *Saarinen*
University of Pennsylvannia, Philadelphia (PA), **L**, *Saarinen*
Mrs Arthur Hooper, Baltimore (MD), **L**, *Breuer*

1958

George Laaf, Andover (MA), **L**, *Breuer*
University of Chicago, Chicago (IL), **L**
Max Berking, Rye (NY), **L**
University of Vermont, Burlington (VT), **CM**
Stuart Scott, Dennis (MA), **L**, *Breuer*
Rockefeller University, New York (NY), **L**
B. V. Zamore, Nashua (NH), **C**
Sugarloaf Mountain Ski Lodge, Kingsfield (ME), **RP**

1959

University of Chicago, Chicago (IL), **CM**, *Saarinen*
Mrs Brooks, Minneapolis (MN), **S**
City Hall, Jersey City (NJ), **C**
Currier Farm, Danby (VT), **L** [see page 44]
Kurre Lmeyer, Shelburne (VT), **L**
Brookline URD Project, Brookline (MA), **S**
Clarence Hamilton House, Columbus (IN), **L**
Pittsburgh URD, Pittsburgh (PA), **S**
Baltimore URD, Baltimore (MD), **S**
New Rochelle URD, New Rochelle (NY), **S**
Archbishop's House, St Paul (MN), **L**, *Cerny & Thorshor*
Wilder Foundation, St Paul (MN), **S**
Maurice Filister, Minneapolis (MN), **L**, *Len Parker*
Mrs Carl Jones, Lake Minnetonka (MN), **L**, *Bliss*
Mr and Mrs George Pillsbury, Lake Minnetonka (MN), **L**
Austin Briggs, Ridgefield (CT), **S**, *E. Noyes*
Connecticut Jr Republic,

The site is very steep, with a rounded prominence which faces south and east. This dual orientation inspired the lay-out of two self-contained units connected by a curved gallery. As one passes through the house into the gallery, a dramatic view unfolds. We used an elevated space-column frame so as not to interrupt the sweep of ground and to solve difficult topographic issues.

DAVIS RESIDENCE WAYZATA, MINNESOTA, 1957   L

The site plan is a balanced composition of two primary volumes, an equilibrium of square courts delineated by honey-locust rows (arrival) and hedge walls (play lawn). Linear massings of flowering trees provides further definition. Existing trees interrupt – and free – the plan's rational geometry. A third volume, an existing living-room terrace, completes the house's 'L' formation; from it an *allée* extends out and connects to a pavilion. With architect Philip Johnson.

DAYTON RESIDENCE MINNEAPOLIS, MINNESOTA, 1957   L

An elegant house by Aldo Giurgola, overlooking Lake Minnetonka, this property was relatively free from constricting design conditions. We therefore took the decision to leave the site as a simple lawn with its existing large maples. The small parterre beds enliven the terraces close to the house.

HOOPER RESIDENCE BALTIMORE, MARYLAND, 1957   L

The scheme's focus, a delicately ordered courtyard just off the living-room's south face, is a space to be viewed from within as much as to be inhabited. An existing sculpture, willow tree and pergola contributed to the initial diagram; we added a second willow, a weeping cherry and a Japanese maple. English ivy, vinca and boxwood clumps fill in and overflow the stone paving for a lush but controlled effect. Espaliers cover the back wall.

NATIONAL ACADEMY OF SCIENCE WASHINGTON, D.C., 1957   L

We designed a small planting to accompany a new south entrance off Constitution Avenue. Twin pairs of American beech flank the walkway, with four magnolia set at the doorway in a bed of vinca. The circulation route appears to be cut out of banks of cotoneaster and boxwood.

LAAF RESIDENCE ANDOVER, MASSACHUSETTS 1958   L

The client and architect Marcel Breuer asked us to simplify the existing site plan and to create a scheme more in tune with Breuer's concise architectonic language. We replaced a bluestone entrance area with grass to create a soft contrast to the house's stone walls. A cobblestone ramp up to the front entrance is planted with ground covers and low, creeping flowers. Over time, footsteps left by visitors will wear a pattern of use into the vegetation.

CUMMINS ENGINE CO. COLUMBUS, INDIANA, 1955–77   S,L

For three decades, I worked on various sites for the Cummins Engine Co. (owned by the Miller family) in and around Columbus, including research labs, a distribution centre and fabrication and components plants. Each project strove to link the building and programme to the site and city via strong spatial arrangements. Other Columbus projects in the same era included several churches and schools, a shopping centre, company headquarters, a courthouse, a medical centre and several residences.

Litchfield (CT), **S**, *Breuer*

1960

Lincoln Center for the Performing Arts, New York (NY), **L**, *Johnson, Harrison & Abramovitz; Saarinen* [see page 56]
University of Minnesota, Minneapolis (MN), **S**
Bankers Trust Co. Park Ave., New York (NY), **L**, *Dreyfus*
Sugarloaf Inn, Kingfield (ME), **L**, *Pfeifle*
First National Bank, St Paul (MN), **L**, *Cerny*
Alpine Inn, Waitsfield (VT), **A**
Morton Bender, Washington (DC), **L**, *S & S*
Rutgers College, Newark (NJ), **CM**, *Kelly & Gruzen*
Yale University, New Haven (CT), **CM**, *Saarinen*
Dr Bergamini, Lake Placid (NY), **S**

1961

Derick Webb Shelburne (NY), **S**
Bankers Trust Co. Wall St, New York (NY), **L**, *Dreyfus*
Columbia Coliseum, Columbia (SC), **L**, *Lyles*
Bankers Trust Co., Lincoln Sq, New York (NY), **L**, *Dreyfus*
Pittsburgh Arts Center, Pittsburgh (PA), **L**, *Skidmore, Owings & Merrill*
Harbor Square Project, Washington (DC), **L**, *S & S*
Church of the Holy Name, Minneapolis (MN), **L**, *Cerny*
Lithonia Housing, Lithonia (GA), **L**, *Toombs*
Richmond Civic Center, Richmond (VA), **UD**, *Ballou & Justice*
Garrison Development, Garrison (NY), **L**
Rohm & Haas, Philadelphia (PA), **L**, *Ewing*
Point Bay Marina, Charlotte (VT), **A**

1962

University of Pittsburgh, Pittsburgh (PA), **S**
Harcourt Brace Inc., New York (NY), **L**, *S & S*
Piedmont Park, Atlanta (GA), **S**
New England Exhibit World's Fair, Flushing (NY), **L**, *Campbell*
Nurses' Residence Memorial Hospital, New York (NY), **L**, *Harrison*
Michael Straight, Martha's Vineyard (MA), **L**, *Keyes*
Louville F. Niles, Hingham (MA), **L**
I.B.M. Research Lab, Armonk (NY), **L**, *Skidmore, Owings & Merrill*
Stanley Bender, Washington (DC), **L**, *S & S*

CHRISTIAN THEOLOGICAL SEMINARY   **L**
INDIANAPOLIS, INDIANA, 1962

Our collaboration with architect Ed Barnes in this project consisted of several detail areas, including the cloister court and an entry sequence, as well as the planting of elements that would relate future additions to the campus. Several decades later, Barnes designed thirty-six apartments across the street from the seminary, for which we provided a landscape scheme which included a grove of poplars.

PENNSYLVANIA AVENUE PILOT BLOCK   WASHINGTON, D.C., 1962–65   **UD**

We developed renovation plans for this historic area (in collaboration with Skidmore, Owings and Merrill), which incorporated L'Enfant's axial avenue into the contemporary urban situation. Along the avenue, we designed a seventy-foot-wide grey-green granite sidewalk and brick roadway, with parallel double and triple bands of littleleaf lindens. Small plazas occur at important intersections.

PILLSBURY HOUSE   MINNEAPOLIS, MINNESOTA, 1963   **L**

The arrival court has a grand and serene air, almost more suited to sculpture than a place for cars. A custom-cut millstone of Minnesota green granite anchors the court's crushed-stone plane; a spout of water bursts out of its flat top, then falls into the encircling basin. The fountain's vertical animation joins with the surrounding airy grove of honey locusts. Other elements of the steep lakeside lot include steps cut into the contours down to an open-air shoreside pavilion.

FREDONIA COLLEGE   FREDONIA, NEW YORK, 1964   **L, CM**

Under Governor Nelson Rockefeller's mandate, the state universities of New York undertook an improvement and expansion programme. We worked with architects Harry Cobb and I. M. Pei to interrelate a new complex of buildings with the existing campus using landscape elements as a tool of connection. The curved entry drive is lined with Lombardy poplars, with a secondary row of pyramidal red maples behind, ready to take over when the poplars die out.

ST PAUL'S SCHOOL CONCORD, NEW HAMPSHIRE, 1964 CM

For this secondary school in the woods of northern New England, we worked with architect Ed Barnes to present a campus plan which included an entry sequence, a chapel green, an amphitheatre and lake-edge treatment. The central green was envisioned as a sunken lawn, surrounded by shade trees and a grass bank on which students could study and nap. A strip of woodland garden, with shadbush, aspens, willow and ferns, separates Lower School dorms from the pond.

WASHINGTON MALL WASHINGTON, D.C., 1965, 1987 UD

In collaboration with Skidmore, Owings and Merrill, I worked on several options to reinvigorate this landscape of intense civic imagery for the National Park Service. We proposed to fortify the edge condition with dense blocks of trees. I later led a Harvard University design studio that focused on the Mall's form and its integration of monumental elements within the Potomac River basin.

Smith Kline & French, King of
Prussia (PA), **L**, *Stonorov*
Southwest Washington Schools –
Syphax, Bowen, Washington
(DC), **L**
Tufts University, Medford (MA), **S**
University of Chicago, Chicago
(IL), **L**, *Skidmore, Owings & Merrill*
University of Lagos, Lagos, Nigeria,
L, *McMillan, Griffis & Milet*
Fredonia Dormitory Phase XIII,
Fredonia (NY), **L**, *Pei*
U.V.M. (Benches, Centennial Field,
Kiosk Sign), Burlington (VT), **L**
U.V.M. (Parking & Traffic, Ski Area,
Water Tower), Burlington (VT), **S**
Virginia Avenue – Contract II,
Washington (DC), **L**
Ansul Chemical Company,
Marinette (WI), **L**, *Murphy*
Yale President's House, New Haven
(CT), **L**
Concordia College, Fort Wayne
(IN), **CM**, *Saarinen*
Weese Office Building, Chicago
(IL), **L**, *Weese*
Wolftrap, Vienna (VA), **S**
Winston Churchill Square,
Edmonton (CN), **L**
Drake University, Des Moines (IA),
S, *Weese*

1967
Minnesota Art Institute,
Minneapolis (MN), **L**
Chicago Inland Regional Parks
Study, Chicago (IL), **MP**
Tenth Street Overlook,
Washington (DC), **L** [see page
68]
Cummins – Fleetguard, Cooksville
(TN), **L**
Cummins – Warehouse, Columbus
(IN), **L**
New Haven Parks – Fort Hale, New
Haven (CT), **S**
Rock Valley College, Rock Valley
(IL), **L**, *E. Kump*
New Haven Parks –
Lighthouse/Bathhouse, New
Haven (CT), **A**
University of Wisconsin, South
Lower Campus, Madison (WI), **S**
New Haven Parks (Wooster St
Playground, Lenzi Memorial
Playground, New Haven,
Jefferson St), New Haven (CT), **S**
Syracuse University Site Work,
Syracuse (NY), **S**
Potsdam – S-6, Potsdam (NY), **L**
Boston Zoo (Franklin Park), Boston
(MA), **S**, *Perry, Dean, Hepburn*
U.V.M. – Animal Research Facility,
Burlington (VT), **S**
Lake Champlain Trans. Co.,
Burlington (VT), **L**
Milwaukee Center for Performing
Arts, Milwaukee (WI), **L**, *Weese*

CONCORDIA COLLEGE FORT WAYNE, INDIANA, 1966   **CM**

Architect Eero Saarinen created an entirely new 190-acre campus in the plains of Indiana. The
lay-out was modelled on a German township, with groups of buildings in their own unified
environment, yet as a cohesive body the college relates outwards to the world. Eero's chapel is
at the heart; we planted lines of trees and blocks of shrubs to link buildings to the main chapel
plaza, and to integrate the campus harmoniously with the land.

OTTAUQUECHEE RIVER STUDY OTTAQUECHEE, VERMONT, 1966   **MP**

Our study, sponsored by Lawrence Rockefeller, investigated the best development scenarios for the
watershed, with an eye to balancing the pressures of promoting natural features which attract visitors
and protecting those same conditions from overuse. We proposed a bike/pedestrian way, a series of
small riverside parks, management of adjacent woodlands for recreational use, and preservation of
abutting historic town centres and their network of dirt roads.

ROYAL BANK OF CALGARY CALGARY, ALBERTA, 1967   **A**

We designed four high-rise
towers, including the Royal
Bank, which was a study of
proportional rhythm and
scale of massings. The
fenestration is restricted to
just the broad faces of the
primary volume, with sheer,
solid walls at each level. At
street level pedestrians are
greeted by floor-to-ceiling
glass. My partner at the
time, Jack Smith, worked
closely on the design and
was responsible for the
project's execution through
construction.

ALTA SNOWBIRD SKI RESORT ALTA, UTAH, 1968   **RP**

I worked closely with my partner Jack Smith on this ski area in the rugged terrain of the Wasatch
Mountains. Two constraints guided the design: the property was limited and the avalanche pattern
permitted just a few sites for building. Accordingly, the original trails are compactly networked and
the lodges are high-rise. The base village is across Cottonwood Creek (joined by a skiers' bridge) on
an elevated platform with parking below. With architect Robert Bliss.

FLOATING CITY BROWARD COUNTY, FLORIDA, 1968   **C**

This project was commissioned by a group of businessmen interested in utilizing low-cost land on
the edge of the Everglades for a golf community. A collection of residential units, each with a service
centre, radiate concentrically to form a mandala. The shallow water table is an asset instead of a
hindrance, as the community's primary circulation is via a Venetian-inspired circular network of
canals. Earth dredged from the canals is used to fill building sites, each with its own dock.

IRWIN UNION BANK COLUMBUS, INDIANA, 1968   **L**

Eero Saarinen designed a modest, delicate and precise building – one of his best, I think. I was called
in a few years later to work out the drive-through portion of the grounds. We envisioned customers
driving up into a shady grove and thus placed a grid of littleleaf linden twenty feet on centre across

S.W. Urban Renewal, Washington
(DC), **L**, *Weese*
Stowe Ski Development, Stowe
(VT), **RP**
Ottauquechee (Presentation, Phase
II) Ottauquechee (VT), **MP**
Calgary Place Buildings Ltd – Mobil
Oil Co, Calgary, Alberta (CN), **A**
Tenth Street Overlook II,
Washington (DC), **S**
Tufts University (President's Drive,
Eaton Hall), Medford (MA), **S**
Carleton College Bridge,
Northfield (MN), **S**
F.B.I., Washington (DC), **L**, *Murphy*
Ansul Chemical Company,
Marinette (WI), **L**, *Murphy*
New Haven Parks – East Rock, New
Haven (CT), **S**
Killington Ski Area, Expansion
Plans, Killington (VT), **S**
Derick Webb – Industrial Park,
Shelburne (VT), **S**
University of Wisconsin – L.C.1,
Madison (WI), **S**
Tufts University (Building &
Grounds, Packard Avenue, Tufts
Green), Medford (MA), **S**
Mulberry Square, Syracuse (NY), **L**,
Ferentino Assoc.
Santa Cruz – University of
California, Santa Cruz (CA), **L**,
Linden, Turnbull & Moore
Baxter Company, **S**, *Skidmore,
Owings & Merrill*
Williams College, Williamstown
(MA), **S**
U.V.M. – Married Student Housing,
Burlington (VT), **S**
Potsdam – Master Plan Updating,
Potsdam (NY), **L**, *Barnes*
Calgary Place Buildings Ltd.,
Calgary, Alberta, (CN), **A**
Calgary Sculpture, Calgary,
Alberta, (CN), **L**
Toronto Bank Roof Garden
Landscaping, Calgary, Alberta
(CN), **L**, *Abugov & Sunderland*
Cinema I & II, Calgary, Alberta
(CN), **A**
Cinema Roof Garden – Calgary
Place, Calgary, Alberta (CN), **L**
Pacific Petroleum – Pacific GG
Plaza, Calgary, Alberta (CN), **A**
Pacific Patroleum Landscaping,
Calgary, Alberta (CN), **L**
Royal Bank of Calgary, Calgary,
Alberta (CN), **A**, **L**
Carleton College – Phase I,
Northfield (MN), **S**
Killington Ski, Killington (VT), **S**
New Haven Parks – Lighthouse
Parking Lot, New Haven (CT), **S**
Potsdam – Stage VIII, Potsdam
(NY), **L**, *Barnes*
Tufts – President's House, Medford
(MA), **L**
Carleton College – Fine Arts

211

the width of the property. Lines of lindens project off the bosque to enclose and screen the parking areas; panels of yew, ground cover and bulbs anchor the trunks.

MT WASHINGTON SUMMIT PINKHAM NOTCH, NEW HAMPSHIRE, 1968 **MP**

For years, the majestic summit of the Northeast's tallest mountain was cluttered with poorly related buildings and obsolete machinery; it was then converted to a state park and cleaned up. My office provided a master plan for this effort, complete with a summit lodge and cog railway study. We examined the most desirable mode of development and public access while keeping in mind the optimum protection of the intrinsic natural values of the place.

WILDCAT MOUNTAIN JACKSON, NEW HAMPSHIRE 1969 **RP**

Since I was an avid skier, designing ski areas was an extra delight. Many of the early areas were laid out by famous skiers, not qualified planners. In this case, the site was generally developed in a conscientious manner, however, I was against cutting trails on the poorly oriented face of the mountain, as it would always be windy. They did it anyway; the trails are frequently icy.

MIAMI RIVER REGIONAL PLAN STUDY DAYTON, OHIO, 1970 **MP**

Our study of the river corridor covered a variety of issues, including evaluating the construction of two dams in downtown Dayton and the creation of a River Front Plaza at the edge of the Dayton business district. We proposed to transform an empty flood plain into a recreational ground. A small park within the city – Deeds Park – was a pre-existing positive element to which we added cafés, a pool and a playground.

WINSTON RESIDENCE LYME, NEW HAMPSHIRE, 1972 **L**

The site is cut into mountainside of field and forest. An entry-garden plinth runs the length of the house front: a solid paved surface leads in from the parking, while an appended carved stone basin holds a small plunge pool. The garden continues with stone edging, its grass panels mediating between interior floor space and fields below. Shade trees are set at regular intervals in the grass panels; the plantings facilitate the house's energy-efficient construction.

CHICAGO WATER TOWER CHICAGO, ILLINOIS 1973 **L**

We studied the water tower's potential as a civic landmark/commercial attraction and its pre-eminent position off Michigan Avenue on several occasions. My office produced sketches to illustrate the strength of the tower as a terminus of an open axis from downtown to the lake; we also produced plans for interior plantings at the tower plaza. There, a series of descending plant boxes became an 'escalator garden', with weeping fig, schefflera, ferns and ivy.

Wildcat Mountain, Jackson (NH),
 RP
St Paul's Lower School, Concord
 (NH), **L**
Baltimore Big Survey, Baltimore
 Co. (MD), **S**
Waubeck-Kilkenny Study, Kilkenny
 (NH), **S**
British Petroleum – Pilot Project, **L**,
 Nelson
West River Route 34 Lagoon, New
 Haven (CT), **S**

1970
Charlotte Nature Museum,
 Charlotte (NC), **S**, *Wolf*
Carrabassett, Sugarloaf (ME), **S**,
 Sasaki, Dawson & Demay
Fort Lawton, Park Seattle (WA), **S**
Industrial Medical Center of
 Columbus, Columbus (IN), **L**,
 Hardy, Holtzman & Pfeiffer
Miami River Regional Plan Study,
 Dayton (OH), **MP**
Toronto Site Studies, Toronto
 (ON), **S**, **UD**
Columbus Bank, Columbus (IN), **S**
Federal Reserve Bank, Philadelphia
 (PA), **L**, *Ewing, Cole Erdman*
Fredonia College, Fredonia (NY),
 L, *Pei*
North American Rockwell,
 Campton (NH), **L**
Rockefeller University – Tower
 Parking Lot, New York (NY), **CM**
Xerox–Engineering Complex,
 Rochester (NY), **MP**

1971
Stony Brook, Stony Brook (NY), **L**,
 Damaz Porkorny Wiegel
Crown Center – Hotel, Kansas City
 (MO), **L**, *Weese*
Columbus Shopping Center,
 Columbus (IN), **L**, *Gruen
 Associates*
Richardson – Merrill, New York
 (NY), **L**, *Roche*
Smith Richardson, Southport (CT),
 L
Scaife Gallery, Pittsburgh (PA), **L**,
 Barnes
Xerox–Buildings 200, 334, 214,
 210, 147, 300, Rochester (NY), **L**
Welfare Island – Blackwell Park,
 Welfare Island (NY), **L**
SUNY Buffalo, Buffalo (NY),
 L, *Pei*
Sugarloaf Farms – Phase #1,
 Warren (VT), **MP**
Columbus Court House Square,
 Columbus (IN), **L**
Cummins Components Walesboro
 Plant, Columbus (IN), **L**, *Roche*
GAC – Beebe R., Camden (NH), **L**
National Gallery of Art,
 Washington (DC), **L**, *Pei*
[see page 80]

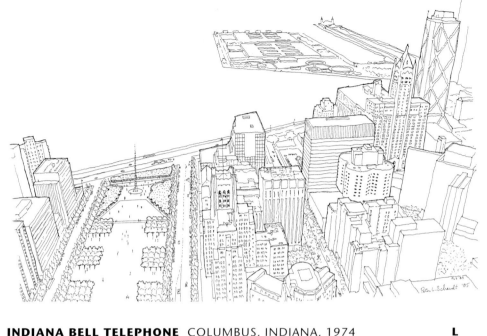

INDIANA BELL TELEPHONE COLUMBUS, INDIANA, 1974   **L**

The building is a four-storey glass edifice on a small-town street of low-rise mixed use. As a gesture towards being a good neighbour, the architect erected a tetrahedonal screen (on which we collaborated) on both street frontages. The screen is covered with five species of vine to create a living, green curtain. We planted shady street trees along the sidewalk, in plant beds of ground cover; these aid the transition to the scale of the neighbourhood's architecture.

Oberlin College Library, Oberlin
 (OH), **L**
Black Grove, Miami (FL), **C**

1972
St Paul Parking, Minneapolis
 (MN), **UD**
Baltimore Inner Harbor II,
 Baltimore (MD), **UD**, **PR**
Eldridge House, Lake Placid
 (NY), **RP**
Walter Thayer Residence,
 Manursing (NY), **L**
Parcel 6, Welfare Island, **L**,
 Johansen & Bhavnani
Newhallville School, Newhallville
 (CT), **L**, *Stull Assoc.*
Winston Residence, Lyme (NH), **L**

1973
Sugarloaf – Phase 2, Warren (VT),
 A, **RP**
New York Botanical Gardens,
 Bronx (NY), **L**, *Barnes*
R.P.I., Troy (NY), **L**
Chicago Water Tower, Chicago
 (IL), **L**, *Loebl Schlossman Bennett*
Columbus Bank – State Street,
 Columbus (IN), **L**, *Caudill Rowlett
 Scott*
City College of New York, New
 York (NY), **L**, *Warnecke*
Berkshire Medical Center, Pittsfield
 (MA), **MP**, *Perry Dean & Stewart*
Ft Lawton – Phase I, Seattle (WA),
 CM
Miller Town House, Columbus
 (IN), **L**
McLean Hospital, Belmont (MA), **S**
Tufts University – College Street
 Relocation, Medford (MA), **CM**
Rockefeller University – Tower
 Building Plaza, New York (NY), **L**
Delta Plantation, Jasper County
 (SC), **L**
Cummins Engine Co. (New
 Storage, Anechoic Facility,
 Charleston Plant, Columbus
 Fabrication, Distributorship
 Prototype), Columbus (IN), **L**
Otterside, Middlebury (VT), **L**
Ridgedale Shopping Center,
 Minneapolis (MN), **L**
Blake School, Minneapolis (MN),
 L, *Hammel Green & Abrahamson*
Pine Ridge School, Pine Ridge
 (SD), **L**, *Marcel Breuer & Associate*
St Paul Capital Area Site Study, St
 Paul (MN), **L**, **MP**
Top Notch Inn, Stowe (VT), **RP**
Robert Cummings Garden,
 Montreal, Canada, **L**
United Engineers & Building
 Constructors, Philadelphia (PA),
 L, *Welton Becket & Associate*
Stone & Webster, Boston (MA), **L**,
 Welton Becket & Associate
Mystic Museum, Mystic (CT), **L**

213

Old Federal Court Building, St Paul (MN), **MP**, *Stahl Bennett, Assoc.*

1974
Indiana Bell Telephone, Columbus (IN), **L**, *CRS*
CAAPB – Master Plan, St Paul (MN), **MP**
Smithsonian Institution, South Garden, Washington (DC), **L**
Springfield Park, Springfield (MA), **MP**
Dayton Residence, Wayzata (MN), **L**

1975
Detroit Institute of Arts, Detroit (MI), **UD**, **L**
Cummins Engine-Route #46, Columbus (IN), **L**
Stern Residence, Rochester (NY), **L**
Coca-Cola Master Plan, Atlanta (GA), **MP**, *FABRAP*
New York Botanical Gardens Carey Arboretum, Bronx (NY), **MP**, *Barnes*
Ringling Museum of Art, Sarasota (FL) **MP**
Robert Winshup Woodruff Plaza, Atlanta (GA), **L**, *FABRAP*
Burlington Cathedral, Burlington (VT), **L**, *Barnes*
CAAPB – Competition, St Paul (MN), **P**, *Design Review Board*
Federal Reserve Bank, Philadelphia (PA), **L**
Landmark Center, St Paul (MN), **MP**, *Perry Dean Stahl & Rogers*
Discovery Park, Seattle (WA), **L**

1976
Tufts Fletcher School of Diplomacy, Medford (MA), **CM**
'Sol y Nieve' Ski Resort, Granada, Spain, **RP**
Smith College, Northampton (MA), **CM**
William Burton House, North Hero (VT), **L**
Washington Cathedral, Washington (DC), **L**
Dumbarton Oaks, **MP**, **PR**
George Newlin House, Columbus (OH), **L**
Belle Isle Promenade, Detroit (MI), **MP**
Jervis Janey Residence, Grand Isle (VT), **L**
Sangsar Town Development, Sangsar, Iran, **UD**, *Perry Dean Stahl & Rogers*
Faulkner Hospital, Boston (MA), **L**, *Perry Dean Stahl & Rogers*

1977
David Rockfeller, Tarrytown (NY), **L**
East Shore Park, New Haven (CT), **MP**

214

BELLE ISLE PROMENADE DETROIT, MICHIGAN, 1976   **MP**

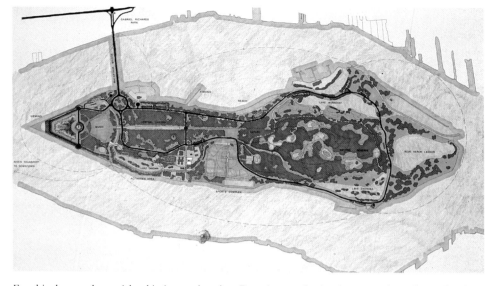

For this thousand-acre island in intensely urban Detroit, we submitted a renovation scheme for the park, a well-worn, massive complex of open playing fields, golf greens, bike paths, picnic grounds, wading pools, boat docks and cafés. The island's existing amenities were in a poor state; our proposal included a new pedestrian promenade, a central activities area, a boat basin and a face-lift for the maintenance area.

DETROIT INSTITUTE OF ARTS DETROIT, MICHIGAN, 1981   **UD**

As part of a downtown urban-revitalization programme, we were engaged by the museum to redesign its main entrance and to create a sculpture garden. With shimmering water flowing over the front steps and two generous fountains on the street-level plaza, the entry celebrates activity, movement and an open relationship with the city. Rodin's *Thinker* overlooks the waterworks and attracts passers-by.

BRYAN RESIDENCE BALTIMORE, MARYLAND, 1985   **L**

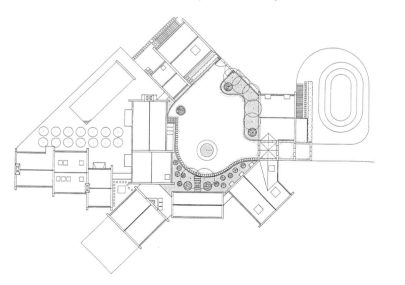

For architect Hugh Jacobsen's house – a poetic aggregation of eleven pavilions on the crest of an eighty-acre site – we designed a simple, secluded entry court of crushed stone with a solitary European beech on axis with the entrance. An *allée* strikes out along the west face of the house as a

Yale Center for British Art, New Haven (CT), **L**, *Kahn*
National Gallery of Art – Phase I & II, Washington (DC), **L**, *Pei*
McLean Hospital Loop Road, Bowditch Parking, Belmont (MA), **MP**, *Perry Dean Stahl & Rogers*
U.V.M. – Library, Burlington (VT), **CM**
New York Botanical Garden Conservatory Surround, Bronx (NY), **MP**, *Barnes*
Lake Champlain Yacht Club, Shelburne (VT), **MP**
Irwin Miller Garden, Columbus (IN), **L**
Manor Woods Condominium, Burlington (VT), **L**
Berkshire County Mental Health Center, Pittsfield (MA), **MP**, *Perry Dean Stahl & Rogers*
Gallaudet College, Washington (DC), **CM**

1978
Amalgamated Transit Union, Bethesda (MD), **MP**, *Hellmuth, Obata & Kassaba*
CAAPB – Cass Gilbert Park, Lief Erickson Park, St Paul (MN), **UD**
Cambridge Redevelopment Study – Kendall Square, Cambridge (MA), **UD**, *Safdie*
Jack Cummings Residence, Stowe (VT), **L**
Cummins Engine Company – Michelen, Brussels, Belgium, **L**, *Roth*
Cummins Engine Company – Jamestown Plant, Jamestown (NY), **L**, *Adams*
Cummins Engine Company – Component Plant, Walesboro (IN), **L**
Cummins Engine Company – Main Plant, Columbus (IN), **L**, *Adams*
Dalle Centrale, La Défense, Paris, France, **L**, **UD** [see page 74]
Robert Elliot Residence, Washington (DC), **L**, *Jacobsen*
John F. Kennedy Library, Boston (MA), **L**, *Pei* [see page 84]
Kensico Plaza, Valhalla (NY), **MP**
Kentucky Courts, Justice & Law Complex, Frankfort (KY), **MP**, *Bennet & Tune FABRAP Join*
Doug Miller, Montpelier (VT), **L**
Nuclear Use Systems Corporate Headquarters, Rockville (MD), **MP**, *Hellmuth, Obata, Kassabau*
Overlake Condominiums, Burlington (VT), **A**
Trout Brook, West Hartford (CT), **MP**
Winooski C.B.D., Winooski (VT), **UD**
Winooski Chace Mill Dam,

Winooski (VT), **UD**
Winooski River Park and Plaza,
Winooski (VT), **UD**

1979
Piedmont Office Building, Atlanta
(GA), **L**, *Amisano*
Trapp Family Lodge, Stowe (VT),
RP, *Robert Burley Assoc.*
Winooski West Allen Street,
Winooski (VT), **UD**
Franconia Notch I-93, Franconia
(NH), **C**, *Daniel, Mann, Johnson &
Mende*
London Standard Chartered Bank,
London, England, **L**, *Fitzroy,
Robinson* [see page 88]
Irwin Union Bank, Columbus (IN),
L
Wheaton College, Mansfield (MA),
L, *Gourley, Mitchell*

1980
North Branford Condominiums,
North Branford (CT), **A**
Arrowhead, Vail (CO), **RP**
East Shore Park – Phases II, III and
Running Track, New Haven (CT),
MP
Hamilton Residence, Boca Raton
(FL), **L**
Scarbrough Residence, Savannah
(GA), **HP**
Mint Museum, Charlotte (NC), **L**,
Harry Wolf Associates
Winooski Block, Winooski (VT), **UD**
DIA – Entry Plaza, Sculpture Court
Grounds, Detroit (MI), **L**
New York Botanical Garden –
Phase II, Bronx (NY), **MP**, *Barnes*
Cummins Engine Co. – South
Mapleton Building, Columbus
(IN), **L**
East Shore Park, Phase IV, New
Haven (CT), **MP**
Julia Field Residence, Coconut
Grove (FL), **L**
Maynard Residence, Southampton
(NY), **L**

1981
McLean Gardens, Washington
(DC), **L**, *Weese*
Sedgewick: Gardiners Corner,
London, England, **L**, *Fitzroy
Robinson*
Carma Towers, Seattle (WA), **UD**,
McKinley Architects
Lincoln West Development, New
York (NY), **UD**, *Gruzen & Partners*
Detroit Institute of Arts (including
African & Ethnographic
Galleries), Detroit (MI), **UD**
Bucksbaum Residence, Des Moines
(IA), **L**
Bruce Smith Residence, Walnut
Creek (WA), **L**
Duncan Symes Residence,

orienting element which links house to land. The swimming pool extends off the *allée* at forty-five
feet, and aligns itself with a series of smaller garden terraces.

CRISWELL RESIDENCE DALLAS, TEXAS, 1985   L

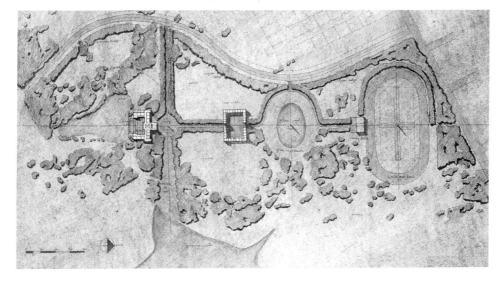

This client was the original developer of Fountain Place. His estate was envisioned as a viniculture
and horse farm. We used a long *allée* of shade trees to establish important circulation routes and
connections within the site diagram. The main house, a checkerboard of square pavilions and open
terraces, was a response to the Texas climate.

BRICKELL AVENUE MIAMI, FLORIDA, 1987   PR
For this unbuilt proposal, we created a patterned boulevard of colour and activity to reinvigorate
Brickell Avenue. Our scheme called for a checkerboard of ground cover and water down the median
traffic-lane division, with towering royal palm trees at regular ten-foot intervals along the sidewalk.

PIERPONT MORGAN LIBRARY NEW YORK, NEW YORK, 1988   L

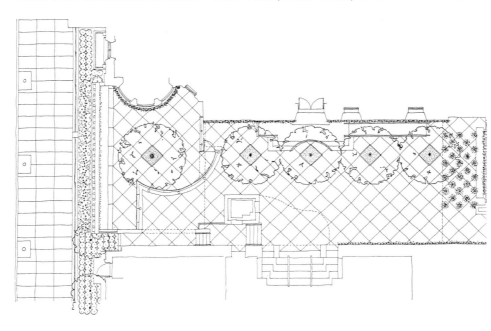

Norwich (VT), **L, P**
San Antonio Museum of Art, San
Antonio (TX), **MP**
British Rail/Liverpool Street Station,
London, England, **UD**, *Fitzroy
Robinson Partners*
Flint Residence, Oyster Bay (NY), **L**
Two Dallas Centre, Dallas (TX), **L**,
Cossutta & Associates
Shelburne Museum, Shelburne
(VT), **L**
K & B Plaza, New Orleans (LA), **L**
Cummins Engine/Madison
Components Plants, Madison
(IN), **L**, *Eisenman & Robertson*
Bank of Korea, Seoul, Korea, **CO**,
Prentic & Chan, Ohlhausen

1982
Crutched Friars, London,
England, **MP**, *Chapman, Taylor
Partners*
Arcade Center – Tower I, Seattle
(WA), **UD**, *McKinley/Gerron
Architect*
Villa Philbrook, Tulsa (OK), **MP**
Mud Island, North Memphis (TN),
L, *Walk Jones & Francis Mah*
William Gregory – New Site,
Wayzata (MN), **L**, *Robertson*
Port Authority Bus Terminal, New
York (NY), **MP**
Kensico Plaza, Phase II, White
Plains (NY), **L**
New Hospital, Memphis (TN), **L**,
Walk Jones & Francis Mah
Ethan Allen Homestead, Winooski
(VT), **PR**
Wherry Housing, Memphis (TN),
L, *Walk Jones & Francis Mah*
East Shore Park – Phase III, New
Haven (CT), **MP**
Irwin Management – Various
Projects, Columbus (IN), **L**

1983
Topnotch at Stowe, Stowe
(VT), **PR**
Trinity University/Stieren
Sculpture, San Antonio (TX), **L**
Stamford Atrium, Stamford (CT),
PR, *Safdie*
Cummins Engine Company,
Indianapolis (IN), **L**, *Hisaka*
Centrum Marine World Executive
Park, Redwood City (CA), **L**,
Gensler Associates
Candlestick Point Park, San
Francisco (CA), **PR**
The Dallas Museum of Art, Dallas
(TX), **L**, *Barnes* [see page 94]
Vasiliou Residence, Fisher's Island
(NY), **L**, *Beckhard*
Schwartz Residence, **L**, *Beckhard*

1984
Middlebury College – Master Plan,
Middlebury (VT), **MP**

215

Harvard Lecture, Cambridge
(MA), **L**

CTS – Housing, Indianapolis (IN),
L, *Barnes*

Reynolds Residence, Peacham
(VT), **L**

Two Bellevue Center, Seattle (WA),
UD, *McKinley Architects*

333 Bush, San Francisco (CA), **UD**,
Skidmore, Owings & Merrill

Purchase University, Purchase
(NY), **L**, *Barnes*

Dulles/CIT, Washington (DC), **MP**,
Davis Buckley

Heritage Landing, Minneapolis
(MN), **UD**

Silicon Valley Financial Center, San
Jose (CA), **UD**, *Skidmore, Owings
& Merrill*

1985

Vanderbilt University, Nashville
(TN), **CM**

Old Stone Building, Providence
(RI), **L**, *Barnes*

Kensico Plaza – Pavilion, Valhalla
(NY), **A**

Criswell Residence, Dallas (TX), **L**,
Welch

Fountain Place, Dallas (TX), **L**,
Weese, Pei [see page 106]

East Rock Park, New Haven
(CT), **MP**

National Sculpture Garden,
National Gallery of Art,
Washington (DC), **PR**

Mahogany Run, St Thomas, Virgin
Islands, **RP**

St John's Seminary, Collegeville
(MN), **MP**, *Jacobsen*

Faith Trust, Potomac (MD), **L**,
Jacobsen

Ethan Allen Estates, Brandon
(VT), **MP**

Joslyn Art Museum, Omaha
(NE), **MP**

Lakeshore Park, Chicago (IL), **MP**,
Powell/Kleinschmidt

U.S. Embassy, Amman, Jordan,
CO, *Perry, Dean, Rogers*

Bryan Residence, Baltimore (MD),
L, *Jacobsen*

Heath Residence, Charlotte (NC), **L**

Centrum, Redwood City (CA), **L**,
Gensler & Associates

Chevron, San Francisco (CA), **MP**

Minnesota History Center, St Paul
(MN), **CO**, *TAC*

1986

Jobs Residence, Woodside (CA), **L**

Elliott Residence, Stonington (CT),
L

Lewis Residence, Rockport (ME),
L

Lewis Farm, Essex (NY), **L**

Minnesota State Capitol Comp., St
Paul (MN), **CO**, *Wolf*

Located in mid-Manhattan just off Madison Avenue, the library is a cluster of brownstones renovated to include an Atrium Court with a curved glass roof by architect Bart Voorsanger. We selected four Shady-Lady black olive trees for the atrium's primary spatial structure. Vine cables are bolted onto the walls as an armature for bougainvillea, glory bower, Boston ivy and jasmine (the mix of vines reflected the experimental nature of the initial plantings).

POST OFFICE SQUARE BOSTON, MASSACHUSETTS, 1988   **CO**

Our entry into this popular competition contains an arrangement of articulated spaces, concise blocks of trees and a play of open/semi-protected spaces (pergolas, trellis, canopied plaza versus open lawn).

BUCK CENTER FOR RESEARCH NOVATO, CALIFORNIA, 1988, 1998   **L**

Our original scheme was a series of triangular terraces derived from architect I. M. Pei's bold geometric forms. In a second go-around, Pei used a pentagonal framework to accommodate multiple research and office wings which revolve around a central court. Court plantings of parkinsonia and star jasmine play into the pentagonal modularity; the outer site is planted with native live oaks and field grass.

DASH RESIDENCE CHICHESTER, ENGLAND, 1990   **L,N**

Over the past few years, it has been a pleasure to observe and advise architect and friend Kevin Dash on the development of his lovely place in the country. One of my favourite elements is a walk bordered by a thirty-six-inch-high hedge, clipped precisely into a green grid out of which rises a second grid of crab trees. The scheme's highly articulated form is an exciting exploration of geometric potential.

Dayton Main Street, Dayton
(OH), **MP**

Hammond Downtown
Improvements, Hammond (LA),
L, **UD**, *Gewalt*

K&M Properties, Washington
(DC), **L**

Carnegie Center, Charlotte (NC), **L**

Lewis-Hobart House, Short Hills
(NJ), **L**

Bostwick Property, Shelburne
(VT), **L**

IBM Purchase, Purchase (NY), **L**,
Wolf

Celanese Building, Charlotte
(NC), **PR**

St John's College, Collegeville
(MN), **MP**, *Jacobsen*

1987

Greensboro Art Center,
Greensboro (NC), **L**,
Cambridge 7

U.S. Judiciary Building Quadrangle,
Washington (DC), **CO** , *Pei*

Vila – Barrett Residence, Brookline
(MA), **L**, *Forbes*

Gulfstream – Jacaranda Park, Ft
Lauderdale (FL), **L**, **PR**, *Pei*

Pelham Greem, Greenville (SC), **L**

Gateway Center, Charlotte (NC),
L, *Trible*

Pemberton Square, Boston (MA),
L, *Cambridge 7*

Alexander Residence, Bloomfield
(MI), **L**

Hillberry/Kandrian Residence,
Birmingham (MI), **L**

Hunter Residence, Manchester
(VT), **L**

Brickell Avenue, Miami (FL), **PR**

Speilman Residence, Chicago (IL),
L

Shorenstein Projects San Fran &
L.A. (CA), **UD**, *Gensler*

Charlotte I-85 & Harris Boulevard,
Charlotte (NC), **UD**, *Odell*

Centrum, Redwood City (CA), **L**,
Gensler

Sheldon Residence, Shelburne
(VT), **L**

1988

Forrestal Master Plan, Washington
(DC), **MP**

Fox Residence, Clayton (MO), **L**,
Jacobsen

Buck Center for Research, Novato
(CA), **L**, *Pei*

Rose Residence, Lake
Memphramag, Canada, **L**,
Rose

Ball Residence, Canada, **L**, *Rose*

Topnotch, Stowe (VT), **L**

Post Office Square, Boston
(MA), **CO**

NationsBank, Tampa (FL), **L**, *Wolf*
[see page 106]

TURNER RESIDENCE WESTMOUNT, QUEBEC, 1989   **L**

The narrow city lot slopes up from the street so steeply that architect Peter Rose chose to divide it into five terraces. The first level is a yew hedge and shadbush glade to screen the house. A ramped stone path leads to a grotto pool and herb garden on the second level. The third level is a smooth *tapis vert* with perennial borders, just below a swimming pool on the fourth level. A woodland garden with meandering paths fills the uppermost level.

GETTY CENTER LOS ANGELES, CALIFORNIA, 1990   **L, MP**

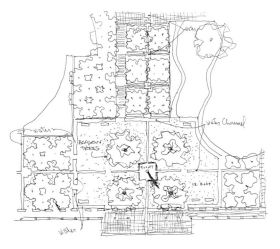

For a time, we worked on the campus plan for Richard Meier's white 'acropolis' of art on the hills over L.A. We recommended that the dry hillsides which surround the white complex be planted with a continuous grid of live oak, a native material which aids stabilization. We proposed a water stair and a banyan court at one entrance, with a Moorish tone of simplicity of form and relationships. Our involvement did not extend past initial schematic plans.

GUAM LEGISLATIVE BUILDING GUAM, 1990   **L**

In tune with the hot climate and heavy rains of Guam, the landscape scheme revolves around water features and drainage elements in this proposal. We designed a grand entry court of stately, arching banyan trees set in etched black granite paving. A series of canals collects run-off and conducts it to the Little Court and eventually into a discharge channel. A bougainvillea trellis brightens the pedestrian connection between old and new buildings.

NAVY PIER CRYSTAL PALACE CHICAGO, ILLINOIS, 1990   **L**

Although just remnants of our proposal were realized in the project's eventual construction, we pursued dozens of iterations of the plan to achieve an interior courtyard of elegance and public appeal. A centrepiece of the Navy Pier's reinvention as a high-traffic commericial/entertainment development, the palace was a glass-enclosed space of light and air. We placed a grid of palm trees across a glass floor, interspersed on a rhythmic interval with fountain pools.

217

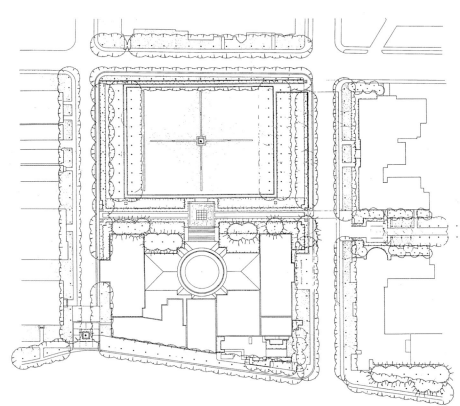

UNIVERSITY OF OTTAWA OTTAWA, CANADA, 1991 L

For this urban campus, we proposed a highly structured network of outdoor rooms, corridors and plazas. Landscape elements function both to define the inner working of campus circulation and to initiate connection and continuity with the enveloping city. With architects Murray & Murray.

GEFFEN RESIDENCE BEVERLY HILLS, CALIFORNIA, 1992 PR

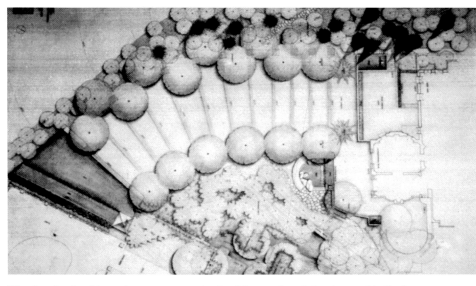

The site plan for this opulent estate contained a rich complex of plantings and built elements. The most stunning feature we proposed was an immense earthen stair which would descend from the south-east face of the house, to open up the view, down to the pool, so that its grass surface would almost seem to flow down the hill. We were involved just through the schematic phase.

LLOYDS OF LONDON HEADQUARTERS LIPHOOK, ENGLAND, 1993 **PR**

To complement Richard Rogers's architecture of sustainable design and energy-efficient systems, we devised a landscape plan of native materials and simply organized exterior spaces, and incorporated existing features (as yet unbuilt). Between parking and building, visitors cross over an eight-foot canal backed by evergreen hedge. The multi-volume building is unified by a grand, sloping lawn on its front which terminates at a circular pool and high water jet.

MASHANTUCKET PEQUOT MUSEUM AND RESEARCH CENTER   **CT**
LEDYARD, CONNECTICUT, 1996

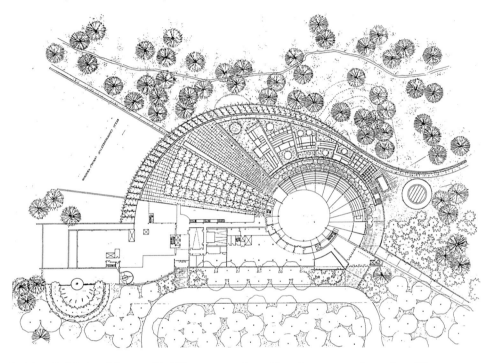

Architect Polshek and Partners' building presented us with an immense roof-top plane (fifty thousand square feet) upon which to design a series of culturally and historically inspired gardens. Although little of our work appears in the built version, our dozens of schemes included masses of clipped lowbush blueberry with sculpture/gathering spaces cut out; an *axis mundi* with a ceremonial ring; a tiered water garden and an herb mandala.

SUFFIELD ACADEMY SUFFIELD, CONNECTICUT, 1996   **S**

In coordination with a new art centre, I was invited to consult on renovation of the heart of the campus. The site is on a slope, with the student union at the top and gymnasium at the bottom, so much of our work focused on the complicated intersection of ramps, walks and steps. A gathering terrace with seat walls and a honey-locust grove extends off the arts centre. We proposed a tulip-poplar *allée* to call out the walkway connection to the rest of campus.

219

A DESIGN MANIFESTO
GARRETT ECKBO, DAN KILEY, JAMES ROSE
Excerpts from the 1939–40 articles in Architectural Record

'LANDSCAPE DESIGN IN THE URBAN ENVIRONMENT'

Generally speaking, man's central effort – the exploitation of all mineral, plant, animal, and insect forms for his own social welfare – has taken two forms, industrial and agricultural production. Where one of these production forms predominated, a characteristic type of environment resulted – *urban* for industry, *rural* for agriculture, *primeval* for those areas either untouched or only superficially exploited (trapping, lumbering, etc.).

But as productivity rose, necessary labor time decreased: time for play as well as work became a reality for the average man. This, in turn, posed a new problem: the *absolute necessity* for and the *real possibility* of man's controlling his environment for his pleasure as well as labor, for recreation as well as production.

This wide and expanding need of society for planned recreational environments offers tremendous new opportunities to landscape designer and building designer alike.

The farmer was the first landscape designer. However remote from reality they may have since become, the great schools of landscape design sprang from the agricultures of this period. Most advances – new plant forms, new fertilizers, new construction equipment and methods – were developed to increase agricultural production, not to make possible a Tuileries or a Kensington Garden.

The farmer has no preconceived ideas of form; he uses all available knowledge and technologies to meet a given need: he plants and cultivates without abstract theories of design or beauty. He is interested in the maximum production for the minimum expediture of time and effort. His forms are not static, but change constantly with the seasons, with advances in farming methods and plant materials.

Cities redesigned for living
The day of passive acquiescence to the given environment . . . is drawing to an end. Certain it is that the city today stands between man and the source of recreation, consuming his free time in travelling to and from those areas which provide a means of restoring vitality dissipated in work.

Yet leisure and recreation, in their broadest sense, are fundamentally necessary factors of human life, especially in the industrial age. Recreation, work, and home life are fundamentally closely interdependant units, rather than entities to be segregated by wastefully attenuated transportation facilities, as they are today.

In our poorly mechanized, over-centralized, and congested cities the crying need is for organized space: flexible, adaptable outdoor space in which to stretch, breath, expand, and grow.

Trend towards recreational systems
The urban dweller requires a complete, evenly distributed, and flexible *system* providing all types of recreation for persons of every age, interest, and sex. The skeletal outlines of such systems are emerging in many American cities – New York, Cleveland, Washington, New Orleans, Chicago – although usually in a fragmentary and uncoordinated form.

And nearly all these systems, or parts of systems, still labor under antiquated concepts of design, seldom coming up to the contemporary plane of formal expression. Nevertheless, the trend is more and more toward considering a well-balanced system essential, such a system including the following types:

1. *Play lot* – a small area within each block or group of dwellings for pre-school children.
2. *Children's playground* – for children 6 to 15 years.
3. *District playfield* – for young people to adults.
4. *Urban park* – large area which may include any or all of the above activities plus 'beauty of landscape.'
5. *Country park and green belts* – for 'a day in the country' – larger area, less intensive use, merely nature trimmed up a bit.
6. *Special areas* – golf course, bathing beach, municipal camp, swimming pool, athletic field, stadium.
7. *Parkways and freeways* – increasingly used (1) to connect the units listed above into an integrated system and (2) to provide quick, easy, and pleasant access to rural and primeval areas.

But quantity is not enough . . .
The problem is qualitative as well as quantitative – not only *how much* recreational facilities, but *what kind.* Here the element of design is vital, and success is dependent upon accurate analyses of the needs of the people to be environed. These needs are both individual and collective.

Design in the recreational environment of tomorrow must (1) integrate landscape and building, (2) be flexible, (3) be multi-utile, (4) exploit mechanization, (5) be social, not individual, in its approach.

The great parkway systems of America are the best example of new landscape forms evolved to meet a purely contemporary demand. The sheer pressure of a mobile population forced their creation; and archaic design standards fell by the wayside almost unnoticed. The landscapings of the New York and San Francisco fairs are other examples. Throughout America, advances in agriculture, silviculture, horticulture, and engineering are constantly being employed by the landscape designer.

Man reorganizes materials consciously; their form effect is produced consciously: any effort to avoid the problem of form will produce an equally consciously developed form. Nothing in the world 'just happens'. A natural scene is the result of a very complicated and delicately balanced reaction of very numerous natural ecological forces. Man, himself a natural force, has power to control these environmental factors to a degree, and his reorganizations of them are directed by a conscious purpose toward a conscious objective. To endeavor to make the result of such a process 'unconscious' or 'natural' is to deny man's natural place in the biological scheme.

Landscape – like building – moves forward
Plants have inherent quality, as do brick, wood, concrete and other buildings materials, but their quality is infinitely more complex . . . It is necessary to separate the individual from the mass, and arrange different types in organic relation to use, circulation, typography and existing elements in the landscape. The technics are more complicated than in the Beaux-Arts patterns, but we thereby achieve volumes of organized space in which people live and play, rather than stand and look.

'LANDSCAPE DESIGN IN THE RURAL ENVIRONMENT'

The irreduceable requisite of any successful planning is that the forms developed will direct the flow of energy in the most economic and productive pattern. This is the criterion in the design of the power dam, the automobile, and the modern cotton field: it should also hold in landscape and building design, where the energy and vitality directed is that of human beings. But to organize the rural areas into the most productive pattern requires an intimate knowledge of the characteristics, rhythm, and potentialities of rural life.

Special characteristics of rural life

First and foremost *the country must be redesigned for country people* – i.e., neither from the viewpoint of nor for the benefit of the urbanite. Second, in view of constantly changing social and economic conditions, that such systems should provide a plastic and flexible environment for both local and migratory farmers. Third, that such systems should be closely integrated with both urban and primeval areas, providing the greatest possible intercommunication between all three.

In general, one can say that whereas in the cities the need is for *more free space* (decentralization), the rural need is for *more intensive use of less space* (concentration) to permit and provide for the social integration of a widely distributed population. But the latter does not imply mere urbanization of the country any more than the former means mere ruralization of the city.

Roads are first

The first and most essential element of any rural recreational environment will necessarily be an adequate highway system.

Consolidated communities mean better recreation

Closely allied with the problem of transportation is that of rural housing. As long as the traditional pattern remains – thinly scattered houses, one to each farm – it is quite possible that a genuinely satisfactory recreational environment will not be evolved … There is already a general trend towards consolidation and reorganization of schools districts. And the recent western projects of the Farm Security Administration – while of course designed for the landless immigrants – clearly indicate the physical advantages of a similar concentration of housing facilities.

What types of recreation are required?

WPA research reveals that the average rural community needs provision for the following types of recreation:

1. Crafts and visual arts, graphic and plastic.
2. Recreational music
3. Dancing
4. Recreational drama
5. Childrens' play center
6. Sports and athletics
7. Other activities and special events

Although there is perhaps no single form which meets so well the various needs of the rural community, the outdoor theater has never been satisfactorily reinterpreted as a present day recreational form in its own right. Developed as an integral part of the rural park, and in a dynamic, three-dimensional pattern, it provides for almost constant use by all age groups.

Many opportunities are overlooked, by sticking too closely to arbitrary and static concepts of recreational planning. For example, the local airport is a form which deserves attention because of the interest and activity which surrounds it … The same thing might be said about the old canal, the abandoned railroad engine, and the automobile junk pile – all of which hold an endless fascination for small children.

Urban invasion – in the form of commercialized amusements, billboards, suburbanzation and the 'naturalism' of 'preserving rural beauty' by screening out rural slums with a parkway – prevents an indigenous and biological development of rural beauty. It is thus that we handicap ourselves with a static and inflexible environment, and lose the opportunity for developing forms which express the needs of the people and the qualities of the region.

[Some are] afraid of destroying the 'delightful informality' by intelligent and straightforward reorganization of nature for the use of man. They resort to 'rustic' bridges, and 'colonial' cottages which will 'blend' with nature. Obviously this point of view can be held only by those who do not live on the land.

We may as well accept that man's activities change and dominate the landscape; it does not follow that they should spoil it.

'LANDSCAPE DESIGN IN THE PRIMEVAL ENVIRONMENT'

The American people had and largely still have a natural environment which is unsurpassed in both scale and variety. But only within the last decade or so have they begun to view it as anything other than an inexhaustible storehouse of material wealth – of minerals, timbers, and furs. Far-sighted Americans long ago realized the cultural, social, and scientific potentialities of the wilderness … Now – with a population largely concentrated in or near an urban environment – the problem becomes one of *establishing and then controlling an environmental equilibrium* – urban, rural, primeval.

The importance of the primeval – its integral relation and the extent to which we are dependent upon it in modern life – is apparent in both a physical (or material) and emotional (or recreational) sense.

The main factor which distinguishes both the urban and rural from the primeval is that, although the primeval may be exploited by him, *it is not inhabited by man.*

Design for primeval inhabitants

As all design of the urban environment is based primarily on the needs of the city dweller, and that of the rural environment on the inhabitants of the country, any intelligent planning of the primeval must be based on *the needs of its native 'population' – beasts, birds, insects, and plant life.* It is the adaptation of the wilderness to the needs of its own 'population' – either by man or nature or both – that provides its chief recreational value to man. Thus, when he controls the survival and selection of the primeval 'population,' he is at the same time providing for his own.

A primeval system must first establish and then control a dynamic equilibrium between man and nature. This means that we must build up the primeval itself, creating the best conditions which science can provide for the native inhabitants, and protecting them against ruthless invasion and destruction from any form or source (human, animal or insect, fire, flood, etc.).

Science shows the way

Recent technological advances at once reveal the complexity of the problem and indicate a trend toward more scientific control of the wilderness.

Clearly, it is not enough to 'establish monuments and reservations' and 'preserve the natural scenery.'

The majority of our 'resort' areas and too many of our parks, although planned to provide man with *access* to the primeval, actually defeat their own purpose – the primeval *retreats* before this advance.

As Lewis Mumford points out, 'It is precisely those of us who recognize the value of mechanization and standardization and universalization who must be most alert to the need for providing an equal place for the complementary set of activities … the natural as opposed to the human … the lonely as opposed to the collective. A habitat planned so as to form a continuous background to a delicately graded scale of human feelings and values is the genuine requisite of a cultivated life.'

The National Resources Board has divided the primeval into four classes to meet the varying needs of the population.

DEVELOPED – specific areas especially equipped for concentrated human use.

1. camping and picnicking
2. summer sports
3. winter sports
4. recreational drama
5. arts and crafts

SCIENTIFIC – areas which contain special zoological, botanical, geological, archeological, or historic values especially.

MODIFIED – areas where man has made alterations with emphasis on the needs of the native population.

1. nature tours
2. camping
3. practice of arts and crafts
4. some sports

PRIMITIVE – mainly unexplored or partially explored areas with conditions of transportation as well as vegetation or fauna unmodified by man.

Design implications . . . access

It is true that the primeval resources and their ultimate value to man depend upon scientific control, but the extent to which the recreational value thereby created can be used by man depends upon its accessibility.

Towards 'the remodelling of the earth'

But the problem is more qualitative than quantitative since wholesale invasion of the wilderness is by no means desirable. On the other hand, access which is necessary to make the primeval useful in satisfying the varying degrees of human needs cannot be camouflaged out of existence by 'styles' of architecture which are supposed to retain the 'feeling' of a particular section, or by 'rustification' which is supposed to 'blend' with nature, and simulate the honest craftsmanship of the pioneers. There is no reason for abandoning the scientific and rational methods of building and construction simply because we come close to nature. The clean cut, graceful forms of the T.V.A. [Tennessee Valley Authority] constructions are certainly less destructive of nature than the heavy, often purely ornamental forms used mainly for their association with primitive technics, rather than because they are the best solution of the problem . . . Harmony is the result of contrast: opposites that complement one another.

The design principles underlying the planning of the urban, rural, and primeval environments are identical: *use of the best available means to provide for the specific needs of the specific inhabitants; this results in specific forms.* None of these environments stands alone. Every factor in one has its definite influence on the inhabitants of the other, and the necessity of establishing an equilibrium emerges. To be in harmony with the natural forces of renewal and exhaustion, this equilibrium must be dynamic, constantly changing and balancing within the complete environment. It is this fact which makes arbitrary design sterile and meaningless – a negation of science. The real problem is the redesign of man's environments, making them flexible in use, adaptable in form, economical in effort, and productive in bringing to individuals an enlarged horizon of cultural, scientific, and social integrity.

BIBLIOGRAPHY

L'Architecture d'aujourd'hui (September 1988)

'1991 Awards Issue: Merit: Henry Moore Sculpture Garden', *Landscape Architecture* (November 1991), p. 57

'Academic Center at Fredonia', *Forum* (1969)

'Allied Bank Tower at Fountain Place', *Places* 4/4 (1987)

Amidon, Jane, 'Dan Kiley: Going Strong', *re/alignment* (January 1994), p. 1

'Architecture as Art', *Burlington Free Press*, 5 October 1995

Bailey, Reade, 'Last Run', *Ski Magazine* (January 1997), p. 146

Barna, Joel Warren, 'Two Dallas Towers', *Texas Architect* (July–August 1987)

Barrett, Jacky, *Terrasses jardins* (Cordoba, 1988), pp. 35, 52, 111

Bassett, Charles, 'Return to Columbus', *AIA Journal* (1984)

Beeson Turner, Carol, 'A Quiet Interlude', *Interior Landscape* (Fall 1993), p. 20

Bleam, Gregg, 'Modern and Classical Themes in the Work of Dan Kiley', in *Modern Landscape: A Critical Review*, ed. Marc Treib (Cambridge, MA, 1993), pp. 220–39

Brown Gillette, Jane, 'Dan Kiley Revisited', *Landscape Architecture* (August 1998), p. 58

——, 'Western Civ', *Landscape Architecture* (December 1997), p. 52

——, *Lanning Roper and His Gardens* (London, 1987), p. 100

Bruegmann, Robert (ed.), *Modernism at Mid-Century: The Architecture of the U.S. Air Force Academy* (Chicago, 1994), pp. 110–20

——, 'The Stanley McCormick Memorial Court', *Museum Studies* (1988)

Built Landscapes: Gardens in the Northeast, ed. Michael van

Valkenburgh (Danby, VT, 1984)

'Un Clasico en el SXX', *El Jardin en la Argentina* (Spring 1998), p. 32

'Changing Times', *Kiplinger Magazine* (1955)

Cooper, Guy and Gordon Taylor, *Paradise Transformed: The Private Garden for the Twentieth Century* (New York, 1996), pp. 124–31

Cottom Winslow, Margaret, 'Seasons and the Golden Mean: Renaissance Revisited', in *International Landscape Design* (New York, 1991), pp. 72–78

Cultural Landscape Report: Jefferson National Expansion Memorial (1996)

'Cuts and Fills', *Landscape Architecture* (1962)

D'Addario, Ray and Klaus Kastner, *Der Nürenberger Prozess* (Nuremberg, 1994), p. 15

'Dance Structure and Landscape' (review of lecture given at Architectural Association), *Urban Design* (January 1995), p. 5

'Dan Kiley: Marcher à Pas de Sioux', in *Pages Paysages* 6 (1994–95)

'Dan Kiley Demands Perfection of Himself and Others', *Calgary Development Digest* (1968)

'Dan Kiley in Person', *SCC/ASLA News* (March 1987)

'Dan Kiley: Land Art', *Peninsula* (April 1986)

'Dan Kiley: Landscape Design II – In Step with Nature', *Process Architecture* no. 108 (January 1993)

Darnall, Margaretta J., 'Roof Gardening on Grand Scale', *Pacific Horticulture* (1991)

Dean, Andrea Oppenheimer, 'Modern Master', *Landscape Architecture* (February 1996), p. 74

'Designer's Symposium: Landscape Architects', *Unique Homes* (April–May 1987)

Dillon, David, 'Constantly Changing Minimalist Tower', *Architecture* (November 1986)

——, 'Fountain Place – Plaza Remains Urban Treasure', *Dallas Morning News*, December 1996

——, 'Fountain Place – The People Commandeer a Plaza', *Landscape Architecture* (January 1991), p. 44

Dunlop, Beth, 'Louisiana Lightness', *Architectural Digest* (June 1996), p. 142

Eckbo, G., D. Kiley, and J. Rose, 'Landscape Design in the Urban Environment', *Architectural Record* (May 1939); reprinted in *Modern Landscape: A Critical Review*, ed. Marc Treib (Cambridge, MA, 1993), pp. 78–82

——, 'Landscape Design in the Rural Environment', *Architectural Record* (August 1939); reprinted in *Modern Landscape: A Critical Review*, ed. Marc Treib (Cambridge, MA, 1993), pp. 83–87

——, 'Landscape Design in the Primeval Environment',

Architectural Record (February 1940); reprinted in *Modern Landscape: A Critical Review*, ed. Marc Treib (Cambridge, MA, 1993), pp. 88–91

Ellis, Kevin, 'Kiley Style: One with the Land', *Burlington Free Press*, 1 March 1990

Flanagan, Barbara, 'The Other Palm Beach', *New York Times*, June 1997

'Fountain Place', in *The Socially Responsible Environment: USA/USSR 1980–1990* (1990)

'Fountain Place, Dallas, Texas', *Designers West* (1987)

Freed, Stacey, 'When Design Compels Movement', *Garden Design* (Autumn 1986), p. 64

Gerron, Gerry, 'Exploring the Landscape of Imagination', *Commentary Magazine* (Spring 1982), p. 4

Gill, Brendan, 'Portrait: Dan Kiley: Landscapes of Joy', *Architectural Digest* (March 1993), p. 34

Goldberger, Paul, 'Architecture: Hugh Newell Jacobsen', *Architectural Digest* (July 1988)

Goldblatt, Lawrence, 'The Nelson-Atkins' Henry Moore Sculpture Garden', *Inland Architect* (July–August 1989)

——, 'The Nelson-Atkins' Henry Moore Sculpture Garden', *Museum News* (September–October 1989)

Goldsmith, Margaret O., *Designs for Outdoor Living* (New York, 1941), pp. 218–19, 283

Graf, Don, 'An Artist Makes the Most of Vermont Hills', *Houses for Family Living* (1951)

Hammer, Lawrence, *Interior Landscape Design* (New York, 1991)

Hammer, Nelson R., 'The Trends of Tomorrow', *Interior Landscape Industry* (June 1989)

Harper, Timothy, 'At 72 Kiley Still Brings Zest to Landscape Architecture', *Boston Sunday Globe*, 9 June 1985

Hewitt, Geoff, 'Interview with Dan Kiley', *Harvard Magazine* (1991)

Higginbotham, Julie S., 'The Landscape Designer Who Influenced Me the Most', *American Nurseryman* (1987)

Holden, Robert, 'Natural Palette for an Urban Landscape', *Independent*, 19 October 1994

——, 'No Sign of Failure at Seventy', *Building Design*, 6 October 1989

'Improving on Nature', *Connoisseur* (1983)

Johnson, Jory, 'Innovations', *Landscape Management* (March 1993)

——, 'Man as Nature', *Modernism at Mid-Century: The Architecture of the U. S. Air Force Academy*, ed. Robert Bruegmann (Chicago, 1994)

——, and Felice Frankel (photographer), 'The Miller House', in *Modern Landscape Architecture: Redefining the Garden* (New York, 1991), pp. 112–27

Karson, Robin, 'Conversation with Kiley', *Landscape Architecture* (March–April 1986), p. 50

——, 'North Carolina National Bank Plaza, Tampa', *Landscape Architecture* (December 1988)

Kassler, Elizabeth B., *Modern Gardens and the Landscape* (Garden City, NY, 1964), pp. 39, 54

Keathley, Barbara, 'H. Moore Sculpture Garden', *Landscape Architecture* (1991)

Kiley, Dan, 'The Emerging Landscape of Peace', in *The Emerging Landscape of Peace* (New York, 1987)

——, 'The Landscaping', in *Oakland Museum: A Gift of Architecture* (1989), p. 11

——, 'The Square and the Park', *Urban Design* (January 1995), p. 23

——, 'Vermont 20–20', *Vermont Magazine* (May–June 1995)

——, and Susan Littlefield, *Garden Design* (New York, 1984)

'Kiley Lecture in Landscape Established', *Harvard Gazette* (1985)

'Kiley Shares Memories of his Education and Developments as a Landscape Architect', *Harvard Graduate School of Design News* (1984)

Killinger, Amy, 'Designed for Discovery', *Gannett Suburban Newspapers*, 31 July 1991

——, 'Designer Dan Kiley Draws on Vermont', *Burlington Free Press*, 12 May 1991

Korab, Balthazar, *Columbus, Indiana* (Kalamazoo, MI, 1989), pp. 70, 72

Kulski, Julian Eugene, *Land of Urban Promise* (introduction by Dan Kiley) (London, 1967)

Lambert, Craig (with photographs by Heinrich Hermann), 'Space and Spirit', *Harvard Magazine* (March–April 1995), pp. 34–41

Landscape Design: Works of Dan Kiley, *Process Architecture*, no. 33 (1982)

Lawrence, Sidney, 'Henry Moore: In America's Heartland', *Landscape Architecture* (April 1989), p. 79

Leskela, Pekka, 'Dan Kiley: Molder of Modern Landscape Architecture' (in Finnish), *Arkkitehti* 4–5 (1992), p. 82

Levine, Michael, 'Kiley Receives Governors Award', *Artsletter* (March–April 1991)

Lewis, Roger K., 'In the Sculpture Garden, Construction Melds with Nature', *Museum News* (September–October 1989)

Lindgren, Hugo, 'Kiley Retrospective at N.Y. Urban Center', *New York Times*, March 1996

——, 'News: Kiley Retrospective at N.Y. Urban Center', *Architecture* (March 1996), p. 34

'The Links as a Landscape', *Connoisseur* (March 1983)

Longstreth, Richard, *The Mall in Washington 1791–1991* (Washington, D.C., 1991), p. 296

A Look at Architecture: Columbus, Indiana (Columbus, IN, 1998)

Major, Leslie, 'Dan Kiley: Making Tracks in the Land', *Vantage Magazine* (July–August 1993), p. 30

'Man is Nature – Thoughtful Planning', *Echo Magazine* (Summer 1973)

Marshall, Robert, 'A Famous Professional's Advice to Home Owners', *The Kiplinger Magazine* (1955)

Masters, Kim, 'The Gallery's Fallow Sculpture Garden', *Washington Post*, August 1992

McClurg, Helen, 'Circle Civic Hall Nixed: Expert Kiley Offers Suggestions', *Hollywood Sun-Tattler, Florida*, 24 May 1968

Merkel, Jane, 'In the Galleries' (review of Architectural League exhibition), *OCULUS* (April 1996)

Mitchell, Henry, 'Landscaping the Urban Jungle, the Right Way', *Washington Post*, 10 October 1971

Moore, Bob, *Urban Innovation and Practical Partnerships: An Administrative History of Jefferson National Expansion Memorial 1980–1991* (1994)

Morris Dixon, 'Geometer's Tower: The NCNB Building', *Progressive Architecture* (February 1989), p. 59

'Most Influential Landscapes: Dan Kiley', *Landscape Journal* (1993), p. 177

Muschamp, Herbert, 'Homage to Dan Kiley', *Corcoran – Day & Night* (May–June 1996)

——, 'If Not Utopia, What Is It? The World by Dan Kiley' (review of Architecture League exhibition), *New York Times*, 1 March 1996

'Natural Man', *Mountain Living Magazine* (1996)

'Nature, the Source of All Design', *ASLA Journal* (1963)

'No Sign of Failure at 70', *Royal Institute of British Architecture* (1989)

Oneto, Gilberto, *Rigoroso in Indiana, di Dan Kiley, Architetto*, Giardini di Villa (Rome, 1989)

Owings, Nathanial, *et al.*, *Pennsylvania Avenue: Report of the President's Council on Pennsylvania Avenue* (1964)

Paris La Défense (Paris, 1987)

Pendergast, Mark, 'Office of Dan Kiley, Charlotte, Vermont', *Business Digest* (May 1987)

——, 'Reminiscence: Trial and Error (Designing the Nürnberg Trials)', *North by Northeast* (July 1988), p. 6

Perry, Michael, 'Coda: Houses on Hills', *Orion* (Summer 1996), p. 72

Persico, Joseph E., *Nuremberg: Infamy on Trial* (New York, 1994)

'Plans for a Garden', in *Second Festival of Contemporary American Arts* (1946)

Pollack, Sally, 'Keeping Up With Glenn (Staying Active, Having Fun; Older Residents Say Good Health Perk of Lifestyle)', *Burlington Free Press*, 29 October 1998

——, 'The Natural', *Burlington Free Press*, November 1997

Price, Martin, 'Dallas Oasis', *Place* (1988)

Racknow, Paula, 'Henry Moore Sculpture Garden Debuts in Kansas City', *Vis-à-vis* (June 1989)

Raver, Anne, 'Cherishing Landscapes as Living Art', *New York Times*, 30 November 1995

'Renowned Landscape Architect Here to Give View on Moving Monument', *Lancaster News Era*, 23 June 1997

Robertson, Jacquelin, 'Step Lightly on this Earth', *Inland Architect* (March–April 1983), p. 10

Rome, Richard, 'The Dallas Waterworks', *Cite* (Fall 1992–Winter 1993), p. 31

Roper, Lanning, 'Coordination and Restraint: The Gardens of the National Gallery', *Country Life Journal* (1981)

Saarinen, Susan, 'A Modernist Garden: The Miller Garden', Ph.D Diss., 1995 (University of Colorado, Denver, Colorado)

Sasaki, Yoji, 'The World of Dan Kiley', *Japan Landscape* no. 17 (1991), p. 92

Schmertz, Mildred F., 'The Oakland Museum', *Architectural Record* (April 1970)

——, 'R.I.T.'s New Campus – A Unique Design Collaboration', *Architectural Record* (November 1968)

Simons, Tom, 'Life is Important, Not Design', *Arkkitehti* (April 1992)

——, and Pekta Leskela, 'Dan Kiley –Trogen Modernist Sedan 1930-Talet' (in Finnish), *Landskab/Review for Garden & Landscape Planning* (August 1992), p. 96

Slesin, Suzanne, 'Prairie Home Companions (Shapiro Residence)', *House & Garden* (November 1996), p. 196

'South Stanley McCormick Memorial Court', *The Art Institute of Chicago: Museum Studies* 14 (January 1988), p. 73

'Spring Blooms at the Kennedy Library', *John F. Kennedy Library Newsletter* (1989)

Stires, Arthur McK., 'Dan Kiley', *Vermont Life* (Summer 1967), p. 46

Sullivan, Karen, 'Free the Steg', *Hartford Courant*, 19 March 1989

Symmes, Marilyn, *Fountains: Splash and Spectacle; Water and Design from the Renaissance to the Present* (New York/London, 1998), pp. 173–87

Temko, Allan, 'Evaluation: A Still-Remarkable Gift of Architecture to Oakland', *AIA Journal* (June 1977), p. 30

Tenny Brogna, Laura, 'Composition of Currier Farm', *Japan Architect* (May 1996)

'To Mold Nature in Man's Image', *Kansas City Star*, 23 August 1987

Tompkins, Calvin, 'The Garden Artist', *New Yorker*, October 1995, p. 136

Tores, Manuel, 'Urbanisme, La Surprise sans fin de Tampa – Un Entretien avec Dan Kiley', *Payagiste* (June–July 1993), p. 52

'Urban Design, The State of the Art', *Harvard Magazine* (1986)

Van Valkenburgh, Michael, 'Two Views of Landscape Design', *Orion Nature Quarterly* (1984/85)

Walker, Peter, and Melanie Simo, 'The Lone Classicist', in *Invisible Gardens: The Search for Modernism in the American Landscape* (Cambridge, MA, and London 1994), pp. 170–97

'A Way with Water: Dan Kiley', *Landscape Design* (March 1992), p. 33

Webster, Susan, Alan Goodheart, and Michael Laurie, 'A Conversation with Dan Kiley', *Landmark* (1965)

'Who's the Favorite', *Architectural Journal* (1988)

Winokur, Julie, 'Moore is More', *Travel and Leisure* (June 1989)

'The Work of Dan Kiley: A Dialogue on Design Theory', *University of Virginia, School of Architecture* (Annual Symposium of Landscape Architecture) (1982)

INDEX